# Edwardians on Screen

# Edwardians on Screen

## From *Downton Abbey* to *Parade's End*

Katherine Byrne
*University of Ulster, UK*

palgrave
macmillan

First published 2015 by
PALGRAVE MACMILLAN

Palgrave Macmillan in the UK is an imprint of Macmillan Publishers Limited, registered in England, company number 785998, of Houndmills, Basingstoke, Hampshire, RG21 6XS.

Palgrave Macmillan in the US is a division of St Martin's Press LLC, 175 Fifth Avenue, New York, NY 10010.

Palgrave Macmillan is the global academic imprint of the above companies and has companies and representatives throughout the world.

Palgrave® and Macmillan® are registered trademarks in the United States, the United Kingdom, Europe and other countries.

ISBN 978–1–137–46788–1

This book is printed on paper suitable for recycling and made from fully managed and sustained forest sources. Logging, pulping and manufacturing processes are expected to conform to the environmental regulations of the country of origin.

A catalogue record for this book is available from the British Library.

A catalog record for this book is available from the Library of Congress.

Library of Congress Cataloging-in-Publication Data
Byrne, Katherine, 1978–
Edwardians on screen : from Downton Abbey to Parade's end / Katherine Byrne, University of Ulster, UK.
pages cm
ISBN 978–1–137–46788–1
1. Historical television programs—Great Britain—History and criticism.  2. Great Britain—History—Edward VII, 1901–1910—On television.  3. Television and history—Great Britain.  4. English fiction—Adaptations—History and criticism.  I. Title.
PN1992.8.H56B97 2015
791.45'658410823—dc23                                        2015014615

Typeset by MPS Limited, Chennai, India.

*For my parents, and for James, with love*

# Contents

# Acknowledgements

Many people have offered help and support while I have been writing this book. Firstly thanks to my colleagues and friends at the University of Ulster, in particular Frank Ferguson, Jan Jedrzejewski, Leanne McCormick and Nerys Young. Most of the manuscript was written with Kevin de Ornellas sitting beside me keeping me company, so special thanks to him. Andrew Sneddon, Matthew O'Neill and Dominic Williams have given me invaluable advice, as have James Leggott, Julie Anne Taddeo and Robin Blood. Earlier versions of Chapter 3 have appeared in the journal *Rethinking History* and in the edited collection *Exploring Downton Abbey*: many thanks to Taylor & Francis and to Scott Stoddart for allowing me to reproduce this here. Alun Munslow's patience, as editor, with my first work on *Downton*, which started me off on this project, is still much appreciated. Thanks also to my editor Chris Penfold, at Palgrave Macmillan, and to Felicity Plester there for her early interest in the project. I am really delighted to have picture of Rebecca Hall and Benedict Cumberbach in *Parade's End* on the cover of the book: many thanks to them and to *Mammoth Screen* for allowing me to use the image, and especially to the wonderful Charlotte Frings at *Mammoth Screen* for all her help.

My family have had to put up with my anti-social behaviour these last months, so thanks for that, and for everything else you do for me, to Suzanne, Mal, Miranda, Eden and Ellis. Most of all I must show my appreciation to my parents, who have seen every period drama from the 1960s onwards, and know as much about them as I do. My father is the best reader and research assistant anyone could hope to have. And finally to James Ward for his wise advice and kind support through endless conversations about heritage television – even though he doesn't actually like *Downton Abbey*.

# Introduction: Neo-Edwardian Television, and "Heritage" Today

This book will explore one of the most popular and influential trends in contemporary television: the representation on screen of the early years of the twentieth century, leading up to and including the First World War. From mainstream period soap operas like *Downton Abbey*, to more "academic," critically acclaimed productions like Tom Stoppard's recent BBC adaptation of *Parade's End*, the small screen has revealed an ongoing preoccupation with the period over the last 15 years. If we can judge the established nature of a genre by the existence of its satire, then the BBC suffragette comedy *Up The Women* (2013–), currently on its second series, is one indicator of how recognisable the Edwardian period has become[1]. This monograph sets out, then, to examine why the Edwardians should have become so popular with today's television audiences – who have of course been avid consumers of all period drama, but seem to have a particular fascination with this era – and what kind of resonance the first years of the twentieth century have for the first years of our own. It will also explore what these programmes can tell us about the state of what I term in this book as "post-post heritage" drama today, and what they reveal about contemporary attitudes toward class and gender, and the ways our television reflects and constructs both.

In order to do this I have concentrated upon a selection of twenty-first century versions of the Edwardian period, all shown on terrestrial television in Britain in recent years, and which all enjoyed subsequent success when rebroadcast in the United States (my main focus here will be on their reception in Britain, but I will make reference to American responses and reviews where appropriate). All are, to greater or less degrees, popular, mainstream fictions. Two of these, *The Forsyte Saga* and *Parade's End*, are adaptations of early twentieth-century novels;

*Mr Selfridge* is an adaptation of a recent biography of the famous Edwardian shopkeeper; and *The Village* and *Downton Abbey* are original screenplays written for television. The latter is really the dominant text in this book, for its success has been such that any following neo-Edwardian fictions are compared to it, try to emulate it or react against it. *Downton* has become a phenomenon on both sides of the Atlantic, but is far from unique: it itself borrows greatly from the style and format of a number of costume dramas which were made in the second half of the twentieth-century, perhaps most directly *Upstairs Downstairs*, but also *The Forsyte Saga*, *The Duchess of Duke Street* and *Edward the King*. These dramas have become iconic television history and have been instrumental in shaping our contemporary ideas about the Edwardian period, and so the first chapter of this book revisits them and examines their politics and their legacy. They are diverse fictions about which it is difficult to generalise, but they offer an intriguing mix of progressive feminist ideas, pro-monarchist agendas and a pro-Thatcherite neo-liberal work ethic, alongside a commitment to representing working-class life in some cases, and a fetishisation of wealth and consumerism in others. They also communicate the sense of a strong sense of identification between the ordinary people living and working in the early twentieth century, and those watching them in the 1960s and 1970s. Many of these tensions and contradictions are, of course, still at the heart of the next generation of costume drama on our screens today.

Chapter 1's main purpose is to provide a sense of how the Edwardian period has been constructed, viewed and remembered in our culture, to provide a context for the reading of more recent television drama in the rest of the book. With this in mind I explore some of the ways in which the period has been revisited in recent years, many of them associated with the "celebration" of the centenaries of the sinking of the Titanic and the outbreak of the First World War. Indeed, the commemoration of such events raises interesting questions about why and how we choose to remember, and what those cultural memories tell us about society today. As well as tracing the trajectory of the Edwardian television serial through the decades, this chapter also examines some representations of the Edwardian period on the big screen, exploring some of the most famous films about the period by, amongst others, Merchant Ivory. The focus of this book is on television, but it is impossible to ignore the huge part which so-called "heritage film" has played in constructing our views of the early twentieth century and influencing the televisual fictions under investigation here.

This brings me, of course, to the heritage debates, which have dominated criticism of period drama, on both the big and the small screen, over the last 25 years. Much has been written about the complexities that surround this genre: there has been a great deal of debate about the word "heritage" since the term passed into common usage in the 1980s and 1990s. Many critics before me have explored and revisited this in detail, and so I will provide only a shortened summary of what I consider to be the main points here, for they are necessary context for the issues of representation of class and nationality which dominate this book. I have just been noting the fascination that the early twentieth-century past exerts over today's society, but this is only the most recent manifestation of a longer standing and more wide-reaching obsession with the consumption of history, which many historians consider deeply problematic. For example, Robert Hewison wrote passionately in 1987 about the newly flourishing museum culture, which he considered a threat to Britain's cultural life – his comments about the past as industry are worth recalling here. For Hewison, Britain is in danger of becoming:

> a country obsessed with its past, and unable to face its future ... I criticise the heritage industry not simply because its products are fantasies of a world that never was; not simply because at a deeper level it involves the preservation, indeed reassertion, of social values that the democratic progress of the twentieth-century seemed to be doing away with, but because ... if the only new thing we have to offer is an improved version of the past, then today can only be inferior to yesterday. Hypnotised by images of the past, we risk losing all capacity for creative change (1987: 9–10)

Via a discussion of such nostalgic obsessions as the cult of the country house, Hewison expresses the same kind of anxieties here that critics of period drama would identify as the problems of the "heritage" film. A term first used in this context by Charles Barr in his 1986 book on British cinema, "heritage" was adopted by Andrew Higson, Cairns Craig, Tania Wollen and Richard Dyer as a description of the quality costume dramas which became so popular on the big and small screen in the 1980s and 1990s. This is an umbrella term which has been used to cover a large variety of historical fictions, including, among others, films by Merchant Ivory (like *A Room with a View* (1985), *Maurice* (1987) and *Howard's End* (1992)); other classic novel adaptations like *Brideshead Revisited* (1981) and *A Passage to India* (1984); and other nostalgic period films like *Chariots of Fire* (1981). Later, it would include Austen adaptations like *Pride and Prejudice* (1995) and *Sense and Sensibility* (1995). What these have in common, Higson has suggested, is the way in which they act as marketing for the British heritage industry, which transforms "the past into a series of commodities for the leisure and entertainment market" (Higson in Friedman, 1993: 112) To this end, they usually present the English landscape as a tourist attraction, for scenery and location is key to these texts, and they also frequently reinforce the Great Tradition of English literature as well, many of them being adaptations of "classic," canonical novels.

As Claire and Amy Sargeant have discussed, these "early discussions of the heritage film tended to deploy the term negatively" (2000: 302): beginning with Higson's well-known, much-quoted and "vigorously contested" views of period drama from the 1980s, some left-wing critics have found such productions ideologically problematic (Dave, 2006: 27). Common criticisms that Higson and others directed at 1980s heritage include their fascination "with the private property, the culture and values of a particular class" (Higson, 1993: 114) and indeed what almost all these films and television programmes have in common is their focus on the more privileged members of society: usually the land-owning gentry, or at least the wealthy upper middle class, as in *Howard's End*. Also of note is their problematic determination to squash "Britain into the south-east corner of England" and subsume "British identities ... under a particular version of Englishness" (Wollen, 1991: 180). Certainly most of these texts are set in, or are about, the English countryside, or other select parts of the country, namely Oxford, Cambridge or suitably gentrified parts of London, and most are uninterested in racial or even regional diversity among their characters. With this in mind, Higson and Cairns Craig, among others, have suggested that certain heritage films sanitised, polished and marketed the past as a commodity, in a way which reflected the aspirations and values of the Conservative Thatcherite government (Wollen, 1991: 183). They can be considered, in fact, a response to some of the issues confronted by 1980s society under Thatcher: "disturbed traditional notions of national identity, which were further upset by the recognition that British society was increasingly multiracial and multicultural ... high unemployment, marked inequalities of income and standards of living" (Higson, 1993: 109). The answer offered by these films is not a confrontation of these problems and changes, however, but frequently an avoidance and turning away from them. Hence, at the same time as they reflect the politics of contemporary society, traditional period dramas can be viewed as offering an escape route from modern life, "seeming to turn their backs on the iconography values of postmodernity, post-industrialisation, and multiculturalism." Higson cites Derek Jarman's argument that these films were "nostalgic, obsessed with the past ... feeding illusions of stability in an unstable world" and that they allow the viewer to ignore certain gritty realities about history (2003: 70). As David Lowenthal puts it, "heritage reshapes a past made easy to embrace" (1998). This is partly achieved by the visual construction of the past on screen as an desirable, glamourous space, without any judgement apart from the aesthetic: "the evocation of pastness is accomplished by a look, a style, the loving recreation of period details – not by any critical historical perspective ... they render history as spectacle" (Higson, 1993: 113).

Subsequent scholarship on heritage (including Higson himself) has revised and moderated these ideas, however, pointing out the dangers of a "monolithic" approach to all films that come under the "heritage umbrella," and articulating the complexities of position and point of view in those 1980s productions (Monk, 2002: 183). As Paul Dave notes, "both Higson and Hill have since argued convincingly that it is the contradiction between narratives aspiring to progressive, liberal sentiments and an indulgence in the spectacle of a socially conservative Englishness that give these films a characteristic ambivalence" (Dave, 2006: 31). Perhaps the most important figure in this rehabilitation of costume drama is Claire Monk, who has critiqued not only the limitations of the leftist approach to heritage but has also pointed out that the condemnation directed towards period drama was as much about the political climate of the 1980s and early 1990s as it was about those films themselves. She argues that "the binaristic simplifications of the heritage-film critique began to make more sense if understood as a defensive response to the terms of debate activated by the Right at that moment:" a moment in which certain art forms were under attack. Monk locates the origins of this confrontation in a 1988 *Sunday Times* article in which historian Norman Stone attacked a number of British independent films, while praising three period dramas which had come out that year: *Hope and Glory, A Passage to India,* and *A Room with a View.* Monk argues, then, that the reductive ways in which critics on the Left responded to heritage film was "initiated in the 1980s by the New Right, only to be reactively replicated by anti-Thatcherite critics and filmmakers ... in a climate in which it was necessary to defend films set in the present and featuring working-class protagonists, it became a corollary that all films set in the past and which focused on the comfortable bourgeoisie or upper classes must be bad" (Monk, 2002: 189–190). Hence heritage criticism, according to Monk, is unfair and reductive in its judgements. Most of these films are after all chronicling the struggle of the individual against an oppressive society, and display their personal freedoms being restricted by severe social codes and financial pressures (Dave offers *Another Country* (1984) as a good example of this). This is especially true from a feminist perspective, for even the most faithful Austen adaptation represents its heroine asserting choice and agency in a patriarchal world. Monk and Pam Cook have addressed the ways in which these films are directed at a female audience and engage with sex and gender in important ways: the content of these fictions may be radical even if the form is not. As Sue Harper has pointed out, the "input of [Merchant Ivory] scriptwriter Ruth Prawer Jhabvala was crucial ... her sense of structure and female character struggles for dominance over the décor" (2000: 148). Moreover, there is a case to be made that some groups of people are reintroduced back into history by these period dramas: they have made women's history mainstream, for example, reminding the viewer about the realities of (admittedly usually upper-class) women's lives. Women are not the only ones of which this is true, however: it has been argued that period drama also reintroduces other groups marginalised by our conventional histories back onto the narrative centre, including the gay community (Higson, 2003: 28). The homoeroticism in *A Room with A View* and *Brideshead Revisited*, and the central love story between men in *Maurice* offer a reminder that history is not just a narrative about heterosexuals. And even that celebration of patriotism, *Chariots of Fire*, does feature "an ethnically diverse middle class seeking not the favours of privilege but to assert this pre-eminence of a meritocratic, open society" (Dave, 2006: 31).

Moreover, Monk has argued that, even if we do accept that period drama under a Conservative government may promote the kind of Victorian values that Thatcher herself identified with (Friedman, 1993: xiii), this was no longer true of those historical fictions produced after New Labour came to power in 1997. She suggests that "the ideological character of heritage film since the mid-90s [has] mutated in response to changed cultural conditions," often progressive in form and generally responding to the "'New British' identity promoted by the new Labour government" (2002: 195). This identity was characterised by multiculturalism, a commitment to social mobility and public investment, and a new spirit of optimism, which encouraged artistic experimentation (within limits) made possible by a prosperous economy. Monk uses the term "post-heritage" to describe such newly innovative fictions of the later 1990s, examples of which might include Patricia Rozema's politically aware 1995 *Mansfield Park* and the decadent version of *The Wings of the Dove*, which I will discuss in Chapter 1. *Mansfield Park* has been identified as significantly post-heritage in that, rather than being a faithful rendering of Austen's novel, it highlights narratives about slavery and imperialist exploitation, which are only hinted at in the source text. Monk also points out that conventional heritage criticism threatens to construct period dramas as the main bearer of conservatism on our screens, while ignoring the fact that mono-cultural heritage agendas abound in recent films which aren't historical. Monk cites the version of middle-class Englishness constructed by films like *Notting Hill* (1999) and *Bridget Jones's Diary* (2001) as an example: they project "a vision of the nation so uniformly young, white, wealthy, narcissistic and implicitly conservative, within a mis-en-scene cleansed of the urban poor, the homeless and ethnic minorities, that by contrast the 1980s heritage film looks like a paragon of socially inclusive, low-budget liberal filmmaking" (2002: 195). As I will discuss in Chapter 4, patriotism and nostalgia on television is not confined to period drama either.

One of the most important recent theorists of historical fictions is Jerome de Groot, whose influential books *Consuming History* (2009) and *The Historical Novel* (2009) have addressed the multiple different forms that "public," non-academic history has taken in recent years. De Groot examines a wide variety of popular historical texts, which range from reality shows like *The Edwardian Country House* (2002) to mainstream Hollywood blockbusters like *The Da Vinci Code* (2006), and argues for the importance of considering all the diverse form of engagement with the past. "History permeates popular culture, and its manifestations are wider than historians often allow for. Popular understanding, use and consumption of 'pastness' are powerful models and paradigms for the ways in which society thinks of history" (De Groot, 2009: 6–7). The classic British costume drama is, then, only one of the genres De Groot examines, but he reminds us of the post-heritage idea that, despite their very recognisable format, period drama "can invoke complex models of historical subjectivity, confound expectations, and consider key political issues of the past in order to educate the viewer" (2009: 184). De Groot was the keynote speaker at a conference I attended several years ago, and in the questions following my paper about *Downton Abbey*, he suggested that there was a real need for scholars to move away from the terms of reference provided by the heritage debate, in order to finding new ways of approaching the – now increasingly diverse – body of historical fictions on our screens. After all, Jane Austen's *Pride and Prejudice* has now been reimagined as a time-travelling romance (*Lost in Austen*, 2008), Bronte adaptations have been skilfully parodied in *Hunterby* (2012) and the ever popular *Dr Who* (1963–) mixes history and science fiction every Saturday night. I have tried to indicate throughout this book the ways in which recent period drama on television is innovative, post-modern, dynamic and self-aware, but I still find it impossible to completely leave behind the concept of "heritage" criticism, which for me is not only part of a particular, Thatcherite cultural moment but is still applicable to neo-Edwardian television today. This is especially true of contemporary television's representation of social class, Englishness and nationhood, regarding which the ideas of Higson and others from the 1990s seem still frighteningly relevant. With the significant exception of *The Village*, the period dramas I examine in this book are still, to varying degrees and with undoubted complexities, still largely nostalgic, mono-cultural, patriotic and fixated on the lives of the upper classes. With this in mind, it seems more accurate to describe them as "post-post-heritage": they are interesting, and often experimental, but still ultimately conservative views of a glossy, sanitised past.

That is not meant, however, to underplay the significance of these dramas or the insights they offer both about their past and our present: all are complex and often conflicted comments on different versions of history. It is also not meant to be reductive about the ideologies each represent: there is no one simple agenda in any of the series I explore here. The subject of Chapter 2, *The Forsyte Saga* (2002) is itself in thrall to an earlier adaptation of Galsworthy's novel – its famous 1967 predecessor – but nonetheless contains notably anti-nostalgic, anti-heritage elements, from its interest in modernist architecture and art to its troubled and troubling anti-hero, Soames, who might make any female viewer grateful to be living in a more enlightened time. With Monk's comments in mind, this is much what we might expect from a drama made at the beginning of a new century and under the changed cultural conditions created by a New Labour government, which was still in its honeymoon period. Thus this is a liberal, bourgeois drama, preoccupied with individual freedom and expression, and strongly advocating the resistance of repressive social structures and conventions. It is, however (perhaps rather like Blair's Labour government), only interested in these rebellions as experienced by its middle-class characters: it shows no interest in the struggles and oppressions of the servants who are perpetually present but largely ignored by the plot. Moreover, it strongly criticises the materialism of late nineteenth and early twentieth-century society, but simultaneously invites the audience to enjoy the sumptuous products of such materialism: clothes, jewels, houses and art. Perhaps more than any other drama explored in this book, however, *The Forsyte Saga* is anxious about the future, drawing clear parallels between the ending of innocence in the Edwardian period, and in our own after 9/11. The terrorist attacks on the World Trade Centre are, I argue here, informing and shaping this drama, which would like to allow us to escape into the past for refuge, but is too cynical, too "post-heritage," to indulge us with a happy ending.

The same cannot be said about the text I examine in Chapter 3, *Downton Abbey*. The most watched programme in this book – indeed the most popular period drama in the world – it has concocted a winning formula (or, more accurately, borrowed it from *Upstairs Downstairs*): it sets out to remind us that history can be about, and for, ordinary people, too. Arriving on our screens in the years following world-wide economic depression, a banking crisis and a housing price crash, it portrayed a charmed world where employers were responsible and generous, servants were hard-working and respectful, and houses were both stately and a home. This drama and its soap-like plotting, was clearly designed as an escape from the hardships of twenty-first century living: some bad things did happen here, but ultimately everything could be sorted out by the patriarch, Lord Grantham. This show states that everyone has their place in the world, and is strongly didactic about the need for obedience and loyalty, while reassuring that both will be rewarded. As a fable for modern society, it did seem to be acting as a mouthpiece for the Tory-led Coalition government, which had come to power in May 2010, just a few months before *Downton* first aired on ITV. The links between the two were further strengthened by the show's creator, Julian Fellowes, who is a Conservative peer, and by the way it was embraced by the right-wing press in Britain. Partly as a result of this, many critics expressed distaste for *Downton's* rosy view of history and deliberate invoking of traditional heritage values. But while is it is easy and tempting to condemn *Downton*, it does represent an important attempt to write the working classes back into history and it also makes that history more accessible and watchable, for a wide audience, than it had been on television for decades.

As I will discuss in Chapter 4, *Mr Selfridge* attempts to follow in the footsteps of *Downton*, by also concerning itself with those who work for a living, alongside the more glamorous lives of their employers.

Interestingly, however, it is much more cynical about the aristocracy and the British Establishment, and much more determined to reject certain types of nostalgia and to embrace modernity, in a way that is the very antithesis of the *Downton* ethos. *Mr Selfridge* also feels more relevant, more deliberately modern, than any other of the dramas under investigation here, for its central characters are not servants but the urban white-collar workers who may be expected to make up a good proportion of its audience. The meritocracy it advocates has a similar value system to *Downton*'s, however: in both shows, hierarchies give security, loyalty is rewarded and the patriarch knows best. In this regard, the liberal illusion that talent will be recognised and encouraged is also problematic. This show offers a fascinating attempt to sanitise capitalism and consumerism, at a time when both had recently been severely threatened by a "double-dip" recession in Britain (from 2008 to 2012). Most revealing, however, is its commentary on nationality and patriotism: if *Downton* is a symbol of, and advertisement for, an idealised, united Britain (where Scottish, Irish and Welsh characters work peaceably side by side) *Mr Selfridge* is much less inclusive, its regional actors losing their accents while occupying a London-centric world. This series portrays a state which ostensibly embraces Europe and America, but in which everyone, even the eponymous employer, aspires to be English, and are prepared to go to any lengths to prove it – even if that includes supporting the Empire and the First World War in ways that are highly unusual for a contemporary show.

The War and the change it brings plays a crucial part in the next drama I examine here, *Parade's End*. Quite aside from whether or not it is "post-heritage," this show is clearly "post-*Downton*." Hence it represents a deliberate movement away from the soap-opera style versions of history offered by Fellowes's show, *Mr Selfridge* and even the slightly more highbrow *The Forsyte Saga*. Like the latter, it displays an interestingly anti-nostalgic preoccupation with modernism; unlike it, it allows this modern experimentalism to shape its form as well as its content. Hence, a complex narrative structure and unusual camera techniques sit alongside deliberately ambivalent morality, which refuses to tell the audience what to think. In this regard *Parade's End*, although in many ways a faithful adaptation of its source text, is much more innovative than the usual neo-Edwardian fare: difficult and demanding, it is not at all like comforting, escapist Sunday night television. Nonetheless, in its unrelentingly focus on the upper classes it is less interested in class tension and commentary than any of the others I explore here, and indeed, with its deliberately highbrow approach it could be said that it is elitist in regard to its target audience too. This drama is, however, another example of an individual struggling against the confines of his society, and seems to remind us that even the upper classes can be outsiders: privilege is no guarantee of happiness or of belonging. And the pointless and often cruel conventions and performances of this world are destructive to all the central characters, just as much as the War, which is its most grotesque manifestation. However, even while it condemns this aristocratic society, this drama legitimises the upper class, public school-educated control of Britain in the twentieth century and indeed the twenty-first century, through the intelligence, sensitivity and morality of its hero, Tietjens. The War and the humiliations and horrors it brings must be endured by Tietjens, but he comes safely out the other side, making an unconventional but fitting union with his intellectual and social equal, Valentine. So, even in this highly self-conscious exploration of social change and modernity, a conservative agenda is apparent: history is still a narrative of rich, intellectual, privileged white men and women.

The final text I explore here attempts to redress this balance. Like *Parade's End*, *The Village* is a reaction against, and rejection of, *Downton Abbey*, but, unlike it, chooses to focus primarily on the working classes. As a result, it is the most post-heritage, or even anti-heritage, drama in this book. An exploration of the life of a farming community from 1914 onward, there is no glossing over or sanitising of the past in this drama: the homes of the poor are dark and bare, and violence and disease is a daily reality, as is constant anxiety about poverty and economic failure. There is no kindly patriarch here who will look after his tenants, and indeed those in positions of power are either corrupt and abusive, or distracted and uncaring. As a parable for modern life, it is scathing: it is unsurprising that the right-wing press disapproved strongly of its political implications. As a picture of the past, it has a gritty authenticity which most period dramas lack. *The Village* sets out to insert the working classes properly back into history: not as inaccurately contented employees of the rich, but as people in their own right. There are difficulties with its representations, however: conversation is kept to a minimum, as is character interiority, and plotlines are deliberately unresolved and unexplained in a way that recalls *Parade's End*. As a result, *The Village* does not seem designed to be popular viewing. Moreover, it does not offer the viewing pleasures we associate with historical fictions. *Downton Abbey* and other dramas succeed in immersing us into history by entertaining us and making the past seem very close, very familiar and rather comforting. Of course there are ideological problems with this, but it is successful both in terms of ratings and in making history accessible. *The Village* does not seek that soap-opera familiarity with its characters and cannot establish the same closeness with its audience, remaining an intellectual effort rather than a pleasure. After all, apart from the stunning scenery – which still markets England as tourist attraction – there is little to enjoy about this bleak world, and we as viewers are merely thankful that it is not ours.

With the notable exception of *The Village*, it is apparent here that, for me, most Edwardian period drama is still politically conservative, whether or not it is adapted from a highly experimental, anti-establishment novel or is written for television by a twenty-first century production team. That said, these programmes are not only about class. And most of them are as progressive about gender concerns as they are reactionary about privilege and social hierarchies, and becoming more so as the years pass. My comments about *The Forsyte Saga* in Chapter 2 imply some reservations about that series' sexual politics: this drama is ambiguous about the morality of rape in a way that seems to me highly problematic (and which I do not think we would see on television today, only 13 years later). But it is after all fundamentally a sympathetic exploration of women's social and economic vulnerability. By the start of a new decade *Mr Selfridge* is preoccupied with the ambitions and appetites – physical, financial and even sartorial – of its female characters, and confronts the problems they face as working women in the modern era. *Parade's End*, too, foregrounds female sexual desire and intellectual frustration, focusing on its complex and angry female lead even at the expense of marginalising its hero, Tietjens. In terms of their politics these dramas are much more sympathetic to women and women's issues than most other dramas on television (at a time when detective shows like BBC2's hugely successful *The Fall* (2013–) have been accused of making misogynistic violence against women more mainstream than ever before (Cooke, 2014)). *Downton* could be considered the exception to this, however, for while the majority of its most central characters are female and the plot follows their movement towards modernity, it chooses to be disparaging about the women's movement and is as anxious about sexuality and desire as the other dramas here are positive. That said, it never forgets the pleasures of its female viewer, catering for their desiring gaze with its sumptuous costumes and handsome male actors: it is just that looking, in *Downton*, is much safer than action.

There are other ways in which these dramas can all be considered progressively post-heritage. For example, they are all self-conscious, meta-fictional and often tongue-in-cheek in the ways in which they acknowledge their debt to period television in earlier decades, and indeed to each other. In this way they actively engage with "heritage" criticism, too. *Downton Abbey* borrows from EM Forster and Jane Austen adaptations, and from *Upstairs Downstairs*; *Mr Selfridge* applies *Downton's* winning formula to a department store and recalls the *House Of Elliot* in doing so; *Parade's End* has the love/hate marital relations of *The Forsyte Saga* and the war-torn anguish of *The Shooting Party*; *The Village* sets out to be a British version of the German drama *Heimat* (1984–2013). All are in dialogue, one way or another, with a tradition of period drama which stretches back to the earliest days of cinema and television, becomes hugely popular in the late 1960s and 1970s, and has continued to evolve since. They are also, in some cases, experimental with their camera techniques, from *Parade's End* Vortican-style split screen to *The Forsyte Saga's* use of uncomfortable close up. But these are within limits: with the exception of *Mr Selfridge*, all these shows, including *The Village*, are still fond of nostalgic long shots of the stately home or the English countryside, which has become so typical of heritage television. Yet even that is problematised: in *The Forsyte Saga* and *Parade's End*, the audience's view of the houses in question is frequently interrupted, obstructed or incomplete. This is a nice metaphor for the ways these shows both offer and thwart what we expect from costume drama, indulging us with visually captivating television, but withholding escapist emersion in the past by reminding us of its flaws. Once again *Downton* is the exception here, by offering a world we might indeed like to inhabit. Hence *Downton* is at once the most conservative and yet the most popular show in this book. This is only true of its earlier, idyllic Edwardian years, however: by the time it moves into the 1920s, even this show has lost its innocence, with plotlines which include the rape of one much-loved character and the death of another.

I have been selective with the texts picked here: they represent most of those neo-Edwardian fictions screened since the start of the twenty-first century, but are not exhaustive: some others are only discussed briefly. I have endeavoured, however, to mix the types of text I examine. All period dramas are considered to be essentially middlebrow, but *Downton* and *Mr Selfridge* offer a type of history that sets out to be rather less intellectually demanding, and watchable and accessible to all. The emphasis is on plot and character, and they aim to entertain, and even educate, through identification with familiar characters like those from our favourite soap. *Parade's End* and *The Village* are rather different, for they set out to make history into art, and to problematise questions surrounding the representation of the past. *The Forsyte Saga,* the earliest and in some ways the most "classic" show explored here, falls in complicated ways between the two approaches. My focus is on drama, and so I have not discussed comic representations of the period, like *Up the Women* and the First World War sitcom *Chickens* (2013–), deeply revealing though they undeniably are. I should also say that I have been flexible with my definition of "Edwardian": Edward VII was on the throne from 1901 until 1910, but I have included the First World War in my consideration of the period, as many historians have also done. I have also included series which begin and end either side of this time frame, given that most of the texts here are deliberately covering a transitional historical period extending over several decades. Hence *The Forsyte Saga* begins in the late Victorian era before moving on into the twentieth century, and has been considered by Iris Kleinecke-Bates to be an example of Victorianism on screen, in her book on the topic (2014). My interest in this drama focuses upon its movement towards, and anticipation of, modernity rather than its portrayal of Victorian life, however, and as the novels were written by Galsworthy between 1906 and 1920, *The Forsyte Saga* can be considered in itself an early neo-Edwardian text, as Sarah Edwards has discussed (2011). As a further complication, as most of series two is set in the 1920s I will focus here mainly on series one. Similarly *Downton,* as I have indicated, is currently continuing on well into the 1920s, as is *The Village* and *Mr Selfridge,* which is now in its third season, and all show no sign of stopping there. I have considered these too late for inclusion in an exploration of the Edwardian period on screen, and only discussed the pre-1920 series, though I have discussed the later seasons of *Downton* – with plotlines which include the rape and death of key characters – elsewhere (Byrne, 2014). It will be interesting to see, however, if *Mr Selfridge* follows *Downton's* and *the Forsyte Saga's* pattern of arguably losing momentum, and certainly losing viewers, as it moves into the 1920s. There is something about the Edwardian period which captivates audiences in ways which the – more recognisably modern – post-War world does not. What it is about those years that so appeals to our contemporary tastes, and how they relate to our own, I will now set out to consider.

# 1
# The Edwardians in Popular Memory

In *Downton Abbey*'s Christmas special for 2014, the Dowager Countess, Violet, is reliving her past to Isobel Crawley and, for once departing from her usual very proper persona, is remembering the passionate affair she had with a Russian prince as a younger woman:

> "At the royal wedding we fell madly in love. And after weeks of balls and midnight skating to the stains of the balalaika ... we resolved to elope ... to set sail on the Prince's yacht..." [Isobel] "And you've never strayed again?" [Violet] "I've never *risked* everything again." [Isobel] "That's not quite what I asked."[Violet] "And it's all the answer you'll get. Remember, we were the *Edwardians*." (*Downton*, Christmas 2014, emphasis Violet's)

No more details are given, but as Violet smiles suggestively and smugly, the implication of her enigmatic response is clear. Her generation may have looked like the respectable, buttoned up successors to the Victorians, and were always discreet about their wrongdoings, but they knew how to have a good time. The upper-class life Violet describes here is one where intrigue and adultery are set against a backdrop of luxury and parties. There are strict social rules, but there is also indulgence and the beginnings of modern sensibilities about sexuality. This seems to sum up our contemporary view of the Edwardian period: as a transitional time when Victorian repression was beginning to give way to modern permissiveness, and where life was very pleasant – if only for a select few, like the characters in *Downton*. But those few are those whose lives we know most about, and who we choose to remember.

Almost every recent history of Edwardian England begins with a reference to the first years of the twentieth century as something warm, sunlit and peaceful: "a long summer afternoon" (Powell, 1996: vii) or "the sunshine days of the twentieth century" as Rowland describes it (1968: ix). This is not just a late twentieth-century perspective: by the time the First World War ended, the years I will describe as the Edwardian period had already become preserved in popular memory as "the last brilliant phrase and expression of a golden age of peace and prosperity ... of stability and imperial splendour before the cataclysm of the first world war and all the problems that followed in its wake" (Brooks, 1995: 1). England was at this point still "the country that other nations wanted to imitate": the world's major financial power, stable – free from threats external and internal – and head of a vast empire (Lloyd, 1970: 2). This image of those pre-War years has stayed with us ever since, with very little reconstruction; it was consolidated by the Merchant Ivory films of the 1980s and, thanks to *Downton Abbey* and its like, now endures into the twenty-first century too. These are only a fraction of the many fictions which portray and construct the Edwardians, however. Many of these are conflicted and ambivalent, especially from the 1970s on, and are torn between competing views of the era. This chapter will consider some of the ways the period has been portrayed and understood in popular memory, on and off screen, throughout the twentieth century, as context for the exploration of recent television in the rest of this book.

Of course, as Brooks has noted, this idea of the period as a peaceful and golden "Indian summer" was and is a sanitised idealisation of years of transition and turbulence. In fact, it was the "interval between the outbreak of two wars" – the Boer war and the First World War – in which feminism, trade unionism and problems with Ireland contributed to a state of flux and conflict (Brooks, 1995: 1). However, as the change such issues finally resulted in – female suffrage, greater class equality and the beginnings of the welfare state – were positive steps on the road to modernity, perhaps the instability of these years has been overshadowed by the sense of them as a time of progressive social improvement. Certainly many of the famous literary figures of the time were positive about the changes taking place in their world – while still aware of the social problems – and felt that their age was laying the groundwork for a better future. In the years before the First World War, writers like Shaw, Wells and the much-adapted Galsworthy displayed "an optimism as to the social fruits of the liberal and rationalistic thought which they expressed" (Coates, 1946: 1). From the suffragette movement to the 1911 National Insurance Act, their age seemed full of possibility for, and willingness towards, change. The literature of the era hence has a part to play in the construction of the Edwardian era as a golden age. Moreover, the opening years of the twentieth century contrasted favourably with what came before and after. JIM Steward, writing in 1963, saw the Edwardian world as one of serenity compared to the turbulent nineteenth century: in 1904 "the Victorian age, in its departing, seems obligingly to have taken most of its anxieties in its baggage. The solvents glimpsed and dreaded by our grandfathers have flooded in and done their work, yet the large and liberal fabric of modern European civilisation triumphantly stands" (Steward, 1963: 9). And, of course, the war-scarred generation who followed the Edwardians were only too aware of the crumbling of that civilisation, and were not at all "hopeful about the world's political future," as I shall discuss further in relation to *Parade's End* (Coates, 1946: 1). For them, the first years of the twentieth century were the last in which the world seemed a certain and civilised place, and 1914 became a watershed moment in human history in which "the lights went out all over Europe, and will not be lit again in our time" (Grey, 1925: 20).

So, for most, the outbreak of war ensured that the Edwardian era was looked back at, over the chasm of the trenches, as an idealised period of tranquillity and prosperity. For some, however, the existence of the War itself cast a contaminating shadow over those prior years. As Samuel Hynes has convincingly argued, the outbreak of war cast this golden period in a new light in the eyes of some disillusioned writers and critics, who believed that there could be, and had been, too much of a good thing. Man of letters Edmund Gross, for example, reflected in 1914 on the Edwardian era as a period of such pleasure and security that it gave rise to a kind of dangerous complacency which only war could do away with:

> we have awakened from an opium-dream of comfort, of ease, of that miserable poltroonery of "the sheltered life." Our wish for indulgence of every sort, our laxity of manners, our wretched sensitiveness to personal inconvenience, these are suddenly lifted before us in their true guise as the spectres of national decay, and we have risen from the lethargy of our dilettantism to lay them, before it is too late, by the flashing of the unsheathed sword. (Gross, 1914: 331)

The pre-War life of comfort and serenity is here exposed as idleness and luxury, which eroded Britain's values and was particularly damaging (it is implied rather than stated) for English masculinity. As Hynes says, the War becomes "a judgement on that life of indulgent civility: it had all been *too* pleasant" and must therefore come to an end (1990: 12). War was also a cure for the social problems that accompanied this decadence, for, in the eyes of Gross and other writers like Wells, the patriotism, hardship and self-denial which accompanied conflict would drive out the nation's weaknesses. I will return to this understanding of, and justification for, the First World War in Chapter 5: for now I simply wish to note that as soon as it ended, the Edwardian period became, for some, a naïve, transient and self-indulgent dream which brought about its own crude awakening – but which was, perhaps, no less seductive for all that.

All these views of the period, though, were of course only applicable to a certain section of the population: those who were wealthy enough to have enjoyed the delights of this privileged world. There was very little that was golden, or dreamlike, about the pre-war years if you were working class. Despite its potential for change, this remained a time of great social inequality: by 1906, still "half the national capital belonged to one-seventieth of the population" (Rowland 1968: xv). The infant mortality rate, always a good indicator of poverty, remained high (approx. 150 per 1,000 births) and did not drop significantly until the 1920s, after it became the subject of medical authority campaigns. Schooling improved after Balfour's 1902 Education Acts, but it would be after the First World War, and more Acts in 1907 and 1918, before this benefited working-class children in any significant way.

Most of the texts I will examine here are aware of these issues, even if they do not directly acknowledge them: much of the dynamism of such historical fictions is given by that tension between peace and tranquillity on the surface, and the awareness of just what they are choosing to silence, ignore or sanitise about class and poverty. Only the subject of Chapter 6, Peter Moffat's *The Village* (2013–), makes an attempt to represent on screen the grittiness and hardship of lower-class life in these years. This series forms a stark contrast with, and answer to, *Downton Abbey*, portraying domestic violence, alcoholism and poverty, and as a result was embraced initially at least, by many critics. Others condemned its "unrelenting grimness" (Infante, 2013), and as its viewing figures lacked the clout of more glossy programmes it seems likely that public simply do not have the appetite for this kind of "reality" (Glennie, 2014).[1] They do, however, remain hungry for representations of this particular era – perhaps, arguably, even more than other in history. No other period has been the subject, or at least the starting point, of so many highly successful period dramas as the first 15 years of the twentieth century, as the texts I will discuss here reveal. The Regency and Victorian periods have always been popular on screen, since the earliest days of film and television relied heavily on adaptations of nineteenth-century novels, and of course remain so: their latest presence includes BBC adaptations of Dickens's novels *Great Expectations* (2011), and *Little Dorrit* (2008), and the neo-Victorian crime drama *Ripper Street* (2012–). These do, however, lack the mainstream appeal of *Downton* or *Mr Selfridge*:[2] something about thus period attracts and moves huge audiences (*Downton* has of course now moved into the 1920s, but its quality, and its hold over its audience have not quite moved with it).[3] This "golden summer" seems to have exhorted a powerful hold over the popular imagination. Perhaps that is not only because of the class-blind, rose-tinted image of those years, but also because of the deep poignancy and nostalgia which is given by their being the end of an era. As Virginia Woolf famously said, the world changed for ever around 1910, and it is that combination of ending and beginning, at once nostalgic and modern, which may make the Edwardians so appealing to modern audiences.

It is also, of course, currently the centenary of the Edwardian period and this has made this past more present. As I write Britain is in the midst of commemorations of 100 years since the start of the First World War: two years ago it commemorated the sinking of the Titanic. The portrayal in the media of both centenaries have made real, modern and very public, events which a few years ago were simply past. They have also, of course, made history consumable in problematic ways, especially when it is the history of tragedy: popular remembrance has come close to celebration in some instances, and is wrapped up with patriotism in others. Lisa Jardine's comments about the First World War galleries recently opened at the Imperial War museum are interesting to recall here. She suggests that these much visited exhibitions lose much of the horror of warfare in favour of instilling national pride. "There is an atmosphere close to veneration, disturbingly close to celebration of what Britons were prepared to undertake for their nation ... where are the lessons for us as individuals about the consequences of conflict? ... Wars are not heroic" (Jardine, 2014). Jardine notes that while the Museum has been making the history of warfare consumable since it opened in 1920, recently the tone of the displays have changed, becoming less frightening and more pleasurable to view. Similarly, Paul Cummins's and Tom Piper's commemorative art exhibition "Blood Swept Lands and Seas of Red," in which the Tower of London was transformed by 888,246 ceramic poppies to represent fallen soldiers of the First World War, has also caused controversy. *Guardian* art critic Jonathan Jones, for example, condemned the memorial, which he regarded to be xenophobic because it only celebrated British and British colonial soldiers, not those of other nations. In his view this is evocative of "an inward looking mood which lets UKIP thrive" (*Guardian*, 28th October 2014). He also considered the "deeply aestheticized" nature of the installation to be inappropriate, noting that "a meaningful mass memorial would not be dignified or pretty. It would be gory, vile and terrible to see." Jones's comments prompted a furious public backlash, which was in itself indicative not only of the popularity of the memorial but also perhaps of the way the War has come to act as a marker of Britishness, particularly in the right-wing press (see for example the response to Jones in the *Mail Online*). His views were, however, shared by other critics like Jardine, who considered that the "wave of patriotic feeling" the poppies inspired in her must be a dangerous thing, and that memorials should caution against war, not glorify it (2014). Of course, the poppy itself has become the centre of debates even before this year's centenary. Author Ted Harrison and newsreader John Snow have in recent years expressed concern about the power of the poppy: Snow has termed the strength of national feeling about the flower "poppy fascism," after his decision not to wear one on air was widely criticised by those who considered it unpatriotic (Revoir, 2011).[4] The poppy, and the War it recalls, have become really important to British identity.

Popular history, then, serves much more than an academic or didactic function: it has been frequently reclaimed as a source of patriotism and national pride – as I will discuss further in Chapter 4. In the process of this "nationalisation of history," of course, something of that history itself is frequently lost, or at least transformed in problematic ways. The conflating of history and capitalism is one example: this can be seen, of course, in the television industry which makes money from its portrayals of the past in all the heritage dramas I mention in this book. It finds even more direct and undigested forms, however, like, for example, the Sainsbury's Christmas advertisement broadcast on television in December 2014. Jerome de Groot has written about the significant role commercials have played in the exploitation of nostalgia, suggesting that they are "direct ways in which history is experienced as something to be consumed ... history is one of a number of fetishized discourses that can be used to market commodities" (2009: 8–9). In this regard, the First World War is currently particularly fetishised by our culture and thus especially valuable to capitalism. This advert is a collaboration between the supermarket and the British Legion, which dramatises the Christmas truce and football game that occurred in the first year of the First World War. The advert presents the Germans and the British exchanging their supplies from home in the spirit of the season, including a chocolate bar which is currently on sale in Sainsbury's and the profits from which will go to the Legion. The collision between consumable past and consumable present here is striking. Sainsbury's have taken care to ensure the advert is historically accurate; it looks like a short film and is quite moving in its Christmas message of peace and collaboration. Despite this, the attempt by a supermarket to exploit the emotions surrounding the conflict, for its own advertising purposes, is potentially distasteful. It is also, however, a clear measurement of the extent of public feeling about the centenary of the First World War, which triggers such patriotic feeling in so many people and which this supermarket wishes to utilise as a means of constructing itself as a very British institution.

As Jardine indicates, it is difficult to charter the line between commemoration and inappropriate celebration: indeed, we might add, the line between commemoration and capitalist exploitation is also a very fine one. This is not confined to the War: the centenary of the sinking of the Titanic was also an example of Edwardian history made consumable, and of the sense of real horror of the disaster being disregarded in the process. Fellowes continued his plundering of the period with the drama *Titanic*, the most recent of many revisitings of the event on the big and small screen. While it was condemned by critics as little more than "*Downton*-on-sea," it did at least remind viewers of the tragic stories of those on board (Groskop, 2012). More successful, but less genuinely commemorative, was the opening in my home town, Belfast, of a newly gentrified "Titanic quarter" of the city, and various "celebrations" of Belfast's connection with the ship. Belfast firm Harland and Wolff built the RMS Titanic: hardly a connection to be proud of, but one which has been utilised by the tourist industry here and has now become "heritage." Hence the opening in 2012 of *Titanic Belfast*, a museum devoted to the ship, which has now become Northern Ireland's biggest tourist attraction. The sense in which this is an "experience" of, rather than a memorial for, the disaster is potentially unpalatable, but the hundreds of thousands of people who have flocked there would presumably not agree. However, in another commercialisation of history, around the time of the centenary local bars offered "Tangtanics," cocktails with Titanic shaped ice cubes – and these do seem to cross the line into bad taste.

So, at the same time as we view the Edwardian period as a charmed era, we are also determined to revisit and even inappropriately celebrate its tragedies as well. Perhaps we, in our post-9/11, War on Terror world, can identify all too well with catastrophe, and there is safety and perhaps comfort in mourning tragedy which is long past and remote from us. Yet it is interesting that it is the early years of the twentieth century which currently preoccupy us more than, say, the Plague, the great Fire of London, or the Napoleonic, Crimean or Boer wars. Other explanations must also exist for our cultural fascination with the period. It is, for example, tempting to make connections between the Edwardian's sense of their own era and ours of our own. All the neo-Edwardian texts I examine here are deliberately marketing Englishness and are self-consciously aware of their status as "heritage" products. Most exploit and play on this: some, namely *Parade's End,* try to resist it. Either way, this is appropriate given that, as Anthea Trodd has argued, the Edwardians were preoccupied with their own legacy and with its relationship with national identity. The Edwardian obsession with the "invention of tradition" took many forms, from the celebration of the British monarchy to the publishing of a British canon by new publishing houses. The Worlds' Classic series in 1901 (taken over by Oxford in 1905) and the Everyman's library from 1906, "defined the works they published as classics to the new reading generation" and promoted English literature as a valuable contribution towards "imperial dignity" (Trodd, 2-3:1991). The Edwardians were newly aware that Englishness could be at once celebrated and constructed by the establishment of a great tradition of art: they believed that the Empire should be a cultural as well as a physical and economic entity. Now, in the twenty-first century, that Empire may not be able to be unambiguously celebrated in the same way – although *Mr Selfridge* does not seem to agree, as we will discuss in Chapter 3! This kind of cultural imperialism is, however, still perpetuated by our television screens and their countless adaptations of "great" British fiction, and their celebration of the Edwardian "golden age."

## Edwardians in twentieth-century television and film

As Claire Monk has noted, "many past decades were moments of historical/costume drama innovation [but] the terrain of British television period drama in the 1970s ... is of special interest for its simultaneous closeness to and distance from the present" (2015: 36).

That is particularly true for my purposes, for the 1970s was the decade when representations of the early twentieth century really became mainstream popular viewing. Indeed, the decade revealed a wider fascination with the period which was not confined to the media, and has since been identified as an "Edwardian revival." In a way which makes our consumption of Edwardian television and *Downton Abbey* bath products seem relatively modest, it was a cultural moment when "Laura Ashley dresses flew off the rails, *The Country Diary of an Edwardian Lady* topped the bestseller list, and *Upstairs, Downstairs* took over on TV" (York, 2007). The resurgence of rockabilly in the 1970s also resurrected Edwardian fashion for men, as worn since the 1950s by the "Teddy boy" – named, of course, after Edward VII. As regards television, we can date this historical fascination from 1967, when *"The Forsyte Saga* burst onto the scene ... giving BBC2 its first big success" (Cooke, 2003: 112:). Following this, several of British television's most popular and long-running productions were historical fictions dealing with the Edwardian period. ATV's *Edward the King (*also known as *Edward the Seventh*) in 1975, and BBC's *The Duchess of Duke Street* in 1976/77, for example, were both Emmy-award winning, if not especially long-lived, and the hugely successful *Upstairs Downstairs* (LWT) began being broadcast in 1971. These were all, however, following in the wake of *The Forsyte Saga*, which "became a broadcasting phenomenon on both side of the Atlantic" (Baskin, 1996: 83) and which really began the mix of soap opera and "quality" television which recent historical dramas would try to emulate. It set out to combine the new commercial success of the Soap – as epitomised by *Coronation Street*, from 1960 onwards – with the classic novel adaptations which the BBC had traditionally relied heavily upon as a source for its programming. Hence "The Galsworthy saga seemed particularly right for the role: being more middlebrow than highbrow ... having 'quality overtones' (as a literary, costume drama) yet also having enough popular appeal (its soap opera qualities) to attract a broad audience" (Cooke, 2003: 83). As Sarah Crompton has noted, however, that adaptation was not entirely faithful to Galsworthy's text, becoming more sensational and more tolerant of extra-marital sex in order to "appeal to popular taste in the Swinging Sixties." Of course, this combination worked: famously, 18 million viewers tuned in for its (repeated) final episode, and so *The Forsyte Saga* became television history, and despite some poor reviews for acting, "has come to represent every value and standard to which British television has aspired ever since" (Crompton, 2002).

Its long time frame stretches from the late Victorian to the inter-War period, and so it cannot be defined only as an Edwardian drama (though, significantly, its 2002 remake confines itself much more to the early twentieth-century, as I will discuss in Chapter 3). Its focus is perhaps less on the past than on modernity, anyway: its family relationships are timeless, and its twin preoccupations are the acquisition of property and of women, with most of the Forsytes driven by the pursuits of one or the other, or both. Of course, this captures the zeitgeist of the 1960s, reflecting the interests of a post-sexual revolution audience: this drama functions as a critique of bourgeois morality and advocates sexual and personal freedoms. Its focus on family, money and illicit relationships would provide the inspiration for any number of family dramas, contemporary as well as historical, in the years that followed. As Rupert Smith notes, "the success of the show in the States ... led producers to develop new extended formats for high-profile series, thus giving birth to the mini-series and to the Byzantine family dramas *Dallas* and *Dynasty*" (Smith, 2002: 35). These are just some of the inheritors of this formula in the later 1970s and 1980s, and of course period television was irrevocably changed by *The Forsyte Saga*, which inspired Andrew Davies and others to make the past more accessible and entertaining by foregrounding romance and sexual desire.

*The Forsyte Saga*, while having many soap-like qualities, is focused on the upper-middle class: young Jolyon risks social condemnation by loving his governess, but soon rescues her from her position and places her within a more affluent setting. *Upstairs Downstairs* is thus the first period drama to really capture the working-class ethos of the phenomenon that *Coronation Street* had recently become. It is also the point at which the Edwardian era really becomes popular on the small screen. *Upstairs Downstairs* is most interesting for its historical representation of the period: it is carefully detailed, moving, deliberately unhurried, from 1903 to the 1920s, chronicling the sinking of the Titanic, the politics of the period, the outbreak of War and every other significant event along the way. In this way it functions as a kind of history lesson for its viewers – while astutely reminding them that "history" as we are usually taught it is something that happened to the higher classes, not their employees. This long running and hugely successful drama captivated audiences with its portrayal of life below stairs and maintains a focus on the servants class that *Downton*, for all it sets out to follow the same formula, does not quite manage. It was famously conceived of by Jean Marsh and Eileen Atkins as a response to *The Forsyte Saga*, which they noticed ignored the family servants, and hence *Upstairs Downstairs* aims to "correct this glaring fault in British TV's portrayal of the class system" (Cornell et al., 1993: 386). Unlike *Downton* and unlike its recent (2011) remaking by the BBC, this show stays resolutely with the servants' quarters, only venturing "upstairs" for a relatively small amount of its screening time and making no attempt to gloss over the unsympathetic treatment of the staff by their employers. In this way at least, it invites social critique in a way which seems radical and leftist by the standards of *Downton Abbey* or *Mr Selfridge*. The privileged selfishness and snobbishness of Lady Marjorie Bellamy is clearly apparent in most episodes, from the opening moments of the series when she changes the name of the new parlour maid to "Sarah" because the name she already has, Clemance, is too "French" and glamorous for a servant (series 1, episode 1). (Notably, however, none of the other servants question this undermining of identity and she remains "Sarah" for the rest of the series). Even those occasions when she intervenes to assist and protect her servants – something which Lord Grantham in *Downton* regularly does out of paternalism and affection– are born out of self-interest rather than altruism or compassion. Episode 4 of the first series, for example, features the mental illness of the Cook, and her subsequent arrest by the police, but Lady Marjorie's intervention is mostly born out of concern for the important dinner party she is hosting next week. The viewer cannot be other than condemnatory of this lack of social conscience, although we might be inclined towards sympathy if we consider her also a disenfranchised victim of this patriarchal society, as Helen Wheatley does (2005: 145). Significantly, however, the servants themselves do not condemn Lady Marjorie: the Cook is grateful for her support and Rose the always-sensible head parlour maid (played by one of the series' creators) remains supportive and fond of her mistress. It is difficult to say whether viewers are meant to accept that these servants recognise innate worth in their employers, or if those workers are simply blinded to truth about them. As we will see with *Downton*, characters who aspire to rise "beyond their station" are punished, namely the aforementioned Sarah, who dreams of a better life but endures one humbling catastrophe after another. Her eventual marriage to the chauffeur can be interpreted as her restoration to her own class after being repeatedly involved with her "betters" (even if this marriage did go on to become the subject of a successful spin-off, *Thomas and Sarah*, in 1979). Even more problematically, in a significant exchange with a cynical, even Marxist, member of the lower-middle class, the butler Mr Hobson defends his life of servitude and his employer's life of privilege:

> I am proud and honoured to serve a noble and distinguished family, and I know my place ... We all serve a master unless we are King Edward himself ... I work for a man of charm and character. He's a member of Parliament, and married into one of the great ruling families of the land, with 400 years of political influence behind them. And you ask me if I am content with my position in life? (series 1, episode 2)

Hudson – who is perhaps the source for another unquestioningly loyal butler, Carson in *Downton* – is too articulate and intelligent to really be argued with here: his statement seems to function as an answer to any left-wing critic of the show. This kind of justification of the status quo is probably a faithful representation of the feelings of many real life upper-servants of the time, of course. And it need not take away too much from the many ground-breaking aspects of the series, not least the implied homosexual relationship between the two housemaids. However, Lez Cooke sees the popularity of *Upstairs Downstairs* and similar historical fictions of the period as innately conservative, part of a "cultural shift from the 1960s to the 1970s, from liberalism to conservatism and from consent to coercion:

> The plethora of historical dramas arguably enabled an escape from the increasingly bitter conflicts of 1970s Britain. In some cases there were lessons to be learned from history ... [but] in most cases this was not the main motivation – the attraction for the TV companies in producing multi-episode historical drama series residing more their potential for maximising and retaining audiences. (2003: 112–113)

It is undeniably true that 1970s period drama serves a conservative agenda in many ways. This is especially apparent regarding its representation of, and seeming fascination with, the monarchy. Henry VIII, Elizabeth I and Edward VIII all became the subjects of television drama in the 1970s. In keeping with the general draw of the Edwardian era, however, Edward VII was a particularly fruitful source of subject matter to be harvested. *Edward the King* takes him as its central character, he appears briefly in *Upstairs Downstairs*, and *The Duchess of Duke Street* (1976–1977) features him as the heroine's lover. Cooke considers that the "ideological project" of these dramas is "the humanisation of the monarchy," as well as being a strategy to capitalise on the public fascination with the royal family (2003: 113). Such sympathetic representations as these formed part of a BBC agenda to support the monarchy at a time when they were under threat from anti-Establishment forces. The celebrations which surrounded the Queen's Silver Jubilee in 1977 – an event which has been described as "a last gasp of the spirit of Empire" – created an image of national unity which attempted to disguise the unemployment, strikes and social unrest which wracked Britain in this period. Hence the banning of the Sex Pistol's "God Save the Queen" by the BBC has been considered part of a tactical campaign by a media "in which almost no dissent against the Jubilee was allowed" (Cacciottolo, 2012). Certainly the portrayal of Edward (in *Duchess* and *Edward the King*) as flawed but lovable may serve this kind of monarchist agenda, although it could also be argued that his bad behaviour with women in both dramas (in the former he arranges a sham marriage for the heroine so she can be more effectively his mistress) undermines the sense of mystery and the moral respect the Royal family aimed to command.

Both dramas may be pro-Establishment in their focus on, and sympathetic portrayal of, the upper classes, but they also have important gender commentary which make them, if not quite radical, certainly an interesting response to second-wave feminism. In the early episodes of *Edward the King*, Queen Victoria, played – significantly – rather unglamorously by Annette Crosby, struggles to reconcile motherhood with her political ambitions, frustrated by pregnancies which she has no wish for and which necessitate her temporary withdrawal from her public role. Admittedly it is difficult to fully sympathise with the capricious and spoilt Queen, but the difficulties of her position as both woman and leader are foregrounded in interesting ways. So too is her relationship with Prince Albert, who is clearly indicative of a 1970s, post-feminist (in the original sense of the term) crisis of masculinity. The Queen's consort struggles with his marginalised political role and his problematic public persona, as he is less powerful – and indeed, more domestic – than his wife.

Moreover, *The Duchess of Duke Street* is fundamentally a narrative of ambition and determination, following the journey of social and intellectual self-improvement of the working-class heroine. She begins the series as a lowly assistant cook with aspirations, who works her way to become the manager of a hotel, overcoming sexism and encountering various hardships (including the aforementioned adulterous affair with the Prince of Wales, bankruptcy, illegitimate pregnancy, depression and various other scandals) along the way. Like Crosby's Victoria, her outspoken and single-minded personality is sometimes abrasive: it seems ambitious women are never entirely charming on television in the 1970s (or indeed today). However, her determination to overcome class and gender constraints – and help others, namely her friend and assistant Mary, to do so too – construct her as a likable feminist heroine, and one who also never loses her Cockney accent. Her arrival at the Norton's upper-class home in the first episode is strongly evocative of "Sarah's" first day at the Bellamy's in *Upstairs Downstairs*, but unlike Sarah, she is eventually rewarded rather than punished for her aspirations to be more than a servant. Hence by the end of the first episode she has become skilled enough to be successfully cooking for Prince Edward, and a promising career beckons: by episode 3 she is single-handedly running the Bentinck Hotel. Claire Monk has described – or perhaps dismissed – this drama as a "proto-Thatcherite narrative of upwardly mobile female enterprise" (2015: 48), and indeed it is. For Louisa, hard work and determination can overcome all obstacles. The high cost of this success is not underplayed, however: we see Louisa collapse from exhaustion in one scene, and romantic happiness is ultimately denied her. This drama is also remarkable for its gender politics and particularly its take on motherhood. In a key plotline in series one, the heroine becomes pregnant by her aristocratic lover Charlie, but refuses to marry him in terms which would simply not appear, unjudged, on television today:

> I'm just not cut out to be a wife, anyone's wife. I mean, look at that baby. It's a nice enough little baby but I don't love it. It could be anyone's as far as I'm concerned. Dunno why, I am just made like that. I'd be no good as Lady Haselmere. I'm best left as Louisa Trotter. Best to be honest about things, eh. Not to pull the wool. Just leads to trouble later on. (series 1, episode 5)

Again in a link with the gender dynamic in *Edward the King*, Charlie is more interested in the child that Louisa – and it is he who takes charge of it. The challenge to conventional gender roles is apparent here and is particularly interesting because there is no condemnation, either from her lover or the plot, about Louisa's unsentimental attitude towards motherhood. She is simply determined to get back to work and not to allow her considerable sexual appetites, and their consequences, to distract her from it again.

This was not the only example of strongly feminist Edwardian television made in the 1970s. The 1974 six-part series *Shoulder to Shoulder* was a "landmark BBC drama documenting the history of feminism" (Ball and McCabe, 2014), which chartered the rise of the suffragette movement at the beginning of the twentieth century, as shaped by the Pankhurst family. It is exceptional for its almost entirely female cast and single-minded devotion to political issues, and is unglamorous, with gritty portrayals of imprisonment and hunger strikes, and a general sense of anger directed at the Establishment and especially the police. All this, as McCabe and Ball have noted in their recent revisiting of the series, "chimed in with Britain in the early 1970s. The IRA bombing campaign (with the Price Sisters on hunger strike in Holloway prison – and forcibly fed), industrial strife and economic crisis meant that the series carried more than a whiff of controversy" (2014). *Shoulder to Shoulder* thus establishes clear links between the Edwardian period and the 1970s, but it differs dramatically in tone from most neo-Edwardian series of then or today. It does have some echoes of *The Forsyte Saga* in its portrayal of the tensions and jealousies of a powerful family, but it is careful to represent working-class characters alongside its representation of the privileged Pankhursts. It is significant, then, that today it has been almost forgotten, rarely-repeated by the BBC and never released on DVD, to the annoyance of feminist critics who are aware of the importance of rewriting the Woman's Movement into our past:

> Remembering *Shoulder to Shoulder* isn't only about reclaiming our stories, but about who has the power to tell them. Even within the production of the series there was a feminist struggle (of sorts) between an ideal and a challenging of power from the margins – Mackenzie, and a shattering of the glass ceiling and ability to change the script but from the inside – Lambert. This remembering of the earlier fight for emancipation happened in the early 1970s at a time when a new feminism was struggling over questions of inequality, images of woman as Other and the culturally awkward position of women within the public sphere and their right to speak. Forty years later and we remain preoccupied with similar questions. (Ball and McCabe , 2014)

As McCabe and Ball note, these issues are still with us in the twenty-first century, and perhaps partly as a result of this there are ongoing

issues with the representation of first-wave feminism in contemporary costume drama. As we will see, most of the texts I explore here
do not give the suffrage movement as much narrative space as they
might, given its importance to the political atmosphere of the period.
Instead they prefer to engage with Edwardian gender politics via more
accessible and less controversial means, namely sexual and marital
plots, which take centre stage. Moreover, they are far from idealistic
about relationships between women, who are usually represented as
rivals or even enemies: June and Irene in *The Forsyte Saga* and the
older Crawley sisters in *Downton* are two examples of this, Grace and
Martha in *The Village* are another. *Shoulder to Shoulder*, in contrast,
places an emphasis on female solidarity and support: "hate can unite
us, but so did friendship" as Sylvia Pankhurst observes in the closing
moments of the series (*Shoulder to Shoulder*, episode 6). Hence this
drama remains exceptional in its concentration on the feminist struggle untampered by romance – though the story it tells is becoming
more "mainstream": a new retelling of the history of the suffrage,
directed by Sarah Gavron and starring Meryl Streep, is coming to the
big screen later this year.

This study centres upon television drama, but any discussion of
the Edwardians on screen cannot ignore its most influential – and
controversial – representation, the Merchant Ivory films. A result of the
combined skills of Indian producer Ismail Merchant, American director James Ivory and German-born screen writer Ruth Prawer Jhabvala,
this company and its award-winning films – often big adaptations
of canonical Edwardian novels, most usually EM Forster and Henry
James – have dominated public perception of the period. Of course
Merchant Ivory have made many films which are not Edwardian, but
their first big film was the Forster adaptation, *A Room with a View*, which
took over 60 million dollars worldwide – "amazing figures for an art
film" (Long, 1992: 145) – and was nominated for eight academy awards.
Adaptations of *Maurice*, *Howard's End* and *The Golden Bowl* followed,
consolidating Merchant Ivory's reputation as one of the foremost period
filmmakers and also the key depicter of the Edwardian era in the 1980s
and 1990s.[5] The films are famously lavish and beautiful to look at
and often draw upon a highly talented if rather insular cast of actors.
Higson and Dyer and Monk, among others, have been rigorous in
their debate about these films: these were, of course, the productions
which most directly motivated the heritage criticisms of the 1990s
which I discussed in the introduction chapter. In this regard, the whole
concept of "heritage" can be considered to be most directly, though of

course not exclusively, associated with the Edwardian period. Higson notes this in passing, observing that many heritage films "are set in the early decades of [the twentieth century] when the culture of the country house was already in disarray – hence the almost pervasive sense of loss, of nostalgia, which infuses these films" (Higson, 1996: 223). At the same time, however, these adaptations also perpetuate the usual idea of the perpetual Edwardian summer, with England portrayed as a sunny and leafy idyll. There are certain memorable exceptions to this, of course, like the rainy London in which Helen Schlegal first meets Leonard Bast (with ultimately disastrous consequences), but in general it is the beauty and tranquillity of rural England which dominates these films. In this, and in the escapist pleasure this offers the viewer, they follow a visual formula which *Downton Abbey*, and many scenes from *Parade's End* and *The Forsyte Saga*, follow.

Content-wise, Merchant Ivory films, like most late twentieth-century period dramas, are much more progressive regarding their portrayal of sexuality than their source texts. *Maurice* (too risqué to be published in Forester's lifetime) has been applauded for its representation of a homosexual love story, *Room* for its foregrounding of the heroine's desire and *Howard's End* for its unapologetic single mother (who becomes part of an idyllic heritage landscape in the final scenes of the film). Perhaps more true to the novels – but problematically so for many critics – is their class consciousness. In my view, their lack of interest in the working classes is clear and makes *Downton* seem radically inclusive by comparison. Sarah Street has argued that "much of the social critique to be found in Forster's novels does surface in these films" citing the cross-class relationship in *Maurice* and the undermining of upper-class values in *Howards End*, as examples (2009: 118). Certainly, the attitude of these Forster adaptations towards the English upper classes, whose practices and prejudices they chronicle, is satirical as well as affectionate. The behaviour of the Wilcoxes in *Howards End*, for example, is exposed as self-serving greed. That said, however, when Street talks of social critique she really seems to mean towards the upper and middle class. These adaptations may satirise the rich, but tend to simply disregard the poor, showing little interest in the servants who appear in these novels, or indeed in any of the working classes at all. (I am of course excluding from this *The Remains of the Day*, the Oscar-nominated exploration of the repressed romance between two (admittedly upper) servants, as it is an adaptation of a recent novel set in the 1930s and 1950s.) James Ivory has himself acknowledged that his interest, as writer and director, lies with the affluent members of society, even though this may be unpopular with his critics:

> Leonard Bast was an embarrassment – I mean, to have to reproduce his dingy quarters!" "Ruth is speaking humorously – unfortunately she is also providing our critics (mostly American) with more ammunition ... On the other hand, Ruth is right when she implies that I'd soon grow tired of spending too much time reconstructing the world of Leonard Bast ... *I do best with educated upper-middle class people like myself.* (Ivory, quoted in Pym, 86, emphasis mine)

Significantly, this choice is as much aesthetic as political: the working classes are simply much less visually appealing – "dingy" – than the rich, and beauty, for Merchant Ivory, comes first. Ivory has also said that as an American he is absolved from the English class system and should not be judged on his representation of it, but this outsider status does not make his loving recreation of money and privilege any less problematic. That said, these films are complex, and have already been thoroughly discussed and debated by other critics (unlike the rather neglected small-screen period dramas I mentioned earlier). Higson, for example, takes *Howards End* as a case study in his *English Heritage English Cinema*, exploring the film's fascinating "tension between the *narrative* critique of established national traditions, social formulations and identities, and the *visual* celebration of elite culture and a mythic landscape" so fully that there is little further to add (Higson, 2003: 149). All I really wish to do here is to note Merchant's Ivory's contribution to the narrative of beauty and prosperity – undercut by a sense of unease and the poignancy of future loss – which signifies the Edwardian period so persuasively.

Not all 1980s neo-Edwardian films share Merchant Ivory's glossy and sunny vision of the period. *The Shooting Party* (1985), an adaptation of Isabel Colegate's novel of the same name, was released the same year as *A Room with a View,* but is strikingly different in tone and approach. Set at the shooting of the grouse in the October of 1913, its vision of England is still rural, but deliberately grey and autumnal. There is no sunshine and little greenery: even the trees are, significantly, already bare and wintry, stripped of their leaves. This film feels much less about preserving a way of life on screen, than showing its death throes. As it mainly follows the lives of the aristocratic Nettleby family and their guests, it is still, however, mainly preoccupied with the luxurious weekender lives of the upper classes, but also critiques their self-indulgent world and observes their relationship with the working classes who serve them. Indeed, we might recall here Edmund Gross's belief, expressed in 1914, that the idleness and self-indulgence of the upper classes in this period inevitably led to war, for it has resonance in this film which explicitly links this existence with the carnage that eventually destroys it. The voice-over which accompanies the opening scenes of the film shows its social conscience right from its first moments:

life is so extraordinarily pleasant for those of us who are fortunate enough to have been born in the right place. Ought it to be so pleasant? And for so few of us? And isn't there sometimes a kind of satiety about it all, and at the same time, greed?

These questions are explored but remain largely unanswered by the end of the film, given that its melancholy tone implies that the death of this way of life is something to be mourned, even as its unfairness and cruelty are noted. In particular, James Mason's old-fashioned patriarch, Sir Randolph Nettleby, is intelligent and perceptive, as deserving as anyone can be of his privileged status. It is Mason's last role, and he plays it with a "contented civility" which commands the sympathy of the audience and makes it impossible to condemn his way of life (Ebert, 1985) Similarly, the focus on the luxury and beauty of the house, and the physical desirability of most of the cast, make the viewer complicit in this way of life, which is "extraordinarily pleasant" for them as much as for the characters. Yet the film cumulates in the accidental shooting of one of the beaters, which is the result of the competitive and reckless behaviour of one of the guests. This signifies a condemnation of the class exploitation of the time: several of the party resent the interruption to their sport more than the death of a "peasant" (*The Shooting Party*, 1985). The tragedy is also a foreshadowing – a "premonition," as the sensitive Stephens puts it – of the First World War to come, and thus associates and blames the aristocracy and its attitudes for the senseless slaughter that resulted. This is implied by the way in which the grounds of the estate appear reminiscent of the battlefields of France: the grassy space of Nettleby is filmed as though it were a kind of no-man's-land at the beginning and end of the film, both set to military music in John Scott's score, and with the sound of shellfire played over the final scene. The ominous English countryside here is very far from the charming space of *Howards End* or *A Room of One's Own*: even the blue sky, which is visible for the only time in the film, has significant clouds rolling in. Yet there is ideological inconsistency here, for the film seems to imply the condemnation of the careless waste of life – both animal and human, of servants and soldiers – by this privileged society, and yet the viewer cannot help but mourn the passing of those members of the upper classes whose deaths in battle appear in title cards in the final moments. It is hence difficult to decide how the film ultimately wants the viewer to feel about the social change that accompanied the War – but its sombre tone means that this is a film much less concerned with audience pleasure than the others I examine here.

Philip Horn, in an interview with Ruth Prawer Jhabvala, suggested to her that in her 2000 adaptation of Henry James's *The Golden Bowl*, she might have been influenced by the 1998 version of *The Wings of the Dove* (Raw, 2012: 143). This is because this film, like hers, shifted its plot slightly forward to the end of the Edwardian period to embrace modernity more directly: Softley's *Wings* is set in 1910, not 1902 as in the book. As a result Henry James's novel is transformed into "a modernist text" (Gibson, 2000: 120). Jhabvala did not directly answer Horn's question, but it is difficult to imagine that she could not have been influenced by this critically and popularly acclaimed film. *Wings* looks and feels like a Merchant Ivory production in many ways: it is a "lavish visual spectacle" with ornate and luxurious costumes, and the mise-en-scene is beautifully detailed to represent Edwardian interiors at their most glamorous (Gibson, 2000: 121). It is also, however, considered to be an unorthodox, "post-heritage" film, due to its lack of fidelity to its source text, as Claire Monk notes (2002: 284):

> "[*Wings of the Dove*] is acceptable to a certain liberal/left critical taste formation not because of a discernible political stance but because of its liberties with the book, which permit a dark and decadent visual splendour, the depiction of Kate's father" [Michael Gambon] "as a derelict opium addict, and a sexual coupling between Kate [Helena Bonham Carter] and her impoverished lover ..." (2002: 193)

This "dark decadence" seems very different to the typical cinematic Edwardian England I have been describing, and indeed, its gothic overtones make this film more reminiscent of the fin de siècle than anything later. The London it represents is an interesting mix of Victorian opium dens and bustling streets newly populated with motor cars. The past and present are mixed in interesting ways, which invoke the struggle of the heroine, Kate Croy, who is caught between old and new values. More central and sympathetic here than in the novel, she also ensures the female focus of the film, and her struggles with convention and social expectation render her a proto-feminist heroine for a female audience. But the same could be said of *Howards End*, and although this film is interested in modernity, and certainly lacks the sunny feel of Merchant Ivory's Edwardian England, London is as beautiful in every shot as any stately home or rural countryside. Even Densher's very middle-class offices are charming and not at all shabby. Money is the source of Kate Croy's dilemma and anxiety in this film – but it is impossible to take her anxieties about being married to Densher entirely seriously, for poverty is not an actual, visceral reality for any of the characters. The view of the Edwardian period this film offers, then, is still one of privilege and glamour – even if we cannot be entirely nostalgic about the repressive social structures represented there. And that remains the key difference between the representation of the period on the big and small screen: the cinematic version looks more glossy, more stylish, more "heritage." Television from the late 1960s and 1970s is confined by budgetary demands so as to seem more gritty, even when it subject matter is the Royal family itself. Of course that changes dramatically in the new century, when episodes of period dramas can command a million per episode. What *Downton* and *Mr Selfridge* in particular set out to do, then, is to combine the 1970s interest in the working classes, with the luxurious look and feel of a Merchant Ivory film, and please as wide an audience as possible by so doing.

## Conclusion

By the time the First World War, which had rendered it so irretrievably "past," had ended, the Edwardian period had begun to be thought of and about in a certain way. Its construction as a time of peace, prosperity and tranquillity was not entirely historically accurate, but compared to the horrors of war and the deprivation of the years that followed the War – also overshadowed by Spanish 'flu – it certainly did look in retrospect like a charmed era, for the upper classes at least. In the 1920s, changing taxation, the extension of the suffrage for women and the beginnings of the crumbling of the British Empire made the world seem a very different, more unstable and for some more frightening place than it had been just a few years earlier. Hence later reflections on, and representations of, this period are often imbrued with nostalgia and wistfulness, and this endures even today. This is not entirely unique to the Edwardian period, however: some similar things could be said about representations of the inter-war years which appeared after the Second

World War, most famously Waugh's *Brideshead Revisited* (1945). Hence late twentieth-century television and film about the 1920s and 1930s has many points of similarity with that which represents the earlier period. In the 1980s, the television adaptation of *Brideshead* and the highly successful film *Chariots of Fire* (1981), for example, recall 1920s England with a nostalgia akin to that displayed by the adaptations of James or Forster I have considered here. In the last few years, however, it is the Edwardian period which has really dominated our television screens. These historical fictions are not only nostalgic for this golden era of British history, however, but also for the "golden age" of period drama on television: the 1970s. Period dramas look very different now: all those I discuss in the following pages command a big budget, with glossy sets and heritage locations, and hence contrast starkly with the rather claustrophobic studio-bound settings of the 1970s. Yet television shows like *The Forsyte Saga* and *Upstairs Downstairs* directly and indirectly inspire much of our current period drama offering. Both have been remade (with varying levels of success) in the last 15 years, and their influence is clearly apparent in other period dramas as well. Writers like Julian Fellowes and Andrew Davies seem frequently to be harking back – as we all do – to the big television events of their own youth and trying to capture the (perceived) innocence of that decade. So *Downton, Mr Selfridge* and others are trying to escape their present by harking back nostalgically to period drama's first heyday in the years following 1967, to programmes which were in their turn constructing a fictionalised Edwardian past for their own political reasons. Recent neo-Edwardian fictions are hence complicated, post-modern productions: recreating more than one past, while aware that there are multiple versions of those pasts, in political as well as literary terms. It all started, however, with the *Forsyte Saga*, and it is to this, and to its 2002 reworking, that we will now turn.

# 2
# An Adaptation of an Adaptation: *The Forsyte Saga* (2002)

At first appearance the most "classic" of the period dramas under consideration here, Granada television's 2002 adaptation of *The Forsyte Saga* is an obvious starting point for the consideration of the Edwardian age on the small screen over the last decade. Previously a huge popular success when it aired in the late 1960s, its reincarnation in 2002 (and its second series in 2003) can be considered appropriate for the beginning of a new century, given that its key subject matter is the transition from one era to the next. Indeed, given that it was being filmed at the time of the attacks on the World Trade Centre, it can be read as a period drama for a post 9/11 age. Chapters 3 and 4 of this project will argue that the stately home and the department store act as states in microcosm, and I suggest here that the Forsyte family seems to function as a "family politic" in a similar way. Its claustrophobic insularity – the series is entirely focused on the Forsytes' clan and those that marry into it, and almost all its scenes are set within their houses – can be considered reflective of the isolationist, inward looking world view that characterised many of the foreign policies of the Western powers in the first years of the twenty-first century. Similarly its bleak and dark view of human relationships and its refusal to grant redemption and reconciliation to and among its central characters seems reflective of a post-9/11 mindset. It is certainly a departure from the cosy, feel-good nostalgia still usually associated with the Sunday night heritage serial. In this way 9/11 seems to shadow this series, even as the First World War did its source text. Xenophobia, paranoia, distrust and miscommunication are important themes in this drama, in ways which make it feel particularly modern. With this in mind, this chapter will examine the portrayal of change and modernity in *The Forsyte Saga*: change which is symbolised by its preoccupation with modernist and avant-garde art and architecture. From Soames's new house – and Irene's "prison" – Robin Hill, to the paintings which are bought, collected and displayed throughout, modernism and proto-modernism in its various forms are constantly examined and debated by the characters, but are frequently associated with the loneliness and dislocation of the modern world. The gender politics here may make the female characters grateful for the new coming freedoms of the twentieth century, but the contemporary viewer may ultimately identify with the "villain" and patriarch, Soames: isolated, adrift and mourning the security and certainty of the past.

While this chapter will focus on the 2002 Granada adaptation by Christopher Menaul and David Moore, it is impossible to discuss *The Forsyte Saga* without acknowledging its hugely famous and successful 1967 incarnation. As I mentioned in the previous chapter, this was such a crucial moment in television history that much of the format and approach of small-screen drama since – both period and contemporary – can be attributed to it. In that regard it is difficult not to regard the 2002 version as an adaptation of an adaptation: a deliberate attempt to recapture the popularity of the original. Of course, the choice of channels available today means that viewing figures could never be equivalent to the 18 million who tuned in to watch the series when it was repeated on BBC 1 in 1968, but a 40 per cent audience share – almost nine million viewers for the first episode – showed that expectations were high for the remake. The makers of the series have, however, taken pains to assert their difference from the earlier programme. "Despite, or perhaps because of, the BBC version's renown, the producers of the *Forsyte* reboot opted to ignore it altogether rather than compete with memories of the series," as the producer Sita Williams makes clear:[1]

> People kept saying "Granada are remaking *The Forsyte Saga*" but that's a complete misunderstanding of what it is. *The Forsyte Saga* is a set of books, not a TV series. We are not attempting to remake what the BBC did. I watched a couple of episodes just to get an idea of how they'd set about it but I didn't go any further than that because I did not want our production to be influenced by anyone else's work. We've gone back to the source, to Galsworthy, and we are adapting that...What we are doing is reinterpreting Galsworthy for our time... (Williams, quoted in Smith, 2002: 49)

This assertion of separation from the BBC's version is understandable but naïve: for most of the audience, *The Forsyte Saga* is a TV series and that is how it will be remembered. The books have not quite made it as "classics" of the English canon for, as one reviewer notes, "poor old Galsworthy may in his day have won the Nobel prize for literature, but now he is just a footnote in televisual history – the begetter of the most popular classic serial of all time" (Crompton, 2002). Even if we regard the reduction of Galsworthy to a "footnote" as a little harsh, it is undeniably true that, given that there are nine novels and several "Interludes" (only the first trilogy and the first Interlude are adapted here) in total dealing with the Forsyte family, only the most perseverant and dedicated of modern readers are likely to know them at all well. The 1967 adaptation, in contrast, is still remembered by older viewers and hence the 2002 version was much anticipated because it covered ground already familiar to the audience. As Iris Kleinecke-Bates has noted, "media as well as viewer comments and reactions suggest that the ITV's *Forsyte Saga* was generally considered a remake of the earlier BBC version" (2014: 16). Indeed, some reviewers inevitably preferred the version they remembered from their youth and regarded this one as paling "in comparison with the original" (Purnell, 2002), and in particular often criticising the casting of Gina McKee as Irene (Purnell, 2002, Rosenberg, 2002). As James Walton noted in *The Daily Telegraph*: "most viewers over about 45 will have spent much of last night's opening episode remembering and comparing" (2002). And, indeed, this prior knowledge of the plot seemed not only inevitable, but expected, even necessary. Walton felt that "The script seemed to assume that we'd instantly know who everybody was...," and, of course, most of the audience already did (2002).

The ways in which the 2002 version "remakes" the 1967 one form an interesting case study on the process of adaptation, as Kleinecke-Bates has discussed (2014: 15–16). Both dramas share many lines of dialogue and frequently dramatise the same scenes, but this might be inevitable when they are both adaptations of the same novels. However, some visual elements, like the scene in which a jealous Soames watches Irene take off her hat as she thinks of Bosinney, seem lifted directly from the earlier adaptation: the similarities are clear. But while it is clear that the series does pay homage to its predecessor, it is of course true that its priorities and focus are different, for the new millennium. Menaul and Moore do have less time to devote to the plot – ten episodes over two series, not 26 – and rather higher production values to play with (though the BBC version was also very expensive for its time: 10,000 pounds per episode).[2] It is faster paced, much more diverse in its locations ("unlike its predecessor, which was filmed on soundstages, the 2002 *Forsyte* was shot on location around Liverpool and Manchester" (Egner, 2012)). The differences are most apparent in the casting, however: the men in the 1967 adaptation were not as young or as handsome as those we expect to find on our screens today, in a post-Darcy world. As Martine Voiret has discussed, the success of period dramas now depends greatly on satisfying the desires of the audience via a highly attractive male lead (2003: 238). Kenneth More had been a heart-throb in his youth, but he was in his mid-50s and his movie career was dwindling when he played young Jolyon (Jo) in 1967 – famously two years older than Joseph O'Conor who played his father, and with little regard for the novels in which we first meet Jo in his 20s. Eric Porter's Soames was younger but more of a character actor than a sex symbol (he spent most of his career in Shakespearean tragedy: he would, for example, play Lear to great acclaim the year after *The Forsyte Saga* aired). Even John Bennet was almost 40 when he played Bosinney, supposedly a very young man only starting out in life. In contrast, the 2002 casting of Rupert Graves, Damian Lewis and Ioan Gruffudd, all handsome men in their 20s or early 30s, reflects the extent to which contemporary period drama is all about the female gaze (or the homosexual one: Graves, although straight, has been a gay pin-up for years, ever since he frolicked naked in *A Room with View* (Billen, 2002)). Presumably a modern audience might also be less tolerant of the off-screen gender issues implied by the casting of beautiful young women alongside significantly older, male "character" actors than those who watched the show in the 1960s.

The progression of modern sexual politics is reflected in the drama in other ways, too, as critics have noted. Egner reports that the writers "went back to the books, seeking to highlight plotlines that would resonate more with twenty-first century audiences, like the striving of Irene and another Forsyte, June, to redefine themselves as women in a changing England" (2012). It is true that this drama is more sympathetic towards, and interested in, its female characters than its source text. Galsworthy can hardly be described as a feminist even by Edwardian standards, and women in the Forsyte novels are judged mainly on their beauty and tend to be regarded as neurotic and burdensome when they cease to be charming. Jo's second wife Hélène, for example, is a hysteric and an emotional burden to her husband (we are told he looks "younger since she died"!) but is rewritten by the adaptation into a strong and determined woman (Galsworthy, 1950: 365). And June, in particular, is an annoyance to her father because "she had never appealed to his aesthetic sense," and hence there is nothing to soften her "decided" personality (Galsworthy, 1950: 367). June's determined and rebellious spirit is looked on much more kindly by the adaptation, which constructs her as a central and sympathetic character, although her potential as a "New Woman" is never developed as fully as it might be. She does appear as a speaker at a suffragette rally at the start of series 2, but that brief scene is the only real engagement *The Forsyte Saga* has with first-wave feminism, in contrast to the way *Parade's End* would foreground the woman's movement, via one of its central characters, ten years later (perhaps, by 2012, feminism has become "mainstream" enough to be attractive to even the most middle England audience, or perhaps the more highbrow *Parade's End* is more willing to take risks with its material). We might also note that these changes to two of the main female characters did not originate in 2002: both June and Hélène had already been reconstructed as forthright, intelligent and well-informed women in 1967 (although the latter did nod to her unbalanced source character when she descends into mental illness just before her death). The gender politics in the drama have not changed much in the intervening 35 years.

Even if it is not especially interested in writing the feminist movement back into history, however, the Granada production is still concerned with the struggle of individual women. Irene's repression by the rigid and patriarchal codes of her society is, after all, the central theme of this drama, just as it was of Galsworthy's first Forsyte novel, *The Man of Property*. There has been much debate over Galsworthy's social ideology over the years, and the critical consensus generally agrees, with DH Lawrence, that he was a skilled satirist who was just slightly too close to, and affectionate about, the class he critiqued (Lawrence, 1928: 122). We might note here that in this regard Galsworthy is a very typical subject for adaptation, given that the same could be said about much heritage drama. But, certainly, as a young man he was horrified "at the hypocrisy with which his own class, his own family – indeed, to some extent, he himself – buttressed their comfortable lives upon the mass wretchedness of the poor." (Barker. 1963: 45) These socialist tendencies do not really come across much in his most famous work, however. His literary response to injustice was really motivated largely by his own experience of the unfairness of marriage, after he fell in love with his cousin's wife Ada. Galsworthy was appalled to see "how his own class could equally inflict, in the name of morality, the most desperate misery ... upon a young woman..." who had married the wrong man. Hence this love affair and the resulting scandal when Ada left her unhappy marriage "became the dominant fact of his personal life and the basic theme which created the possibility of the novelist" (Barker, 1963: 45–46). As Sarah Edwards notes, "in 1906, when *The Man of Property* was published, reform of the Victorian divorce laws was an increasingly topical issue" (2011: 201) and this was certainly a theme Galsworthy would revisit obsessively throughout his work. This personal sympathy with those who suffer at society's hands is at the core of *The Man of Property*, in which real love is usually extramarital and always controversial, and conventional morality is suffocating and restrictive.

Such a subversive attitude towards marriage was one of the main reasons why the 1967 adaptation was so popular, given that it reflected the anti-establishment thinking of the time (the first novel had been already been adapted in 1949 as the film *That Forsyte Woman*, but it made a loss at the box office: perhaps its audience were not yet ready for the scandalous Forsytes). We might also note that the novel's sympathetic representation of divorce, remarriage and complicated family relationships (Jo, despite being "the moral centre of John Galsworthy's tale" and one of his most lovable characters, has four children by three different partners, for example) is a reminder of the ways in which the Edwardian age reflects our own (Billen, 2002). Family may be fetishised in *The Forsyte Saga*, but it is also a messy, problematic structure, which is constantly under threat: not so very different from how it is in contemporary society today. Our modern, post-nuclear-family world clearly has its roots in this era, and this is represented in the neo-Edwardian drama on our screens. As we will see, adultery and marital breakdown feature strongly in *Parade's End* and *Mr Selfridge* as well (though not, significantly, in the more idealistic and escapist *Downton*). Far from being remote, the period is in this regard very familiar to the audience, and Galsworthy in particular is deeply aware that he is writing about the arrival of a new era. As Edwards points out, divorce "becomes associated with the transition towards modernity and, fittingly, Soames's and Irene's divorce is granted in 1900": it symbolises the new age (2003: 204).

The sympathy for Irene as society's victim comes across very strongly in the 2002 adaptation, which allows her some of the interiority denied her in Galsworthy's novels. Gina McKee's Irene – a "chilly, swan-necked beauty" – reflects her source character in being frequently silent, remote and seemingly impassive, but a scene in which she opens up to her kindly, but uncomprehending, mother-in-law gives the viewer insights that were denied to Galsworthy's readers (Egner, 2012).

[Emily] "Forgive me my dear, but you seem so cold." [Irene]
"I know. I know I do and I am not a cold person. I am not! Emily,
I know I am not! This is not me sitting here. This is…some wife! But
what can I do? I do not love him. I cannot love him. I do not want
to love him." (series 1, episode 2)

In this scene (a sympathetic reworking of a similar, but more intoler-
ant exchange between Irene and Uncle Swithin in the 1967 version)
Irene seems to be answering her audience as much as she is Emily, for
Galsworthy's readers have long noted the impenetrable "strangeness
and unknowability" of this character whose thoughts and intentions are
never really accessed in the source text (Edwards, 2011: 207). This lack of
interiority is a necessary part of the novels, however, for it is necessary
that the reader is somewhat detached from Irene in order that they feel
sympathy with the central character and (anti) hero, Soames.

Soames is a very problematic subject for adaptation, for he is a difficult sell to a contemporary audience: a repressed, avaricious and
mercenary "Man of Property" who is somewhere between monster and
victim. His behaviour to Irene is pathologically possessive and oppressive, and cumulates in her (horrific but legal) rape, followed by harassment and threats which continue long after their separation. Yet at the
same time he is a devoted son, loyal brother and affectionate father
to Fleur, and is motivated by the desire for love as much as money.
Moreover, it is his consciousness the reader follows throughout much
of Galsworthy's trilogy – not his victim's, as I have noted. The writers
of the adaptation were aware of the difficulties involved in representing
this figure:

> There is a temptation to reign him back a bit and make him more
> sympathetic because for all his faults you do end up loving him. But
> the producer was always pushing for us to go further, to bring out
> his dark side, and I was worried that people would just hate him…
> Soames is a very disturbed individual, and it's difficult for a woman
> to write for him. I mean, he's a rapist! But you can understand what's
> driven him to it. You can see the turmoil in his mind that's twisted
> him into doing a thing like that. (Smith, 202: 58)

To my mind it is difficult, and indeed morally problematic, to represent a
character like Soames in such a way as the audience "ends up loving him."
But in order to capture the spirit of the source text, as this adaptation

clearly intends to do, the audience has to "understand" him and his motivation, for Soames, by the second novel in the trilogy, has become a sympathetic character. *The Man of Property* identified him as a symbol of all that was wrong with late Victorian society, but by the time of *In Chancery* biographers have argued that an essential change took place in Galsworthy's "whole attitude to property, including even property of the person" (1950). By the end of the war Galsworthy had lost the bitterness and anger he felt at Ada's treatment and the ensuing scandal. He was happy and wealthy, had brought Ada back into respectability and returned to the Forsytes with new affection and understanding. Indeed, "his original novel of protest [was] hidden by the huge humanity – sometimes even sentimentality – of the saga of English prosperous family life" (Barker, 1963: 184–185). In this way Galsworthy joins the other twentieth-century writers who, immediately following the First World War, look back at the Edwardian period with an affection and nostalgia which at the time it had not merited: as one of Galsworthy's biographers put it, "there was a considerable feeling just then for continuity, for reaching back and linking up with the Peace we had once known" (Mottram, 1956: 197, quoted in Edwards, 2002: 211).

So the complex attitudes that have always surrounded the character of Soames may have as much to do with his creator's nostalgia as they do with any actual moral ambiguity. Soames is attractive to Galsworthy because he stands for a charmed era which is now irretrievably past. In this determined old-fashionedness we can align him with the – rather more lovable – character of Christopher Tietjens in *Parade's End,* who I will discuss in Chapter 5. And in both men's deliberate "turning away" from the modern world we can see our own reflection, for as nostalgic consumers of heritage television we too desire, even temporarily, to turn away from modernity. In this regard we may be pre-disposed to be sympathetic towards Soames, who shares our yearning for a past which never existed. Even the house he builds at Robin Hill, "aspiring to the apparent permanency of the landed gentry", has its parallel in our desire for the stately home beloved of, and much visited by, viewers of period drama (Hubble, 2011). The 2002 adaptation deliberately builds on this sympathy in a way in which the 1967 version does not. In this it may be responding to the viewer's – especially the female viewer's – reaction to the 1967 Soames, who almost overnight, became a sensation. Far from simply being condemned for his actions, there was a great deal of public debate about whether he was justified or excusable in his rape of Irene (Hargreaves, 2009: 32–33). In the Granada version, these waters are further muddied, as Soames's torment occupies a good deal more screen time, and is carefully presented to move the audience emotionally. As Damian Lewis has suggested, the production wanted the audience to have a complicated, non-judgemental attitude towards the drama's most important character:

> We didn't want a simple villain in Soames. I think it's more challenging for the audience if they're presented with a character they hate but also feel sympathy for, who presents them with moral questions and has them thinking, God, I feel so sorry for Soames, but he just raped his wife! That's far more interesting. (Lewis in interview, 2002)

Particularly important in this construction of Soames as an object of sympathy is the depiction of his mental collapse following his separation from Irene, when, distraught and "past caring" he takes to his bed for a period of some weeks (series 1, episode 4). This is a particularly modern addition to the drama, for there is no equivalent plot arc in Galsworthy's *Saga* (which moves swiftly from Irene's return to Soames at the end of the first book, to his contemplating remarriage to another woman at the start of the second) nor in the 1967 version. In fact it can be read as a reversal of the source text, in which several women – namely Hélène, Jolyon's first wife – are hysteric and prone to mental illness, not the men. Such a mental collapse is of course the antithesis of the kind of dependable, rational late-Victorian manhood Soames has always represented himself to be. Indeed, it is one of several elements in the 2002 adaptation which remind the viewer of the transitional nature of this text, for this breakdown signifies modernism and the crisis of values and certainties which accompanied the new century and would be exacerbated by the First World War. It is too the same kind of crisis of masculinity we will see again in *Parade's End*, though in that novel it is a result of shell shock as well as the more common battleground of modern marriage.

This breakdown serves a more straightforward purpose in the adaptation as well, however. It has the effect of constructing Soames as a victim, suffering and broken, damaged by Irene's abandonment and unable to cope with the demands of life. In this, he seems to demand and deserve our sympathy: certainly he receives plenty from his family, who rally lovingly around his bedside.

> [Emily] "You have to snap out of it. You are young. You can start again. Whatever she did to you – it was dreadful. But it's better to

discover it now ... than when you are up to your neck in commit-ments with a houseful of children." [Soames] "That would never have happened. Children. She took steps to prevent it." [Emily] "Behind your back? Soames, that's wicked!" (1:4)

All this seems designed to complicate the construction of Soames's guilt and undermine the possibility that he might deserve to lose Irene because he has raped her. To Emily, after all, it is Irene who is "wicked" because she has broken his heart *and* denied him the children he badly wants. If these scenes succeed in encouraging the audience to see Soames as a victim of emotional trauma, then, this changes our whole view of him. Fritz Breithaupt's ideas on trauma are useful to note here:

> The most prominent and, so to say, appealing aspect of the ideology of trauma, is, of course, the innocence of the victim.... This idea of innocence can be manipulated.... Once one manages to position oneself as a "trauma" victim, one seems absolved from possible involvement. Yet, this line is blurred: victim of a second attack may have been the aggressors of a first. (2003: 70)

Breithaupt is writing about trauma on a national scale (he is discussing post 9/11 foreign policy, of which more later) but his points are none-theless relevant here. Soames is indeed the "aggressor" in this drama, given that he is the perpetrator of the sexual violence that Irene suffers, but the adaptation does cleverly "manipulate" the audience's allegiance. The attack itself is graphic: contemporary television does not shy away from screening sexual violence against women, and this rape scene is much longer and more violent – though admittedly less eroticised – than its world-famous 1967 predecessor. It is much less interested in its aftermath for Irene, however, revisiting the rape only via a scene in which the focus is really on Bosinney's emotional reaction to her attack. This reaction will shortly lead to his violent death, and the plotline moves swiftly from the suffering of one man back to another: Soames. Instead of keeping Irene at the centre of the narrative, then, the drama focuses on the consequences of the rape on the men in her life – even though one of them is the perpetrator. It is worth noting here that, as John Fiske and Lisa M Cuklanz have argued, rape on the small screen is often represented as being more about masculine identity than about the female victim, and of course *The Forsyte Saga* is no exception to this. (We might also recall here the infamous rape of Anna in series 4 of *Downton*, which follows the same pattern, as I have discussed elsewhere

(Byrne, 2014).) Bosinney in fact, by dying as a direct result of the rape, effectively erases Irene's status as victim: Soames's breakdown a little later ensures that it is not restored. By the time she next appears in the series, several years have passed and the rape is all but forgotten.

The way in which Soames's emotional collapse in episode four is portrayed further contributes to the negation of his guilt, for it follows a pattern familiar to the viewer. We are well accustomed to seeing the emotional turmoil of unrequited love on the screen and the page, from the eighteenth century to the twenty-first: from Marianne in *Sense and Sensibility* to Carrie in *Sex and the City* to Bella in *Twilight*, fiction is full of the suffering of lovelorn heroines who become mentally and indeed physically ill from their passions. These narratives usually chronicle the bedridden suffering of their central character, who withdraws from the outside world, but eventually is coaxed back to mental health by the restorative love and support of friends and family. This is exactly what happens to Soames, but he differs in that these sufferers are usually women. Indeed, the real key to Soames's popularity – and the reason for his identification as an unlikely sex symbol following the 2002 adaptation – is this feminisation of his character, which (only) in matters of the heart rejects conventional expectations about masculinity. Soames is more emotional, more intense and more vulnerable than most heroes in period drama: as his mother Emily tells him following his breakdown: "I should have taught you not to love like that. With all your heart. You feel things too much. You always have" (series 1, episode 4). Lewis himself says of the role which made him a kind of "thinking woman's pin-up", "I think anyone who loves to distraction, or obsesses to distraction, somehow becomes endearing, however badly and gauchely he expresses his love," he says, quickly adding: "Certainly forcing yourself on your wife is not an attractive or forgiveable thing to do" (Anon, 2003).

Lewis' comments here are revealing, implying as they do an awareness that the audience will not only forgive Soames but find him "endearing." All this ambiguity surrounding his character sheds interesting light on the ways in which rape is viewed in our society. The adaptation sets out to make us appreciate the way that marriage, economic dependence and patriarchal legal systems conspired to oppress women until the second half of the twentieth century. In this regard if none other, this adaptation invites us to reject nostalgia and to be grateful for the modern freedoms and gender equality we take for granted. Yet at the same time the presentation of the rape of Irene as understandable, forgivable, even justifiable – perspectives shared by writers, producers, cast members and viewers, a number of whom I have quoted above – undermines the critique of gender politics that underpins the source text and both its adaptations. Some reviewers would go further still, as this analysis of the rape episode in *The Telegraph* reveals:

> How would Damian Lewis, as Soames, ravish his icy spouse? Once inside Irene's chamber last night, Soames loosened his necktie with malicious deliberation. String music played nervily as he took off his dinner jacket, pulled his shirt over his head and slid into bed beside the sleeping form of Gina McKee, clad in what looked like a mail order nightdress. McKee has played Irene Soames with such glacial hauteur for most of three episodes that it would not have been surprising if Soames had discovered he was fondling her alabaster model ... If she is the talk of the canteens, the school runs and the office smoking rooms this morning, it will be because viewers are divided about whether Soames's wife, brittle as glass and unresponsive as a statue, is an artistic soul in torment or whether she had it coming to her. (Grice, 2002)

This review is being deliberately scathing about this famously melodramatic part of the plot – but its playful handling of such sensitive material is remarkable, and problematic to say the least. This is one of the most famous rapes in television history, probably the most influential and memorable aspect of the drama, and yet the discourse it provokes is startlingly anti-feminist. I am suggesting throughout this book that there are certain closenesses and similarities between the Edwardian era and our own, and here it finds its most disturbing manifestation. The construction of, and response to, this significant plotline reveals how little sexual politics have really progressed over the course of the twentieth century Then Soames's behaviour was sanctioned by law, but now, in the post-feminist, "raunch culture" we now inhabit, sexual coldness is enough to explain and justify it. Irene, because she is distant and impassive, has lost her victim status: she has "it coming to her" (Levy, 2005).

## The *Forsyte Saga* and 9/11

I have discussed the rape of Irene at some length, for it is not only the most famous part of the plot, but also, for me, the most controversial. It is far from being the only bleak and cynical aspect of the 2002 *Saga*, however. Galsworthy's *Forsyte* novels have generally been considered to be humorous and comic in their social satire, especially the books which came after *The Man of Property*, which were more lighthearted for reasons I have discussed (Hubble, 2011). In contrast, and despite their claimed return to the source texts, the tone of the 2002 adaptation is much darker. There may still be occasional moments of humour from the observations of the older characters: the Forsyte Aunts, for example, are largely there to provide often humorously tactless commentary on the lives of their nieces and nephews. They only occupy a marginal role in this adaptation, however, which is much more focused on the younger generation. The real preoccupation here is on Irene's miserable marriage, Jo's struggle with conventional society, Soames's pathological obsession and the inevitable decay brought about by time. Even a happy moment (one of few) in which the family is reunited and toasting "new beginnings" with champagne, immediately cuts to the grave of one of them in the next scene, which is set five years later (series 1, episode 4). Soames seems to have a reconciliation with his second wife in one scene, but they are again estranged the next (series 2, episode 3). Deaths and funerals punctuate the series, and at regular intervals different characters express pessimism about the future. This conversation between Soames and his father James is one such example:

> [James] "We've never had a divorce before ... the family's breaking up. All the rules have changed. This Kruger business. There'll be a war in South Africa soon. The empire's going to pot. The family with it."
> [Soames] "The family will be fine. We're taking steps. [James] A man needs his son around him at times like this. A son's the one you turn to." (series 1, episode 5)

This exchange sums up the main theme of the series: a general sense of foreboding about the future is warded off only by the family unit – in particular, by the reassuring and unchanging Soames. It is, however, a very bleak view of the late 1890s, one which could only be voiced by the most pessimistic of the Forsytes, James. Of course there were many social anxieties as Britain approached the *fin de siècle*, but most citizens would not believe that the Empire was really in serious trouble until well into the twentieth century. Sanderson, writing in 1899, would still speak confidently of a "vast and prosperous realm.... an empire washed by all oceans" which "can furnish us with endless supplies" (1899: 352). The BBC adaptation has a version of this scene between Soames and James, but interestingly, in that more optimistic decade, does not have the same prophetic focus on decline (*Saga*, 1967: episode 10). Moreover, this is not the first time in the 2002 series that these sentiments have been voiced. After the death of old Jolyon in the 1880s – an event which is also considered "the end of an era" for the Forsytes – young Jo, in a scene which is not in the source text, mourns not just his father but the age he belonged to and its certainties: "we're full of doubt now. Apologetic. Smaller." "The world's a more complicated place," his daughter June responds (series 1, episode 3). Historical fiction is fond of expressing these kinds of sentiments, but usually locates them around the time of the First World War, as we will see in *Downton* and especially in *Parade's End*. It is unusual, then, to find them voiced in the late Victorian period, especially given that at the time of both the exchanges here, in series 1, modernity has not really impacted upon the Forsytes' world in any way. There are no motor cars here or suffragettes or bicycles or rational dress: the streets are still filled with horse-drawn carriages and even the most rebellious women are still tightly corseted. Hence the kind of apocalyptic anxiety about the future that is so apparent in this series seems to have as much to do with the time in which it was made than when it was set. The drama was being made at the same time as the terrorist attacks on the World Trade centre: the infamous rape scene was filmed the very day that the planes crashed into the Twin Towers (Lewis interview, 2003). By the time it appeared on British screens in 2002 (and in the United States a year later) the audience was inhabiting a recognisably post-9/11 society. With this in mind, the anxiety about the future expressed by a number of characters – from young Jo to old James – in this drama can be interpreted as a as a comment on the frightening new world that opened up after the attacks – never had there been a more desirable time to retreat, even escape, into the past.

As Laura Frost has discussed, in the years following 9/11, the terrorist attacks permeated rapidly into popular culture, as "films of many different genres began to explore the disaster, explicitly or indirectly" (2004: 15). Frost cites the buddy movie and romantic comedy as two unlikely genres which can be seen to represent responses to the destruction of the Twin Towers, but does not include period drama in her analysis, which focuses upon drama and horror as the most recognisable forms through which 9/11 was confronted (2004: 150). Eckart Voigts-Virchow, however, notes that "In November 2002, with the world drifting painfully slowly towards the Iraq war ... the British press felt the need to resort to martial imagery" when describing the tensions between the scheduling of various heritage dramas (2004: 13). Nonetheless there was no explicit acknowledgement of the ways in which these dramas might be a response to those wider political events. One recent (2012) review of the 2002 *Forsyte Saga* did, however, notice – with hindsight – that it appears to be "about" the political landscape of the twenty-first century. This critic hinted that the drama was a kind of cross between a conventional period drama and *Homeland*, the terrorism thriller which in recent years has made Lewis into a big star:

> Among the best drama nominees at the Emmy Awards ceremony on Sunday night, *Homeland*, an of-the-moment political thriller, and *Downton Abbey*, a soapy period drama, could hardly be more different. But a decade ago the dynamics that animate both shows churned within a single mini-series: *The Forsyte Saga*. Based on the John Galsworthy novels, the series ... starred Damian Lewis of *Homeland* as another repressed villain demented by love and loss. Soames Forsyte – like Brody, [Lewis's] character on *Homeland* – is driven by a cause he believes is just and evokes sympathy for his torment if not his misguided actions ... (Egner, 2012)

Egner does not expand on this conflation of the two shows, but we can see the relevance of his suggestion: *The Forsyte Saga* does mix *Downton's* escapism with *Homeland's* paranoid and bleak world view. (It is also entertaining just to note here that even dramas which are made ten years before *Downton* still manage to be compared to that show in the press!) Indeed, *Homeland* also uses a fracturing family unit to express anxieties about twenty-first century society: it and *The Forsyte Saga* share more than their lead actor.

Much has been written about the cultural and social changes that took place after 9/11. Some of these texts identified disturbing new ways of viewing the future as a dark, dangerous place of religious dissent and pre-emptive wars (Gaddis, 2001; Kolko, 2002). Some, significantly, were more about recapturing old fashioned values, ideals and comforts. Elaine Tyler May has noted, for example, that after the terrorist attacks many Americans retreated into, or rediscovered, family life: "Americans also turned to each other for solace and comfort...people reached out to their family members across the world ... requests for marriage licences went up 10 to 15 per cent ... some observers predicted that there might be a baby boom nine months after Sept 11" (May, 2003: 50–51). Dana Heller has also written about the social anxieties that followed the terrorist attacks, and the media's attempt to reassure them. Heller argues that the television industry set out to salvage, via a certain kind of broadcasting, "heterosexual family life ... and paternal continuity ... in an attempt to maintain faith in the solvency of familial – and national – unity" (2005: 16). Similarly, gender roles and expectations also underwent a transformation in the media in the period following the attacks. Coverage of 9/11 had initially focused on the heroic efforts of the fire and police forces, and afterwards the media remained seduced by the image offered by these strong patriarchal organisations:

> the names in the headlines were all powerful men ... As in the Cold War, the time had arrived for an image of reinvigorated manhood. Powerful men appeared as the major players on both sides ... while women and children seemed vulnerable, in need of protection.... of course, these women and children did need protection. But the framing of the media images, focusing on heroic men and dependent women, re-inforced gender constructions that date back a century. (May, 2003: 50)

With this in mind, we can see how the plot of *The Forsyte Saga* might be regarded as reflective of the cultural preoccupations of its audience, both in Britain and in America, whose anxieties it both highlights and reassures. It is a drama about a (mostly) strong, close-knit and supportive family, their homes and their marriages, at a time when people were looking to the domestic sphere for comfort and reassurance. It also represents women as fragile victims in need of chivalrous support, via sexual politics that do, of course, "date back a century." This is most clearly illustrated by Irene, who escapes her miserable marriage thanks to one man; is comforted after his death by another (Jo, in scenes which stress female vulnerability and, significantly, are not in the source text nor the 1967 adaptation); is rescued from poverty by a third; and finally supported in her older years by her son (who sacrifices his own happiness in order to look after her). Most of all, it is a drama in which the outside world, beyond the family, is dangerous: it is safer to look inward than out. The Forsytes are the most insular of families: they buy houses from one another, they fall in love with the same people, they do not seem to have or need relationships outside the family circle, and when one is formed with an outsider – like June's with Bosinney – it brings disaster. We might argue that this reflects both the social politics of a "post-war-on terror" world, and its foreign policies too. In the twenty-first century the West is more paranoid and more xenophobic than it has been for decades, and becoming increasingly anxious about its relations with other nations. For the United States, for example, the world is more complex and more dangerous than it was during the cold war ... September 11 confirmed, if any confirmation was needed, that the United States had abysmally failed to bring peace and security to the world. Instead it has managed to become increasingly hated, placing itself in profound and mortal danger... (Kolko, 2002: 149)

After 2001, in both America and Britain, multi-culturalism came to be viewed with suspicion, and anti-Muslim feeling began to build. Moreover, the vague and indefinite concept of a War on Terror came to stand in for constructive foreign policy. *The Forsyte Saga* engages with many of these issues through the Edwardians' own version of a destructive, controversial, ideological conflict: the Boer War.

The second South African War overshadows the final episodes of series 1. It is a slightly unusual inclusion to a period drama: we are much more used to seeing the First World War on our screens. Here the Boer War clearly prefigures and signifies the 1914 conflict, however, with the advantage of being less well known to the audience and having less clear-cut moral judgements attached to it, but the same problematic jingoism. This is implied by Jo, who is a pacifist and objects to the war. He tells Irene that he has fled England to escape a kind of fervent nationalism and xenophobia which he finds objectionable: "There's a mood abroad in England at the moment against the Boers. It makes me uncomfortable. It's a vengeance ... but I am in the minority so I left" (series 1, episode 5). This conversation is introduced in the Granada adaptation – it is not in Galsworthy's novels – and as such is clearly meant to speak to a contemporary audience. This disturbing desire for "vengeance" against an ideologically opposing group must have resonance for the twenty-first century viewer, but Jo, here as elsewhere in the drama, acts as the voice of reason and compassion, reminding us of the pointlessness of conflict. The irony, of course, is that he cannot escape the War, or remain remote from it. It follows him to Paris when the news arrives that his son has enlisted, and he is personally scarred by it when Jolly then dies from typhoid in South Africa. It is clear that the price of conflict is high and it is the individual who must pay it – but Jo still sets a good example by refusing to be embittered by his loss.

Back in 1909 Galsworthy made clear that he saw the Forsytes as a microcosm of late Victorian society: their fall would be the fall of the century and the old ways, their endurance the survival of capitalism and the spirit of Englishness and family. As the opening lines of the first novel suggest, they have the "mysterious concrete tenacity which renders a family so formidable a unit of society, so clear a reproduction of society in miniature" (Galsworthy 1). Kleinecke-Bates has noted that the opening scene of the ITV *Forsyte Saga* "rather fittingly resembles the entry into a doll's house," to which the audience rather voyeuristically gains access through a window (2014: 38). By establishing the house as a contained space, the drama plays around with public and private histories, using the home as a way of accessing a personalised past which is also reflective of a whole society (as captured by Galsworthy) (2014: 38). We might add that the "family-politic" established here is also a means of commenting on a very public history, 9/11, which most of the British population had also witnessed remotely via their television screens. For them, the inward-looking Forsytes, contained within their secure houses, offer some kind of solution to, and escape from, a changing and a frightening world – but they also bring with them the reminder that eventually that would will catch up with you. By the end of the second series, the home and the family is fractured by a modernity which even Soames cannot keep at bay.

## The 'man of property': heritage and consumerism

Up to this point I have said little about the representation of class in this adaptation. It is well known that Galsworthy' novels are famously class-specific, and deal with the type of society he himself belonged to. Hence the Forsytes are not the aristocracy or landed gentry we are used to seeing on screen throughout the 1990s, in adaptations of Jane Austen or even (the Wilcoxes aside) EM Forster. Instead they are the wealthy middle classes, who are only three generations removed from their farming ancestors, and who are especially conscious about their status and their financial security as a result. This is why the novels are deeply materialist: possessions are bound up with identity here and Galsworthy uses "property as the outward display of inner feeling" (Robbins, 2003: 55). As Edwards has noted, this is one of the reasons *The Forsyte Saga* was a relevant text to be remade for the new century:

> The recent dawn of the twenty-first century led some reviewers to contemplate the saga's Edwardian antecedents and to identify with them. For one critic, "the wheel has turned full circle since then and the values questioned by Galsworthy in the original novels seem very reflective of today's Western society" (Portman 2002: 7). For this critic, then, the novels reflected a cyclical narrative of

history, where the consumer-oriented spirit of the early twenty-first century is a reflection of Galsworthy's own turn-of-the-century society and the 2002 adaptation functions as a cautionary tale. (Edwards, 2011: 218)

Our consumerist age, then, is in this regard as in others close to Galsworthy's own: for him as for us, consumer goods are important signifiers through which our world can be represented and understood. This is true of clothes, jewels and art – more of which later – which all reveal status, wealth and personality, but these are most directly and crucially apparent through houses. All the Forsytes are preoccupied with making money through the acquisition of real estate, and for Soames in particular, finding and owning the right house is one of the main markers of his sense of self. Hence the title of the first novel, while referring to Soames's need to own things (most disturbingly Irene) also indicates his desire for "property" which will become home. In this Soames is once again connected to the modern viewer, for in the twenty-first century we are – at least prior to the housing market crash and worldwide recession of 2007/2008 – a society obsessed with the acquisition of houses. This can of course be seen in the media of the time: the start of the new century also saw the rise of property shows on television, which both reflected and constructed British society's fixation with the housing market and the home. The hugely popular *Location Location* first aired in 2000 and *Property Ladder* in 2001 (the latter was remade in the United States in 2005). It is unsurprising, then, that the 2002 adaptation foregrounds the house that Soames has built at Robin Hill, which we follow from its conception until it is put up for sale in the last episode. There are other properties in the drama, but this house is the most crucial: it is not just a setting for much of the action of *The Forsyte Saga* but also a key part of the plot.

So unusual, and so important was Robin Hill that, for in the 2002 adaptation, it had to be specially built for Granada – or rather half built and the rest filled in by computer graphics. This was a huge and expensive undertaking which took the production "wildly over budget," but they could not find a suitably innovative house to film in (Smith, 2002: 59). Moreover, this determination that the property be perfect reflects an awareness of the fact that "sets and locations have become the stars of TV drama almost as much as the actors themselves." (Smith, 2002: 59) As consumers of heritage drama, we expect to see beautiful, old and valuable stately homes, in stunning locations, on our screens; as consumers of property shows, we also like to see how much they cost and how they take shape. *The Forsyte Saga* sets out to fulfil the latter desire, but subvert the former by presenting us with a newly built house. Primarily Robin Hill functions as a symbol of Soames's increasing wealth and improving social status: he builds a stately home as he does not have one to inherit (and in doing so creates his own form of "heritage"). Soon of course, this attempt to better his position threatens it instead, for the house, and especially its architect, become the catalyst for the breakdown of his marriage and the loss of Irene. Hence Soames is denied actual ownership of, or access to, the house: he spends his money building it, but never really becomes its owner. This might remind us of Higson's point about period drama often posing the question "who is to inherit": the answer here is those who prioritise love and beauty over money, the artistic and subversive half of the family, not Soames.

This house is shot in what we might describe as typical "heritage" style: long shots of the building and its beautiful grounds, always filled with sunlight and tranquillity, repeated at intervals throughout the series. The house itself is notably different from the kind of stately home we usually see in period drama, however. That it was built especially for the series, rather than being a pre-existing national trust property, is itself unusual. So too, of course, is its style: it is meant to be avant-garde in design, "unique" "with clean lines where the eye can rest," and with "the freedom to move and breathe" as Irene longingly says (series 1, episode 2). The conservative Soames, of course, is taken aback when he sees Bosinney's plans for Robin Hill, declaring "it's an odd sort of house!"(series 1, episode 2). Its simple, airy, modernist appearance certainly forms a dramatic contrast to the cluttered late Victorian interiors of the Georgian town houses inhabited by the other Forsytes, and indeed to the more conventional country pile, Mapledurham, which Soames eventually buys (series 1, episode 5). It also, of course, symbolises the adaptation's main thematic concerns: the importance of aesthetics and the coming of modernism, as well as the search for, and construction of, "home." The series designers began their version of the house with reference to the Arts and Crafts movement, but brought together later styles from several different designers of the 1880s and 90s – including Frank Lloyd Wright and Charles Rennie Mackintosh – in an attempt to capture the innovative originality of Philip Bosinney. What is really significant to a modern viewer, however, is its familiarly: both externally and internally, this looks like a building we might construct today. It appears to be an elegant open plan home, not an inherited English country house. This is an interesting example, then, of a house which the characters deliberately construct as "heritage" but which differs from the usual heritage mansion. All who visit it are preoccupied with the knowledge that it will be admired and talked about for years to come: as Galsworthy's narrator speculates, "It might even become one of the 'homes of England' – a rare achievement for a house in those degenerate days of building" (Galsworthy, 1950: 364). Sarah Edwards interprets this longing for heritage as ultimately conservative: "in this evocation of the timeless country house which elides historical change and conflict, the Forsytes are reconciled with Bosinney and modernity is reconciled with tradition. This ... seems to undercut Galsworthy's social critique of possessive materialism..." (2003: 214). In the context of period drama, however, we might regard Robin Hill as inviting discourse about what is to be preserved and cherished about the past. This unconventional house reminds the viewer that heritage can and should be a much broader category than we might think from other historical fictions on screen (a point that would be developed further by *Mr Selfridge* a decade later, when a department store becomes the focus of the nostalgic gaze). As Robert Hewison has discussed, from early in its conception to the present day, the National Trust has been primarily concerned with the architecture of the Georgian period "which is now considered the apogee of the country house manner" (1987: 74). It is apparent that the screen usually perpetuates the same classicist taste: in heritage drama the stately home is almost always pre-Victorian, and thus "keeps the rise of modernism at bay" (Hewison, 1987: 74). *The Forsyte Saga* is exceptional, then, in its representation of a different kind of country house.

If *The Forsyte Saga* is unusual and deliberately "post-heritage" in its very contemporary interpretation of Robin Hill, the way the house is filmed is rather more typical of classic period drama, and indeed specifically of the way in which the Edwardian period habitually appears on screen. The house itself is treasured by its owners in a way which might recall *Howards End* (even if its architecture and style are notably different): it is also shot with a similar Merchant Ivory emphasis on sunshine and rural tranquillity, as also seen in *A Room with a View* (the casting of Rubert Graves of course creates a further intertextual link between the two productions). Even the sad death of "Old" Jolyon is peaceful and charmed because it takes place here, in the garden on a summer afternoon. Indeed, the rural idyll of Robin Hill can be seen to reflect traditional heritage settings, and to perpetuate the idealised views of the Edwardian period I discussed in Chapter 1. It is, however, appropriate that it should, given that I have argued that Galsworthy himself wrote all his later texts looking back at this turn of the century period with nostalgia and affection from a post-War perspective. Indeed, the title of the interlude in which Old Jolyon dies, *Indian Summer of a Forsyte*, might recall those precious, ever-sunny last summers before the War: Galsworthy wrote it in 1915.

All this idyllic agrarianism forms a stark contrast with the sections of the drama which are set in London: the city is associated with the darkness, repression and paranoia which I have already categorised as the dominant tone of – especially – series 1. In the final scenes of the very last episode, however, this bleak world view catches up with Robin Hill – even as the city seems to have spread out and encroached upon it. Again, we are reminded of Higson's observation about so much Edwardian fiction: the question posed throughout the series is "who is to inherit" Robin Hill and finally, here, no-one is. The house's previous owner, young Jolyon, has died; its heir, Jon, has moved abroad, and its current owner, Irene, has put it up for sale. Soames contemplates buying it, but decides against it, and in the final scenes we see it being emptied of possessions as Irene prepares to leave. It is the setting for her final meeting with Soames, and their reconcili- ation, but significantly it is only shown in pieces: its hall interior, its driveway and its front gate with the "For Sale or To Let" notice upon it. The final shot of Soames walking away from it again only shows a fragment of its front steps. There seems to be a deliberate departure here from the conventional heritage long shots which have lovingly captured the house and its luscious grounds up to this point. (We will see a similar technique in *Parade's End* in Chapter 5.) The adaptation reminds us finally of the post-War problems of inheritance – while making the viewer nostalgic for the house's previous, Edwardian existence as a place of life, music and love. The dynasty itself endures, however: among Soames's last words to Irene is the voicing of his triumphant expectation of grandchildren. Family, fractured though it is, is still the future.

## Art and costume

Robin Hill is not the only way in which this drama engages with modernism or even proto-modernism. A preoccupation with late nine- teenth and early twentieth-century painting is apparent throughout both series, once again most clearly manifested through Soames, who collects art and whose taste reflects his personality. Soames again demonstrates the consumerist nature of our contemporary society, as well as of his own: art for him is a commodity to be purchased and hung on his wall. It is this declaration which makes Irene realise they are "unsuited" even before their marriage. Her hasty and unsympathetic judgement of him may also be one of the moments in which the viewer feels she is a little unfair to Soames, but she is soon to be more than punished for this. The drama uses art to signify the way that women function as possessions and objects in Edwardian society, and Irene will soon be purchased, just as Soames buys the picture that takes his fancy. Like them, he wishes to secrete her away where only he can enjoy her: moving to the country is the equivalent of being stored unseen in his basement, like most of his collection. The adaptation uses costume to reinforce this connection between women and art: in episode 2 Irene literally becomes a portrait, when she appears at a ball in a red velvet dress which is a recreation of that worn by "Madame X" in Sargent's famous – and controversial – 1884 painting of the same name (Smith, 2002: 67). This signifies Irene's function for Soames, and indeed for the lecherous Dartie and others for whom she is, at this ball, an erotic focus of the male gaze. She is still, at this point, Soames's possession, a commodity like the paintings he buys, but this scene marks the beginning of her movement away from him and possessive marriage towards attempted freedom, and her dress also has a part to play in the construction of this. I have already discussed the ways in which Irene is a difficult character to portray fully and sympathetically while being at all faithful to a source text which denies her interiority. Gina McKee's interpretation is "chilly" as a result. However, the 2002 adaptation uses Irene's costumes to attempt to portray her emotions: the rich jewel colours she usually wears hint at her passionate interior, and red outfits in particular frequently signify her sexual desire for Bosinney. The red velvet dress is the most memorable of these, given that she wears it while dancing, scandalously, with him following their declaration of love. Needless to say the rest of the Forsytes, who are watching, are shocked at her sudden courage and very modern disregard for convention. Again the portrait from which this dress has been taken adds intertextual meaning here: Sargent's painting too was ahead of its time and caused consternation and horror among the bourgeois public when it was first displayed in the Paris Salon in 1884 (Davis, 2004: 172). By the time he sold it in 1916, however, it was recognised as the masterpiece of one of the greatest artists of the day (Davis, 2004: 239). The scandalised response to Irene's newly found happiness and freedom at the ball echoes the condemnation of that other implied audience, who are also fixed in the past and cannot recognise the future.

This is not the last time we will see this dress, however. It has a rather more sinister afterlife later in the adaptation. In a disturbing scene in episode 4, Soames, who has now been abandoned by Irene and who is becoming increasingly unbalanced by his loss, takes the dress out of her closet and caresses it on the bed. Jane Gaine's comments about the significance of empty clothes are useful to recall here. She points out that "the ghostly garment is too corpse-like and finally reminiscent of the empty space for woman produced by theories of culture" (Gaines and Herzog, 1990: 3). Quoting Roland Barthes on Ertè, Gaine reminds us that "the empty garment, without head and limbs ... is death ... the body mutilated, decapitated" (Barthes, 1975: 26). Attaching significance to previously worn clothes is a common feature of period drama: inhaling the negligees of women, for example, has become a frequent signifier for frustrated desire. Soames presses Irene's nightgowns to his face in this scene, and Tietjens does the same, in a rather less predatory way, with Sylvia's in *Parade's End*. This masturbatory embracing of the empty ballgown, however, is more uncommon and more perverse, and plays up the gothic elements of the series. This scene works on two levels: firstly it reminds us that Irene is a victim of the male gaze, reduced to a synecdochic and superficial surface by Soames, the other Forsytes, and finally the viewer, who all admire her beauty but have no real insight into the mind which lies beneath it. But it is also recalls the sexual violence which Irene has undergone and is still threatened by, for Soames here, as at other moments throughout the series, becomes a version of a gothic villain. If we accept Barthes, he is the necrophiliac embracing "the body mutilated, decapitated" and this is simply an extension of the way he has already slowly negated and effaced Irene's soul and threatened and violated her body. At this moment, he is at once a distraught victim of love and loss, and a dangerous monster determined in his desire to possess and capture what is no longer his.

This construction of Soames as predator reoccurs throughout the series: after the rape of Irene, he attempts to buy back her affection with the gift of a ruby necklace which might recall Bluebeard in Angela Carter's anti-tale *The Bloody Chamber* (this scene is not in the source text). In Carter's version of that fairytale the villain presents a ruby choker to his new wife, which prefigures his attempt to decapitate her later in the story: he is a sadist for whom women are first possessions and then victims. Soames is not such a monster, but he continues to hound and threaten Irene physically and mentally. Most dramatically, he accosts her in the streets of London when he again tries to buy her with jewellery, presenting her with a diamond brooch and then trying to force himself upon her when she refuses it. Irene is saved from him by the intervention of the prostitutes with whom she has been doing charity work, in a scene which is one of the few examples in the drama of female solidarity and support (her friendship with Soame's cousin June, although no longer acrimonious, is presented as much more uneasy here than it is in the more idealistic source or 1967 version). This incident also emphasises, however, the gothic overtones of the series, much of which is set in a London which recalls the late Victorian gothic novel, with dark streets and heavy fogs. In this place of confused identities, Soames becomes a number of different literary monsters. There are overtones here not only of Bluebeard but of Jekyll and Hyde, and Jack the Ripper – except that the woman Soames preys upon is not a streetwalker, but his own wife. There is a striking contrast here between this sinister urban environment, where there is danger for and from the main characters, and the idyllic rural one at Robin Hill. And this is also the contrast between our views of Victorian England (which we access most usually through the Gothic, from *Dracula* to *Sherlock Holmes*) and the Edwardian period: in its modernism and its enlightened occupants, Robin Hill is associated with the latter, and all that goes along with it.

### *"Painfully aware of their place in life"*: servants in *The Forsyte Saga*

Up to this point I have been focusing on the middle-class preoccupations of *The Forsyte Saga*: its fascination with property both architectural and personal; its anxieties and scandals; its fears over inheritance, and so on. I have, however, barely mentioned a group of characters who constantly appear on screen here, but who are not actually allocated a share of the plot: the servants. Indeed, the most revealing thing about representation of the working classes here is the extent to which they are marginalised, even ignored, by the narrative. Since *Upstairs Downstairs* and *The Duchess of Duke Street* in the 1970s, there seems to be no expectation that the working classes in heritage drama need exist on screen for any other purpose than to serve. *Downton Abbey* would, of course, change all that in 2010. But here those employed by the Forsytes are very much in the background, and significantly, it is only the upper servants – the housekeeper, butler and ladies' maid– who have any dialogue at all. Galsworthy's novels were not much different in this regard, but they were aware of a tension between servants and their employers. We are told, for example, that old Jolyon's butler "didn't care a pin about his master," whom he regards him with "contempt": in return, Jolyon considers him a "sneak" and a "slug" but is philosophical enough to acknowledge that the man wasn't "paid to care" (Galsworthy, 1951: 77). In the adaptation, in contrast, servants are loyal to, even affectionate about, those who they serve. They are frequently portrayed as overcoming their better judgement and putting their own feelings aside in order to be faithful and supportive to their employers, who they indulge in their whims. This is most apparent in series 1 episode 2, when we see the elderly Ann Forsyte having her hairpiece brought to her in bed by her maid. Smithers tacitly agrees to be ignored, even to pretend not to be in the room, until the wig is position, and may only greet her mistress once the "false front" is safely in place. The maid's forced coalescence in an old lady's vanity is present in Galsworthy's novel, and functions there as an indicator of the pride of the Forsytes. The adaptation reads it rather differently, however: later in the series, when Anne has died, Smithers is pictured tenderly positioning the false front on her body in the coffin. The viewer is meant to understand the scene as a display of the maid's devotion to her employer, but this is a devotion not all implied in the source text. It after all does not include this scene and is cynical about the relationship between the two women: Ann complains that Smithers is an adequate maid but "very slow." On screen, in a sanitising and sentimentalising of historical class relationships that anticipates *Downton Abbey*, there are bonds of loyalty and affection between these two women otherwise so separate in age and social position. In a drama that is otherwise so cynical about human relationships, and especially about those between women, this is unusual – but the keeping up of appearances has become a feminine secret that cuts across boundaries.

This is not the only secret kept by servants in this drama, of course. Smithers's awareness of her employer's social pretence foreshadows the much darker knowledge to come to (perhaps the most important servant character) Soames's housekeeper Bilson. Bilson acts as a figure of silent surveillance throughout the slow failure of the couple's marriage: she presumably knows well before Soames that her mistress has taken a lover and that she spends her afternoons with him. She is also aware of the rape itself: like the viewer, the housekeeper is a horrified witness to Irene's cries, but is powerless to intervene or, at least, thinks that she is. She hesitates outside their room during the attack – but ultimately goes about her business as normal. Next morning, she serves Soames at breakfast without judgement and as though nothing has happened. Her only further recognition of the assault is again a silent, passive one: when Irene is preparing to leave Soames and takes her cases through the door, a look of understanding passes between the two women (series 1, episode 3). It is, however, a strangely emotionless moment, for no words are exchanged and sympathy itself does not seem to be in evidence. In this way, the housekeeper's sympathies are aligned with Soames, not his wife, even when she is the victim and he the perpetrator of sexual violence. In fact, such is Bilson's loyalty to her employer that it is she who notices his failing mental health in the next episode, and anxiously summons his mother to his bedside. Indeed, she is still his faithful housekeeper 30 years later, at the end of series 2.

It is difficult to know how to read Bilson's behaviour: she is not given enough narrative attention for us to identify whether she is really sympathetic towards Soames, judgemental towards Irene, or simply motivated only by self-interest and the need for financial security. Kleinecke-Bates has suggested that her actions might remind us of "yet another level in the hierarchy of power which Soames's rape of his wife has introduced," that Bilson, too, is a victim of this patriarchal society. Her livelihood, after all, depends on the good will of her employer and her position in life is much lower than his. However, her refusal to condemn Soames does encourage the viewer to do the same: through her moral neutrality we are reminded that what he is done is at this time legal, possibility even commonplace, and – perhaps – comprehensible if not justifiable. And even if Bilson is as unfathomable as Irene, the other servants are clearly bound to their employers by more than duty: young Jolyon's butler Parfitt, for example, is as devoted to his household as the faithful dog Balthasar, and remains so until the final scene of the drama. His loyalty and affection perpetuates the kind of fantasy of mutual respect and support which would be at the core of *Downton Abbey* eight years later, and which glosses over so the social tensions of the time, as I will discuss in the next chapter. But then, Parfitt serves the bohemian, artistic branch of the family and lives at Robin Hill: it is appropriate, then, that their relationship should be viewed with the same nostalgia that imbues that house.

## Conclusion

Most period drama broadcast on Sunday nights can be characterised as escapist, feel-good television. This will certainly be true of the subjects of my next two chapters, but it is not the case with this adaptation of *The Forsyte Saga*, which is an unusual mix of gothic melodrama and political fable, dark in tone and bleak about human relationships. There is no happy ending here: the last episode concludes with the selling of the family home and the fracturing of the family unit, even if there is at last some kind of reconciliation between the lead characters. This can be attributed to the political climate in which this drama was produced, in which anxieties about a new century were given real and concrete form in the attacks on the World Trade Centre and the subsequent "War on Terror." It can also, however, be considered a response to the heritage criticism of the 1990s, which had condemned period drama for presenting a sanitised, glossy, consumable view of history. The Granada production thus presents (in more detail than its 1967 predecessor) a disturbing rape scene, and portrays dark and gritty views about marriage and social expectation which remind the viewer that the past was often a far from a desirable place – especially if you were female. Even the most idealised aspect of the drama – the family home at Robin Hill – is deliberately modernist and anti-heritage in appearance, and doomed to be disinherited by the plot. Indeed the only aspect of the series which is not especially cynical is the representation of servant/employer relationships, which, unlike the more socially conscious 1967 adaptation, gloss over class conflict and legitimise social hierarchies. Kleinecke-Bates has suggested that this refusal to challenge class structures and "an emphasis on competition and money ... situates the drama historically as part of a post-Thatcherite socio-political climate" and we can see how this drama, while post-heritage in many ways, is still resolutely middle class in subject and audience (2014: 47).

Yet while this drama may suggest that money and "property" binds this family together, it also shows the transience and superficiality of both. And if *The Forsyte Saga* is a family politic, we are at least invited to criticise and judge its patriarch, Soames, and to see the emptiness and futility of the power he wields. When and if he becomes a sympathetic character, it is because we pity him, because he undergoes an emotional breakdown, or loses his wife on not one but several occasions. Eight years later, when *Downton Abbey* hits our screens, no such ambiguity or weakness will surround *its* patriarch. No dissent is allowed to challenge the authority of Lord Grantham, who is intended to be as loved and respected by the viewer as he is by his family and staff. But by this time, of course, a change of government, a worldwide economic crisis, and the continuation of those wars which began after 9/11, had made a return to conventional "heritage" values seem highly attractive once again.

# 3
# Class and Conservatism in *Downton Abbey* (2010–)

ITV's BAFTA and Golden Globe winning *Downton Abbey* was, and is still, the television success story of recent years. First shown in 2010 and now on its sixth series, it has been declared the most successful British period drama since 1981's *Brideshead Revisited*, with average viewing figures of around 9 million per episode, and it has also been extremely popular in America.[1] Its success may partly arise from the fact that it represents a departure from most period productions, being not an adaptation of a classic novel but a made-for-TV drama created by the writer of film re-imaginings of the past like *Gosford Park* and *The Young Victoria*, Julian Fellowes. Thus it does not face the challenges of rendering a literary text accessible for a contemporary audience but instead is made with that audience in mind. As such it combines period drama with elements of the soap opera – a large cast of characters, numerous subplots and parallel storylines – and, like *Gosford Park* and in the tradition of (recently remade) *Upstairs Downstairs*, follows the lives of both servants and employers in the eponymous house. Set between 1912 and the 1920s, with lavish costumes and careful period detail, and making a visual fetish of the stately home (a shot of which lovingly appears between every scene in the first series) this production is in many ways a classic example of what Andrew Higson and other critics have termed a heritage production (Higson, 2003): perhaps more than any other drama currently on television, it has displayed the "marketing and consumption of British heritage as tourist attraction" (Sargent, 2000: 301). For example, Highclere Castle, the real-life Abbey, receives more than 60,000 visitors a year. *Downton Abbey*'s success reveals that on television even very traditional notions of "heritage" remain as popular, marketable and significant as ever, but I will discuss here the ways in which *Downton* self-consciously adapts and responds to this through a range of strategies. This utilisation of heritage for the small screen, its undeniable success, and the subsequent creation of something of a *Downton* "industry" (ranging from books inspired by the series, to a British fashion industry influenced by it) also raises interesting questions about the current consumption of history through popular media, something I will use this chapter to discuss.

It has become commonplace now for historians to concede that film has become "the chief conveyor of public history in our culture" (Rosenstone, 2006: 12), although, as Peter J Beck has discussed, debate continues as to how well the visual media can represent "serious history with a capital H" (Rosenstone, 2006: 2, quoted in Beck, 2012: 168). *Downton* inserts itself neatly, and centrally, into these debates in their current form, for since its first episodes has aired it has, perhaps more than any other recent historical fiction in Britain, prompted public response, and divided opinion regarding its "value" as history. Its accessibility and ease of watching seem to be at the source of much of this criticism, as Jerome de Groot has implied (2011). In particular, its deliberate use of a soap opera format might make us recall Dan Carter's comments about historical documentaries as "soap opera substitutes for real engagement with the past" (1998). David Harlan has discussed how historians like Carter, David Lowenthal and Sean Wilentz are uneasy about fictional history as an "essentially passive spectacle, a neon epic of mind-numbing nostalgia ... [it is] seductive and captivating ... it opens the heart but castrates the intellect" (2007: 120). *Downton,* and its satellite show *Mr Selfridge,* can be said to personify many of these anxieties, given that their largely straightforward plot and sumptuous *mise-en-scene* do create a "seductive" and not too-intellectually-taxing spectacle for the audience (although not, as I will argue here, a "passive" one, given that it at once invites and repulses, and implicates and alienates, the viewer, as we will see). Of course the assumption here is that historical fictions are very different from, and generally inferior to, "actual" academic history: *Downton* "is not a history lesson," as one recent blog suggested, but it "certainly inspires an interest in history."[2] Carter quotes the novelist Robert Penn Warren, the author of *All the King's Men,* as saying that the writer of historical fiction and the historian "had equally important roles to play in understanding our past, but they travelled on separate roads toward the truth" (1998). (Carter's criticism, in his article, of any artistic liberty taken with historical accuracy does imply, however, that he might not entirely agree about those roles being "equally important.") The problem with this view, however, is that it presupposes that it is possible to obtain the "truth" about the past, and also suggests that some mediums give a more authentic access to that truth than others. Recent scholarship has convincingly argued that contemporary historians should be uneasy about these assumptions for a variety of reasons. As Alun Munslow has suggested, in a post-modern world we must accept that we cannot hope to really know the past: all we are really doing is considering a number of possible versions of "the past-as history." Given that all history is an "aesthetic, subjective and ironically construed cultural creation," essentially a story about the past, it is also necessary to accept that the evaluation of one as more authentic or true than another is a problematic concept (Munslow, 2010: 6). As all perspectives of the past are subject to the demands of form, the expectations of the readership/audience, the morals and agenda of the author and, in post-structuralist terms, the limitations and problems of language, we might want to consider a historical media fiction on an equal footing as its more "academic" written cousin. After all, all history is a "personal, impressionistic and expressive undertaking that always exceeds the empirical" (Munslow, 2010: 183) and thus it remains "impossible to know if it is the 'right' (hi)story" (Munslow, 2010: 4).

Harlan applies similar arguments regarding the value of historical fictions, which he suggests need to be part of the "historian's newly enlarged territory" (2007: 121) as they are significant in their own ways. He notes that fictions are often engaged with "recovering the details of everyday life – details that are often so minute that academic historians often overlook them" and thus create a more complete and "fully realised" historical world in which the reader or viewer can be immersed (2007: 121). Certainly it can be argued that *Downton Abbey*, with its emphasis on the domestic sphere and its fascination with everyday artefacts, gives the viewer interesting insights into often-overlooked aspects of the past (there have been plotlines dealing with the excitement and anxiety caused by arrival of the telephone and the electric toaster, for example, and a recent series of "behind the scenes" articles in the *Daily Mail* weekend display the endless public appetite for the minutiae of the *Downton* world). However, even within this acceptance of the significance of fictions to "future history" is a value judgement about what constitutes a useful type of fiction. Ann Rigney, for example, when discussing the relative historical merits of different texts, differentiates between "complex novels," and "popular block-busters," giving *The Da Vinci Code* (2003) as a typical example of the latter. In its existence as popular culture, it seems likely that *Downton Abbey* and *Mr Selfridge* can easily be classed with the "hamburger variant of fiction" that Rigney criticises (2007: 155). In the tradition of the most factually careful kind of British heritage, however, *Downton* has made the appearance of period accuracy its priority. Spotting and debating occasional anachronisms has nonetheless become something of a hobby for some factually minded viewers , but these seem mostly to consist of television aerials appearing in shot, and some (generally hotly debated rather than confirmedly wrong) contentious uses of more modern slang. Thus it seems it can generally be accepted that, in the words of an ITV spokesperson, "A great deal of consultation and painstaking research has gone into ensuring the historical accuracy [of the series]" (Copping, 2010): certainly, costumes and legal and medical information imparted by the plot seem to be correct. Does this commitment to detail make *Downton* "good history," however? There are after all much more profound ideological issues surrounding *Downton's* approach; questions to do with the form, rather than the content, of its "historying." My focus in this chapter, then, is to question what Munslow describes as the ethics of representation, most centrally here to do with class, of Downton's presentation of the past. In order to do this we might remind ourselves of the heritage debate I discussed in the Introduction, in which Higson and others posited that many of the period dramas of the 1980s and 1990s served the values of the then Conservative government, namely individualism, neo-liberalism and family values. Of course that was far from the end of the story, as Claire Monk, and others have discussed: as Jerome de Groot puts it, recent period dramas are "post-heritage" in that "they are not dry, conservative mythmakers ... [they] are flexible and innovative" (2009: 184). De Groot does not seem to regard *Downton Abbey* among these fictions, however. Writing about the first series in *History Today*, he suggests that "it is unarguable that it is little more than a lovingly rendered, uninterrogative version of the past" which invites Higson's original criticism of heritage to "linger" on (de Groot, 2011). While I would not agree with de Groot that *Downton* does not "have anything particularly profound to say about the past" – or rather I will suggest that the most interesting things it has to say are about our present – it does seem apparent that this series is, ideologically speaking, in many ways a return to the more traditional notion of heritage, and the media has tended to agree.[3]

Of course, if the "classic" heritage film, as defined by Higson, was a product of Thatcher's Britain, it seems appropriate that *Downton* should become popular in a time of equal comparable unrest, financial crisis and Conservative-dominated government. As a review in *The Guardian* notes, it is "simultaneously escapist and relevant ... *Downton Abbey* has captured the spirit of our own times: it portrays, in microcosm, a society on the brink of disaster" (Groskop, 2010). Fellowes, himself a Conservative peer who is married to the great-grandniece of the first Lord Kitchener, in fact seems to embrace many of the values associated with the genre which have been condemned by left-wing critics. Indeed, he has suggested that the contrived sense of social "stability" Jarman mentions is the source of his drama's appeal for a contemporary audience:

> I think, in difficult and rude-mannered times, it is comforting for people to see a story about a period of British history when everybody had a station in life, whether it was as a footman or an earl. I'm not saying that's necessarily right, but everybody has a role to play in keeping this huge operation going, upstairs and downstairs, and for the most part they got along. And what lies underneath is a seething maelstrom of human stories. (Lee, 2011)

It is clear here that Fellowes sees his work as a fable for social responsibility and order: the individual exists to serve others and is an indispensable part of the running of the whole machine. Such implicit didacticism makes easy to see *Downton* as following, albeit self-consciously, in the tradition of costume drama from the 1980s. Indeed, as this chapter will argue, the Abbey itself deliberately functions as a microcosm for the state, and it is difficult to ignore the implication that twenty-first century Britain would be more successful if it were organised in the same hierarchal and patriarchal way, even if that is not "necessarily right" to the modern mind. In this regard *Downton* may be fairly described as a conservative drama. As its narrative focus is on the servant class as well as the aristocracy, however, it does engage with what Paul Dave calls the "unresolved conflict between a secure, traditional, elite Englishness and a more unstable sense of national identity" (2006: 27). This conflict is presented to us "through the experiences of those whose lives lie on the social margins and who are traditionally mere 'footnotes' in the national past" (Dave, 2006: 27). I will go on to detail how those "footnotes" – the working class, the colonised subject (represented by the Irish chauffeur, Branson) and the homosexual – are, in Higson's terms, "moved ... to the narrative centre" of *Downton* (2003: 28). Furthermore, *Downton* does not "turn its back on post-modernity": it is in fact a drama preoccupied with the post-modern both in terms of narrative technique and identity politics. Its self-consciousness and meta-fictionality are apparent throughout, and its very concept is post-modern in that the creation of a neo-Edwardian text plays around with, constructs, and ultimately undermines, the notion of authenticity. As Sarah Cardwell suggests, critical engagement with period drama is shaped and driven by a desire for an "authentic" and trustworthy view of the past, but this is complicated by programmes like *Downton* which have completely fabricated that past without the assistance of a classic novel (Cardwell, 2002: 114). Unlike adaptations, such texts create, rather than re-create, history: the vision they offer convinces the viewer because it "conceptualised the past as ... a familiar aesthetic trope" which we can instantly identify. *Downton*, for example, deliberately attempts to create the look and feel of an adaptation of Edwardian fiction: some scenes are reminiscent, for example, of *A Room with a View* (1985),[4] which also starred Maggie Smith, and some of *The Wings of the Dove* (1996) which also starred Elizabeth McGovern.[5] In this way it functions analogously to historical fictions as discussed by Jerome de Groot, undermining "its purported genre," subverting by its very existence "the gravitas and cultural worth accorded to the canonical and 'authentic' text" (2009: 192–193). And, freedom from the adaptation business can be liberating as well as problematically "inauthentic," of course: *Downton* can engage with uncensored modernity with those themes – sexuality, feminism and war – which appeal most to a contemporary audience. It can deliberately play around with our interests and preoccupations without having to trouble itself with fidelity to a source text; so long as it looks "authentic," the viewer accepts it as such.

*Downton* is also post-modern, and indeed, post-heritage, in its self-aware and deliberate pastiche of other classic heritage productions: there are echoes not only of EM Forster but also of Austen, as the plots of *Mansfield Park* and most directly *Pride and Prejudice*, are borrowed and reworked here. As Higson has noted, heritage film often focuses on "a crisis of inheritance among the privileged classes, or the threat of disinheritance": we saw that the end of *The Forsyte Saga* represents such a crisis, and *Downton* does too. Here, however, it is *Pride and Prejudice*'s version of this theme that Fellowes adopts. Such intertextuality seems extremely pragmatic, of course, given the highly lucrative success that has been enjoyed by the Austen industry over the last two decades. Using some of Austen's plots makes *Downton* instantly accessible and desirable to an audience likely to be already familiar with *Pride and Prejudice* through Andrew Davies's hugely successful 1995 adaptation for the BBC, a production which has often since been considered the benchmark for quality costume drama (Cardwell, 2002: 135–158). Thus it is with the pleasure of likely viewers in mind that the three Crawley daughters are, like the Bennet family, the victims of primogeniture and of an entail which will see the estate pass to the unknown cousin Matthew Crawley when Robert, the current Lord Grantham, dies.[6] Matthew proves more of a Mr Darcy than a Mr Collins, however, and he allows the series to ultimately shy away from tackling the gender issues which surround primogeniture when he and Mary, after some initial difficulties caused by pride and prejudice on both sides, fall in love. For most of the first series the gendered nature of inheritance is debated by all the characters and always seems on the point of being challenged, but it never actually is. From the Dowager Countess – a character who, being a sharp-tongued, formidable matriarch who criticises primogeniture, is a more likeable version of Lady Catherine de Bourgh – downwards, the female members of the family struggle against the entail, but their attempts, unsupported by Robert's conservatism, ultimately come to nothing. Mary's disinheritance may be due to a "wicked law" (as even the butler Carson is feminist enough to describe it) but the only real solution the series offers is marriage. Hence it is only the romance with Matthew that makes an Austen fairytale ending possible, though such tidy closure is constantly deferred and is only offered at the end of a second series, throughout which Mary's happiness and reputation remains precarious. In this second series, in which Matthew looks elsewhere for a wife, Mary is on the verge of prostituting herself in a disastrous marriage in order to secure a home. The social, economic and (given Mary's fallen status after losing her virginity) sexual vulnerability of women is made clear, but its direct cause – the entail – is not revisited, for, as in *Pride and Prejudice*, injustices are ultimately resolved by the marriage of the hero and heroine, and are not revived even after Matthew suddenly dies. The dowager may observe that she doesn't "want Robert to use a marriage as an excuse to stop fighting for Mary's inheritance" (series 1, episode 3), but that is in effect exactly what *Downton* itself does.

If Fellowes refuses to go much further than Austen in his response to key feminist issues, however, he does make explicit and central the class relationships that are marginalised by his source texts. Like Fanny Price and Elizabeth Bennet, Matthew is an outsider who joins a family of higher rank, and like an Austen novel, *Downton* follows the process by which he and the other Crawleys come to understand one another and reconcile their class differences, although this is only one of many ways in which this drama investigates social hierarchies, as we will see. (Significantly, the character is played by Dan Stevens, whose most high-profile role prior to *Downton* was as the hero Nick Guest in *In the Line of Beauty* (2006), another middle-class outsider and "ideal heritage spectator" who is seduced by the wealth and privilege he sees (Kagan, 2011).) In this respect Matthew is an important figure in terms of *Downton*'s ideology. As a solicitor from Manchester he functions as a representative of the professional, urbanised middle classes who are the programme's target audience. The link between the two is deliberately played out: Matthew's arrival at the Abbey at the start of episode 2 seems to re-enact the viewer's entry into the *Downton* world at the beginning of episode 1, and his initial response – a mixture of admiration and awe at the spectacle it presents, and distaste for the aristocratic way of life – is likely to be that which the modern viewer has already experienced. The audience has previously been invited to be both amused and appalled at such services as the newspaper being ironed by a servant to prevent the ink coming off on his master's hands, and Matthew's reaction to the pomp and ceremony he witnesses at the Abbey seems to be the same. He voices contemporary, anachronistic anxieties about the "ridiculous" trappings of hereditary wealth, especially regarding servants, which he considers an unnecessary indulgence: indeed, the servant-master relationship which is at the heart of *Downton* is considered by him humiliating to all involved. This is indicated mostly by his rejection of the assistance of his new valet, whom he does not allow to dress or serve him:

[Matthew] "I know I'm a disappointment to you, Molesley. But it's no good. I'll never get used to being dressed like a doll." [Molesely] "Only trying to help, sir." [Matthew] "Of course ... But surely you have better things to do?" [Molesley] "This is my job, sir." [Matthew] "Well [chuckles] it seems a very silly occupation for a grown man. (*Downton*, series 1, episode 2)"

Soon we see him ask Lord Grantham if he can get rid of Molesley because the servant's presence is "superfluous to our style of living." Robert's response is significant because it uses paternalism to justify the class system, while at the same time hinting that that system is artificial:

Is that quite fair? To deprive a man of his livelihood when he has done nothing wrong? Your mother derives satisfaction from her work from the hospital, I think. Would you really deny the same to poor old Molesley? And when you are master here is the butler to be dismissed? Or the footman? ... We all have different parts to play, Matthew – and we must all be allowed to play them. (*Downton*, series 1, episode 2)

Robert's words here are carefully chosen: he implies that class is performative, rather than innate, and that aristocratic status is a learned behaviour. The social implications of this are very contemporary – subverting the Victorian and Edwardian ideas of one's class as intrinsic and god-given – and also very self-consciously meta-fictional: the audience watches an actor playing the role of a man who is "playing" at being a Lord. We might be reminded here of Higson and Dave's observations about "a certain model of Englishness ... presented as a role, an act" in films like *The Tichborne Claimant* (Dave, 2006: 40; Higson, 2003: 32). This post-modern interest in, and display of, theatricality and fictionality is further emphasised in the same episode when the butler Carson, a man admired by the other characters for his dignity and excellence at his job, is revealed to be a former actor and performer with a socially dubious past, and not "descended from a long line of butlers" as is generally believed. Carson, too, then is "playing" at being a butler in the same way as his employer plays at being the master, and so *Downton* implies that despite this world's obsession with breeding and permanence there is nothing natural or intrinsic about the ordering of society and its roles.

Despite this, however, Robert's construction of serfdom as social responsibility, and of middle class work and Molesley's service as essentially the same, seems to convince Matthew, who from this point begins to accept his new role, one which he may "play" even if it does not come naturally to him. He indicates his new acceptance of the class hierarchy he has been thrust into through an exchange with Molesley, where he allows the valet to dress him, and over the choice and insertion of a pair of cufflinks they are symbolically "pinned" together in mutual respect and friendship:

[Matthew] "They seem a dull option for such an occasion, wouldn't you agree?" [Molesley] "May I suggest the crested pair, Sir? They seem more appropriate." [Matthew] "Hmm. They're a bit fiddly, I wonder if you could help me? ... I see you got that mark out of the sleeve– how did you manage it?" [Molesley] "I tried it with this and tried it with that until it yielded... (*Downton*, series 1, episode 2)"

Like the mark on his jacket, Matthew's anxiety about the class system may be stubborn but Downton Abbey, its benevolent patriarch Robert, and its desirable daughter Mary will eventually cause it to "yield" and vanish.

He may anxious about becoming a "puppet" of the upper classes, but even though Downton is like "living in a dream," it is apparent that that is much preferable to reality (*Downton*, series 1, episode 7). Where once Matthew was resistant and anxious about being assimilated into the upper classes, remarking "I won't let them change me ... [Robert] wants to limit the damage by turning me into one of his own kind" – by the second series he displays no trace of his previous ideological objections, and his main concerns are about his ability to continue the family line. Notably he does attempt to take a wife – a "little person, an ordinary person" – from the middle classes, but her convenient death from Spanish influenza allows for the final union with Mary which, and whom, of course, he secretly prefers (*Downton* series 2, episode 8). Moreover, by series 3 he is so successfully assimilated that he is clashing with Robert over the management of the estate (episode 5). Matthew thus comes to feel that his class awareness and anxiety about his position can be channelled into paternalism and love, both personal and social, rather than change or equality. There is a clear attempt here to reassure the viewer, through Matthew, that the future of the aristocracy – and by extension the country – is here in good, socially caring hands (at least until the end of the long Edwardian period, for a new decade brings about the death of Matthew and a host of new problems and instabilities).

In fact for the most part the servant/master relationships throughout *Downton* reiterate this assurance of paternalist benevolence. Lord Grantham employs a lame valet, Bates, because he served with him in the Boer War, and insists on keeping him even when the other servants cast doubt on his abilities to do his job; Lady Sybil helps her maid find a clerical position so she can escape service; Carson is defended by Robert against a blackmailer. Loyalty works both ways, too, with the housekeeper and valet both prepared to sacrifice their personal lives for the family's happiness and reputation. The drama validates and sanitises class inequality by framing it in terms of mutual support and even love. The view it presents, of a world in which people work together for the good of the whole, is idyllic and reassuring – for even in one of the few cases when the head of the family does not help out (being unaware of the situation of a servant who is impregnated and then abandoned by a member of the upper classes) the concern and charity of the housekeeper provides her with the means to live (*Downton*, series 2).

## The 1911 Insurance Act

Given its didactic message of mutual help and support, it is unsurprising that *Downton* has risen to popularity at a time when welfare, in particular healthcare, provision is a hotly contested topic in both Britain and the United States. Since 2010 the NHS's role has been the subject of debate and dispute in Britain and major reform is constantly on the political agenda of a Conservative-led Coalition government committed to public spending cuts. In the same period, the Patient Protection and Affordable Care Act, more usually known as "ObamaCare," has brought about the most extensive changes to healthcare in America since the 1960s, and has caused much controversy in the States. In the *Downton* world, illness and disability are a constant presence, but paternalism does away with any need for a welfare state, and this does seems like a clear attempt to reassure and comfort a British audience dealing with public spending cuts on a scale unequalled since the 1980s.

This is a rather manipulative modern representation of the years in which *Downton* is set. As I discussed in Chapter 1, the Edwardian period has been viewed by historians from the 1960s onwards as being one of social reform, which marked the origins of what would become the modern welfare state in Britain. One of the main developments of the time was the 1911 National Insurance Act, Part 1 of which dealt with health insurance, and which provided sick pay, through compulsory contributions, for the working classes. This aimed to "prevent the poverty that would follow from the worker's illness and consequent inability to earn" and also "significantly increased the number of those able to see a doctor, and consequently increased doctor's incomes" (Johnson, 1994: 87). The Act did not instantly bring about radical change, but it did form the starting point for more extensive social reforms which took place after the Second World War, one of the most important of which was the creation of the National Health Service – "a major public health achievement ... comprehensive, inclusive, and free at the point of delivery" – in Britain in 1948 (Baggott, 2000: 45).

The series only references the 1911 Act in passing – Robert mentions "Lloyd George's new insurance measures" conversationally at the dinner table – but class and economic issues provide a subtext to every servant's ailment in the series (1:2). For example, the cook, Mrs Patmore, begins to lose her sight towards the end of series 2, and, like Bates who struggles with his lame leg, her job is under threat as a result. However, the family step in and pay for her to have a cataract operation at

Moorefield's, which is successful. In the *Downton* world, there is no need for an organised, external welfare state: the house and its owners will provide and care for their staff, in ways which are a significant departure from the laissez-faire legacy of the New Poor Law which had in actuality controlled British provision until this point. Paternalism, loyalty and love are more crucial than any insurance, as even the previously independent housekeeper learns when she has a cancer scare in series 3:

> Mrs Hughes, I only want to say one thing. That if you are ill, you are welcome here for as long as you wish to stay. Lady Sybil will help us find a suitable nurse. I don't want you to have any concerns about where you will go or who will look after you, because the answer is: here, and we will. (*Downton*, series 3, episode 3)

Mrs Hughes is surprised, as well as "touched," by the support offered by her employers, but the viewer is not, for her plotline is only a more sombre version of that already experienced by Mrs Patmore and Bates. And, like them, her story has a happy outcome, for shortly after she has the above conversation with Cora, she learns that her lump is benign. Kept secret from her employers, the possible illness has worried her for months: within a day of sharing with them, her worries are put to rest. It is as if she too is healed by the nurturing environment in the household, and this implies that trust, honesty, and communication between employer and employee make further medical intervention unnecessary.

## "Doubting Thomas" and class tension in the Abbey[7]

As we have seen, *Downton*'s view of class relationships is almost always a rosy one. The only dissenting voices in this idealised society are those of the supposedly "bad" characters, Thomas the footman and O'Brien the ladies' maid, who are both viewed with suspicion by everyone else at Downton. "Guy Fawkes and his assistant," as Bates the valet describes them, are considered to be untrustworthy, disloyal and dangerously radical because they frequently voice their frustration with their lot, and don't hesitate to criticise their employers, in private if not directly. Nonetheless, Thomas and O'Brien are the most important and complex characters in the servants' hall, as well as the most relevant to a twenty-first century perspective: their complaints about their working conditions and their employers seem more "modern" than the unquestioning loyalty displayed by most of the others.

Thomas (who, further adding to Downton's soap-opera feel, is played by former Coronation street star Rob James-Collier), is the voice of modernity and equality in the drama, objecting to the lack of freedom and privacy which accompany a life of service: "we can say what we like down here ... there's such a thing as free speech" (*Downton*, series 1 episode 2). For the viewer, however, such subversive willingness to comment on the unfairness of the class system is undermined by the fact that, if there are any villains in *Downton* it is these two, in the eyes of the other servants at least, and that their struggle against the class system is often represented as disloyalty. O'Brien is particularly problematic in these terms, for her rebellion against the system takes the form of curtailing the perpetuation of this dynasty. At the end of series one Cora becomes pregnant with the family's last chance for a direct heir: if the child is a boy, he and not the middle-class cousin Matthew will inherit the estate. In a politically loaded act, however, O'Brien destroys this opportunity. Believing her years of service to Cora are about to be abruptly terminated, she takes her revenge on the "filthy, ungrateful cow" (*Downton*, series 1, episode 7) by orchestrating a fall which causes the child, who was indeed a boy, to be miscarried. O'Brien here reveals the power servants wield: their subservient position is actually potentially very subversive because those in "authority" are so dependent upon them. The family can be damaged, and its future imperilled, thanks to the servant's personal access to Cora at her most vulnerable – in the bath – and it can be done in a way which ensures no blame is attributed (her guilt undiscovered, O'Brien is still Cora's maid by the end of the next series). More than simple revenge, this act has a wider symbolic significance in that it indicates that the aristocracy's future is as fragile as the easily damaged human body (whose vulnerability we are repeatedly reminded of throughout *Downton*, given its thematic preoccupation with illness) and that it is power from below, from those who serve, which will destroy it. This proves a significant ending to the first series, in that it anticipates the "fall" of the old way of life: Cora's miscarriage occurs in the days leading up to the outbreak of the First World War. As I mentioned in the previous chapter, Higson observes that "the idea of heritage implies a sense of inheritance, but it is precisely that which is on the wane in these films ... the problem is generally posed as a question: who is to inherit...?" (2003: 28). *Downton* is clearly preoccupied with the future of the estate/nation and anxious about the part played by the lower classes in this future. The political implications here are played down, and indeed smoothed over, by the personal context, however. This is a tragedy and all the more so because it is born out of a misunderstanding, O'Brien's job never being under threat at all. This necessarily undermines the rebelliousness of the act, O'Brien herself viewing it as a terrible mistake which she immediately regrets, and goes on to atone for with a new devotion and loyalty to her employer. Indeed, her redemption as a more compassionate character in series 2 is largely predicated upon this atonement and her determination to not let her mistress be harmed again, by anyone. Among the servants mourning the lost child, only Thomas points out the futility of grieving for "a woman who scarcely knows his name," but again this is outweighed as political point by his observation that "she'll get over it ... they are no bigger than a hamster at that age." The other characters, along perhaps with the viewer, react to this casual cruelty with horror and disgust, especially as it is immediately followed by an even more uncaring jibe about the recent bereavement of one of the other servants (*Downton*, series 1, episode 7).

It is Thomas, then, who remains the most radical of all the characters in the show, but he is also in many ways the most unlikeable and this serves to question the motive, if not the validity, of his politics. The audience might well agree with his rejection of paternalism: "why must we live through them? They are just our employers, they are not our flesh and blood." They cannot, however, escape his construction as a liar, a thief and a bully. This is especially problematic because, as above, his crimes are not only directed at his employers, but towards the most vulnerable members of his fellow staff. William, the under-footman, is a regular victim of his sharp tongue, and he also exploits the innocence of the kitchen maid Daisy, who is attracted to him and is naïvely unaware that he is homosexual. In fact Daisy's admiration for Thomas, who manipulates her into lying for him, is described as "being under an evil spell" and when William finally is goaded into violence by his taunts, the other characters agree that Thomas "had it coming" (*Downton*, series 1, episode 7). With this in mind it is difficult to view the first series of *Downton* as anything but homophobic, especially given that Thomas is only surpassed in evil by the only other gay character in the series, the mercenary and manipulative Duke of Crowborough. The Duke – a charming rake somewhat reminiscent of *Pride and Prejudice*'s Wickham – attempts to marry Mary for her money, while continuing his secret relationship with Thomas, and their cynical affair ends in mutual distrust, blackmail and bitterness. In this regard *Downton* seems to reverse the tradition of classic heritage, which has been "notably hospitable to homosexual subject matter" by suggesting that "gays belong in what is handed down as cherishable from the past" (Dyer, 2001: 43). Thomas's presence ensures that *Downton* does "put gay men into history," but his homosexuality cannot be described as "cherishable" – given that he is "put into history" as a corrupter of innocence and a stage villain (Dyer, 2001: 45). However, we might prefer to regard Thomas as an example of the kind of complex character Ellis Hanson suggests forms part of a "promising backlash against [the] preoccupation with positive images" of gay characters in film, which he considers a reductive "good-gay cliché" (1999: 9). Citing a number of films from the 1990s, most famously *Philadelphia* (1993), Hanson notes that "instead of accurate or positive images of the gay community, we find predictable types and cardboard role models," which make him "nostalgic for queer villains" (1999: 9). Certainly, in a drama filled with extremely altruistic and morally upright characters, Thomas, *Downton's* "queer villain" stands out as an important and interesting exception: an anti-hero who, with his modern sensibility and the ironic detachment born of his outsider status, functions as an important point of reference for the viewer.

Furthermore, it is important to note that the portrayal of Thomas does undergo revision in the second series of *Downton*. He remains hostile to most of the other characters, but for the first time the viewer has an insight into why. Early in the second series, Thomas attempts to comfort a despairing, recently blinded officer by sharing his own experiences of being marginalised and "pushed around" because he is "different," and that as a result he has had to "fight his corner" throughout life (*Downton*, series 2, episode 1). This scene suggests a link between Thomas's sexuality and his new friend's disability: a politically dubious comparison, certainly, but one which confronts the viewer, almost for the first time in the series, with a sense of the discrimination and prejudice Thomas has endured. The suggestion here (made through a subplot involving a man unable to "see") is that Thomas has been presented as a villain largely because of the ways he has been viewed by the other, homophobic, characters. And of course viewers are implicated in this discrimination because they had previously accepted the characterisation of Thomas and had not recognised that he in fact might be a victim. *Downton* builds on this further in later series plots, in which Thomas is persecuted by the law because of his sexuality, and undergoes traumatic medical "treatment" in an attempt to become heterosexual. Hence from this confessional moment onward we are invited to view his aggression and sarcasm as defiance, and even his bullying of William is understandable as jealously and (justified) resentment: William is loved and protected by the other servants because he is simple, straightforward and heterosexual – a foil to Thomas's complexity, intelligence and darkness.

## Downton at war

The contrast between this representation of the two footmen symbolises many of the ideological struggles and tensions in the drama, especially in series 2, where the prevailing ideology is challenged by the coming of war. Evil or not, Thomas is more perceptive, pragmatic and far-seeing than any of the other characters: he not only anticipates the First World War but plans how to survive it. Before war is even declared he joins the medical corps in an attempt to avoid the Front, and when this fails he allows himself to be shot in the hand in order to be sent home. Such tactics may be the opposite of heroic but *Downton* (which has several sympathetic characters, including Molesley, who are determined to avoid being sent to France) hints that they are a sensible and pragmatic response to the destructive madness of war. For Thomas the conflict is an opportunity for rapid social advancement, in that he orchestrates a return to Downton as a medical officer who oversees the running of the house and is no longer answerable to the hierarchy he had resented so much. William, in contrast, is punished for his blindly devoted patriotism when he is the only member of the household to be killed. In fact William's death challenges the whole ethos of unquestioning service that the first series of *Downton* championed: he is effectively duped by propaganda which glorifies war and so he is willing, even enthusiastic, to give his life for king and country: "I believe in this war. I believe in what we are fighting for and I want to do my bit" (*Downton*, series 2, episode 2). Such a statement seems foolishly naïve to a modern audience who knows the political outcome of the war, as well as how it is likely to end for William. In this regard, it is Thomas who acts as the voice of that audience when he, with his usual cynicism and clarity, anticipates William's death by describing him as "cannon fodder" even before the fighting has properly begun. William's political naiveté is paralleled by his emotional gullibility, for he is also fooled by Daisy's reluctant participation in their romance, which he believes is genuine but which on her side is only born out of pity and guilt. The audience are invited to share in this pity when William saves Matthew – now his commanding officer – on the battlefield, an act which proves his loyalty as both servant and soldier, but which brings about his own death. The implication here – that service equates to death – is surprising given the previous message of the series. We can see here that while William is the epitome of the honest Tommy, his limited intelligence and unquestioning acceptance of all forms of authority make him a character who belongs to the old world and who has no place in the new.

This critique of patriotism and obedience is continued throughout those plots which deal with the War. In this regard, of course, *Downton* offers a particularly modern view of the First World War, as a "futile struggle, directed by dull-witted generals whose only strategy was to waste young lives" (Paris, 1999: 51). Michael Paris, among others, has noted that this has been the popular "negative interpretation of 1914–18" since the 1960s (1999: 52). As both he and GD Sheffield have pointed out, modern understandings of the conflict are epitomised by the 1989 BBC comedy series *Blackadder Goes Forth*, which stresses the carelessness of those in charge and the pointlessness of what they aimed to achieve. Blackadder's critical "portrayal of British strategy and tactics ... is funny because everyone 'knows' that British generals were incompetent and that their battles were inevitably bloody failures" (Sheffield, 1996: 55). Fellowes, perhaps unsurprisingly, follows in this tradition, but, more significantly, his characterisation is also made to fit this ideology. In this regard *Downton* does not seem too concerned with historical accuracy: there is little attempt to portray the Edwardian "patriotic fervour" and the nation's widely held belief, in 1914, "that war would not only be a great adventure, but also a miracle cure for Britain's ills (Clark, 1996: 48)." Sheffield argues that "even in 1918 British military and civilian morale and enthusiasm for the war were probably as high as they had ever been," but there is little evidence of this among the characters in the series – unlike in *Mr Selfridge*, which as we will see in the next chapter takes a very different approach only a couple of years later (Sheffield, 1996: 59). *Downton*, however, is much more interested in reflecting of its audience's feelings, in the twenty-first century, than it is in presenting us with an accurate but for many unpalatable version of the past.

It is through the drama's portrayal of shell shock that this – probably anachronistic – lack of support for the war becomes most apparent. The mental trauma and psychological breakdown inflicted by the Trenches is understood and sympathised with in the Abbey in a way it would probably not have been even by 1917. Lord Grantham, for example, has nothing but compassion for his new valet Lang, who has been sent home from France because of his shell shock and who is troubled by those "who look at me and wonder why I am not in uniform." Robert reassures him by saying "you've been invalided out. That is perfectly honourable" (*Downton*, series 2, episode 2). This compassionate treatment in the Abbey is clearly constructed on modern lines, for, as Peter Leese has observed, in reality "comrades in arms, friends and family frequently saw traumatic neurosis as either cowardice or madness" throughout the war years" (2002: 21). Even though it is only O'Brien who really understands his illness, the Downton community supports Lang in the same ways they do all the other invalids throughout the series. Moreover, given Lang's clearly apparent physical health, he is fortunate to have been correctly diagnosed by the army and not sent back or punished as a malingerer: "military medics and higher ranking officers were usually sceptical about the diagnosis of shell shock, and they turned this belief into official policy" (Leese, 2002: 5). Perhaps a more authentic fate for the traumatised and disturbed combatant – one who is not fortunate enough to come under the protective umbrella of Lord Grantham's patronage – is the example of Mrs Patmore's nephew who, we learn, had been court-martialled and shot as a deserter. "Courts-martial were viewed as a necessary tool in the policing of unmilitary behaviour" and, given the frequent refusal to recognise shell shock as a defence, resulted in the execution of at least 307 soldiers in the British Army during the War, in an attempt to maintain morale and discipline. Once again, however, *Downton* takes the modern perspective and regards the unseen Corporal with compassion, constructing him as a victim, not a coward, as this exchange between Lang and Mrs Patmore indicates:

> "I sometimes feel I'm the only one who knows what is going on over there. You all wander around ironing clothes and cleaning boots and choosing what's for dinner, while over the Channel men are killed and maimed and blown to pieces." "We know more than you'd think. The war hasn't left us alone, it hasn't left me alone, however it may look." "Have you any idea how scared they are? How scared they all are?" "I lost my nephew ... he was shot for cowardice, they said. But I knew him, and he'd never have done such a thing if he hadn't been half out of his mind with fear"." "Don't blame him. It was him but it could have been me. It could have been any of us." (*Downton*, series 2, episode 3)

Lang's comment here "that it could have been any of us" is pertinent given that this series displays some kind of breakdown in almost all of the male characters, whether or not they have fought in France. Copelman has argued that is Lang who is "the primary stand-in for the trauma of the war, representing how the initial enthusiasm ... turned into weariness, disillusion, anger, loss and mourning all around" (2013). Certainly Lang's primary function in the narrative is to manifest the symptoms and consequences of shell shock: after repeated nightmares, failures serving at table, and finally breaking down in tears in front of a visiting general, he is proclaimed unfit for work and forced to leave the Abbey, his story there at an end. Copelman has suggested that "one not-quite-crucial character cannot carry that burden: *Downton's* portrayal of the actual war and its impact is quite sanitized" as a result of being "confined" to Lang (2013). This seems an over-simplification of the complicated ways the programme explores the period, however. It is true that the other survivors of the war do not appear to be traumatised by their experiences in the same way, but shell shock is not the only mental illness under investigation here. In fact, depression, anxiety and loss of identity afflict almost all the male characters. Even Carson, the most reliable and stalwart "guardian of the old order" of all the servants, experiences what can be considered a hysteric illness, collapsing from stress-induced exhaustion while serving at the dinner table. That the formidable Butler is exhausted and unable to continue with his duty, reflects the crisis in masculinity key to the second series, which sees Matthew paralysed from the waist down, and even Lord Grantham become depressed and "wretched" about his life and his family's future (series 2, episode 8).

We will see this challenge to the previously powerful, virile and secure Edwardian male again in *Parade's End*, which also reveals the extent to which the war undermined old certainties. In *Downton*, however, it is one of a number of social changes which take place in series 2, many of which do reflect the coming of modernity. As Matthew puts it while drinking with Thomas, his former footman, at the Front, "War has a way of distinguishing between things that matter and things that don't" (*Downton*, episode 1, series 2). Rank *seems* irrelevant to him in the trenches (of course in actuality it was not) and the number of cross-class relationships – from Lord Grantham's romance with his housemaid to Edith's short-lived fling with a local farmer – at home symbolises a new fluidity there too. Even Branson's (the chauffeur) declaration of love to Lady Sybil, which shocks her at the start of the War, is reciprocated and results – much to the dismay of the rest of the family – in marriage by the end.

In this light, "*Downton* at war" as the second series has been described,[8] is really more accurately "*Downton* at war with itself." Fellowes's creation chronicles a time of rapid transition and suggests that war acts as a social leveller, yet still clings fast to a socially conservative message. For example, the new maid, Ethel, wishes for social mobility and voices her frustration with being a servant, yet her attempt to improve her station and better her life only ends in illegitimate pregnancy, abandonment by the father and, eventually, prostitution. Similarly, Robert's cross-class affair is never consummated and Mary's engagement to new money is eventually called off in favour of marriage to Matthew, the heir (by now thoroughly assimilated into the upper classes). And, of course, the second series closes with Thomas being humbled because his post-war attempt to become a businessman has proved futile, for the present at least. Thomas's escape plans are only ever temporary: he always returns to Downton and to a life of service. The drama makes very clear that it will not reward disloyalty and ingratitude, just as it will not condone adultery (even at the expense of the potentially exciting plot possibilities and moral complexities which might have resulted: the viewer seems likely to be frustrated, as much as reassured, by Robert's sexual self-control and his rekindled devotion to his wife). The Abbey itself reflects this conservatism: the war demands that the house changes its role and so it becomes a convalescent hospital, but one which – despite some debate about admitting soldiers from all walks of life – is only open to officers. When the war is over it once again closes its doors and becomes again a family home – although, as plot developments in series 3 reveal, Downton will not be entirely returned to its happy, secure pre-war existence.[9]

This commitment to continuity and refusal to acknowledge the problems of modernity are reflected in the drama's representation of the War itself. There is a deliberate distancing from the political origins of the conflict: although a drama which has repeatedly come under fire for its right-wing agenda, *Downton* frequently prefers to avoid direct engagement with political events, as though they endanger the escapist qualities of the programme. As Dina M Copelman has suggested, in *Downton*: "World War I is presented as a somewhat abstract affair. There are a few references to specific events, but for the most part we have very little sense of political developments ... the political turmoil ... remains off screen" (2013). So too, of course, does much of the reality of life in the trenches: rats, lice and general squalor are not readily apparent in the war scenes here. Some critics have interpreted this as an historically inaccurate, and indeed ideologically disturbing, white-washing of the War (an accusation which is, of course, based on the generally recognised sanitising of class conflict apparent in the series as a whole), as this journalist notes:

*Downton Abbey*'s depiction of trench warfare in the series 2 has received withering fire from history buffs. "No mud? No blood?" commented one incredulous blogger. The ITV programme's sanitised portrayal of the conflict has irritated historically minded viewers almost as much as the rogue TV aerials, yellow parking lines and modern conservatories that cropped up in the first series (Barrett, 2011).

In fact there seems to me to be plenty of blood in series 2 of *Downton*, for every episode deals with one, or more, different war tragedies: Lieutenant Courtenay's gas blindness, and resulting depression and tragic suicide; Thomas's self-invited gunshot wound to the hand; and Matthew's spinal injury, which once again brings the long-term survival of the Crawley family into question, are just some of these. Certainly scenes set on the Front are kept to a minimum, however. The drama instead chooses to mediate and comprehend the horrors of battle through the bodies of its characters, after they return from France. This is of course typical of Downton's narrative strategy, which with a few exceptions chooses to locate all its plots within the Grantham estate, as though the outside world does not exist (*The Village* will follow the same format, as we will see). The sense of comforting, controlled familiarly this isolationism usually gives is another aspect of the show which is reminiscent of a Jane Austen adaptation, but in this instance there is no rose-tinted escape for the viewer from the damage that trench warfare inflicts on the human body. In this way, *Downton* does not sanitise war, as it does so many other aspects of history, but it does confine and control it by relocating it within a familiar safe environment of the house. And, for the most important (and most upper-class) characters, this suffering has a happy ending, when Matthew melodramatically walks again (*Downton*, series 2, episode 6).

## Conclusion

*Downton* is thus a contradictory text in many ways. Fellowes himself has argued that, in an attempt to be true to "our present zeitgeist" it "gives equal weight, in terms of narrative or moral probity or even likeability" to both servants and their employers (2011: 7). In terms of narrative weight, the series may well devote the same time and attention to all its characters, but it also keeps those who serve in their place and punishes those who are ungrateful. It is bookended with disasters – its first series begins with the sinking of the Titanic, its second closes with the influenza pandemic – yet it reassures viewers that the inhabitants of the house will weather such storms together, with minimal disruption. Throughout both Edwardian series, there is no tragedy which cannot be overcome with togetherness, loyalty and love. As a metaphor for contemporary Britain beset with economic and social difficulties, *Downton* acts as an idealised vehicle of reassurance for its audience. Even devolution and Irish rebellion, as epitomised by the politically minded chauffeur, are safely contained by the narrative: it becomes apparent that Branson is planning an act of terrorism on a visiting English General, but the plan in question is rendered humorous and light-hearted when it turns out to involve rotten soup, rather than murder. Indeed the Abbey itself functions as a unified and inclusive nation, with Scottish and Irish servants working side by side. This symbolic nation may be temporarily split when Branson elopes with Sybil, but it is ultimately reconciled when series 3 has the couple and their child welcomed back into the family and the house. Ultimately this kind of comforting cohesion and inclusion goes a long way towards explaining why *Downton*, despite its complexities, can be viewed as deliberately returning to the heyday of 1980s heritage film in and the "secure world of an earlier Englishness" which that seemed to represent (Craig, 2001). Its critics have received it as an ideological tool of the Right, a conservative nation in microcosm which puts forward traditional values of loyalty and order. Indeed, the ideological links between *Downton* and the current Government have been noted and exploited by *The Guardian*, *Private Eye* and the Leader of the Opposition.[10] Perhaps what is most "post-heritage" about this series, then, is the post-modern way it blurs the lines between real life and fiction – to the extent that, due to its focus on money and privilege, the Coalition in power from 2010–2015 has been nicknamed "the Downton Abbey government" (Freeland, 2012). *Downton*'s most useful and serious message, after all, may be its ability to remind the viewer that, in terms of social mobility, contemporary society is not as far removed from the Edwardians as we might like to think.

I have throughout this essay been trying to suggest that *Downton Abbey* is interesting precisely because of these kinds of complexities and the problems that surround it. Claire Monk has argued, persuasively and influentially, that "heritage film has lost its ideological substance ... or that the heritage-film critique has lost its currency" in recent years, as criticism has redefined its analysis of what period drama is and what it can be (2002: 195). *Downton* seems to indicate that that is no longer quite true, however. As will have been apparent, it seems to me impossible to consider or discuss Fellowes's creation without invoking Higson and Craig's, now contested, comments about heritage film as style-dominated and materialist, and ultimately ideologically conservative. Of course such qualities are by no means confined to period drama or to conventional heritage, as Monk notes (2002: 195). But *Downton* is deliberately, and shamelessly, harking back to the heyday of 1980s and 1990s "classic" heritage, and its success implies that viewers are willing to go along for the ride. Fellowes, himself a highly controversial public figure, has defended his sanitised view of the past by being dismissive of gritty social realism in the media: "people are pleased to see something on television that isn't about a dead prostitute in a dustbin" (Copping, 2010). Fellowes may be being deliberately provocative here, but it is true that his success seems to stem from the marketing of a kind of aesthetically pleasing, escapist and yet loosely educational television to a wide – and not just middle class – audience looking for distraction from world-wide recession. A comparison with the subject of Chapter 5, described as the "thinking person's *Downton Abbey*," makes this clear. Tom Stoppard wrote the screenplay for *Parade's End*, Susanna White's adaptation of Ford Maddox Ford's trilogy, and the result, an atmospheric production with a challenging plot, was critically acclaimed. It did not achieve great popular success, however: initial viewing figures of 3.1 million tailed off dramatically after the first episode, contrasting markedly with the continuing appeal of *Downton*. Historical drama of a more "highbrow" nature still has its audience, clearly, but that audience is a limited one. As David Kamp has expressed it:

> the show is welcome counter-programming to the slow-burning despair and moral ambiguity of most quality drama on television right now. *Mad Men, Breaking Bad, Homeland* – all are about people who succumb to the darkest, most transgressive aspects of their nature. *Downton Abbey*, meanwhile, is largely about people trying to be ... good. (2012)

Both *The Forsyte Saga* and *Parade's End* have this kind of "moral ambiguity," their main characters conflicted and conflicting, and their view of the past bleak and nostalgic at the same time. In contrast, Fellowes's "post-post-heritage" formula, his soap-opera-style makeover of period drama, seems to offer the viewing public its history in the most readily consumable, palatable form. Perhaps this is what is most radical about *Downton*'s pastiche of the heritage mode: it is period drama made familiar and accessible to wide sections of the population, not only the culturally literate middle classes who are the usual consumers of this type of programme. Moreover, Fellowes's dominance of televisual popular history looks set to continue: his other recent Edwardian drama for ITV, *Titanic*, opened with viewing figures of 7.2 million; he has Shakespeare and Agatha Christie adaptations currently in pre-production; and there is already a media buzz around his new, late Victorian, drama *The Gilded Age*, which will begin filming next year, as *Downton* draws to a close. And, as we will see in the next chapter, many aspects of Fellowes's approach have been imitated by Andrew Davies in *Mr Selfridge*. Thus *Downton* may be part of a continuing trend in the popularisation of history and one which is full of contradictions and debates: is it useful as history, being factually accurate, or damaging for being ideologically problematic? Does it stimulate public interest in history in a positive way, acting as a "stepping stone that motivates" the viewer to find out more – or does it just "dumb-down" a past which is reduced to melodrama? (Rigney, 2007: 168). What is certain, of course, is that *Downton* is most significant not for what it tells us about the Edwardian past, but for what it communicates about the cultural appetites of the present, as we re-imagine and consume that past on the small screen.

# 4

# From *Downton* to the Department Store: Sex, Shopping and Heritage in *Mr Selfridge* (2013–)

*Mr Selfridge* appears, superficially at least, to share the same *Upstairs Downstairs* concept and format as *Downton Abbey*, and can be regarded as another attempt on the part of ITV and Masterpiece to combine soap opera and heritage drama, with a view to recreating *Downton*'s success. It cannot be said that it has quite achieved this, but it has been very well received, with average ratings between 5 and 8 million per episode in Britain, and is currently enjoying a successful run in the United States. Moreover, *Mr Selfridge* has beaten BBC's rival shopping show, *The Paradise*, which was dropped after two series: Davies's show has been commissioned for four. The show represents a reboot or evolution of the period drama, given that it exchanges the rural stately home in which *Downton* – among many other costume serials – is set, for the famous London department store. *The Paradise* shares a similar format, although as it is set earlier, in the late Victorian period, it is outside the scope of this book. There are a number of similarities between the two shows, however, which makes a comparison useful, as Andrea Wright has explored (2015: 224–235). Both draw on popular 1990s BBC fashion serial *The House of Eliot*, although their production values are very different from that cheaply made show: *Mr Selfridge* in particular is notable for its glossy appearance, extravagant costumes and impressive set, with a budget of about 1 million per episode (Whitelocks, 2013). Like *The House of Eliot*, however, these shows both explore a female history: both contain narratives of female ambition and charter the entry of women into the workplace and the public sphere. There is a sharp contrast here with *Downton*, which as I have discussed is at best ambivalent and at worst hostile to the progression of first-wave feminism it chronicles. In other ways, however, *Mr Selfridge*, given the hierarchal and ultimately patriarchal organisation of the store, echoes and reinforces the ideology which dominates Fellowes's show. It is these complexities and contradictions, and others like them, which will form the core of this chapter.

*Mr Selfridge* is perhaps the most "lowbrow" and popularly accessible of the texts I examine in this book. It has been described, for instance, as a "poor man's *Downton Abbey*": pretty damning considering that *Downton* itself has not exactly been embraced by many critics, as we have seen (Rackyl, 2014). The plots of *Mr Selfridge* are fairly straightforward and formulaic, and it has been accused of prioritising style over substance in terms of its glossy, feel-good content (Hinkley, 2014) and lack of subtlety: "*Mr Selfridge* isn't the sort of production to risk letting its viewers miss the point" as one reviewer cruelly notes (Tate, 2014). This is not in any way to distract from its interest, however, for it is also more unorthodox and innovative than most other recent period dramas. Its departure from convention is apparent right from its source text: it is not an adaptation of a classic Edwardian novel, but of a biography of the eponymous main character, adapted for the small screen by Andrew Davies. It is not that unusual for period dramas to be based on biographical or auto-biographical texts: BBC1's *Lark Rise to Candleford* was adapted from such, for example. However, the biography in question here, Lindy Woodhead's *Shopping, Seduction and Mr Selfridge*, is more of a factual history of the evolution of the department store than a novelistic account of a man's life. In tone and approach it does not feel like an obvious choice for adaptation for a Sunday-night period drama, or for Davies, dubbed "King of the Adapters" who is well known primarily for his adaptations of big canonical novels for that slot, perhaps most famously his 1995 BBC *Pride and Prejudice* (Moore, 2008). The making of the show, then, reveals a fairly new willingness on behalf of its writers to look for new possibilities and to expand the definition of "heritage" further.

Indeed Davies is at pains to differentiate the show from *Downton*, as he reveals in an interview for *Time Out* (it is ironic that the creators of all the period dramas I discuss here, while clearly influenced by one another, always feel the need to assert their independence):

> At the moment, *Downton Abbey* is the touchstone for populist ITV drama but Davies gently baulks at the comparison. "*Downton* is about conserving tradition," he argues. "We're about modernity and glamour and change. That doesn't mean we don't like *Downton*. But our characters have different values." Davies is right. *Downton* represents the death throes of a bygone era – hereditary privilege, deference and

the status quo are under siege but defending themselves vigorously. *Mr Selfridge*, with its new foreign money, nascent brand culture and emerging consumerism represents a new age being born. Our age, for better or worse. (Harrison, 2013)

If we regard this programme as a deliberate attempt on the part of Davies to write something with different "values" to *Downton* – something less conservative and more democratic, perhaps, as well as more "modern" – this particular department store is an appropriate choice of subject matter. We might, of course, raise ideological objections to the decision to preserve and celebrate the history of consumerism as "heritage," and I will return to this later in the chapter. That aside, however, Selfridges is a good example of a successful long-lived corporation with commendable attitudes and practices, which are worthy of being commemorated and revisited. As Harrison puts it, Selfridge's reward for rising above "London's snobbery, intransigence and limited horizons" is to have "a TV drama made in his honour" (2013). As Sanders has discussed in her exploration of modern shopping, this store, in contrast to its more aristocratic rival Harrods, aimed to be a space "which provided democratic access to all" (2006: 73). She notes that newspaper articles of the time advocated Selfridges as somewhere that "if a rich woman, you may spend £1450 on a sable cloak, or if a poor one, you may buy a yard of ribbon with equal facility" (*Daily Express*, March 1909). (One might observe here that the aims of the store closely follow those of the lower-middlebrow television programme Davies wrote around it. The lightweight and glossy nature of the show is after all designed to be appealing to a wide spectrum of viewers as the Store was to a wide range of shoppers.) Even more significantly, Selfridge pioneered good working practices and fair treatment for his staff in ways which make him a worthwhile figure to revisit and reconsider, especially in our current age of worker exploitation in the private sector:

[Selfridge] consciously fashioned himself as a model manager, emphasising the efficiency and fairness with which his employees were treated ... [he] resisted the perception that his employees were merely cogs in the vast machine of the store ... Selfridges's most marked innovations in staff relations came in the form of classes which were intended to provide education in the business of retailing and to train new recruits for employment in the store. These innovations contributed to a culture of upward mobility which differed significantly from the curtailed narrative of progress provided by Harrods, whose management refrained from actively encouraging the majority of their employees to climb the social ladder of the store's hierarchy. (Sanders, 2006: 76–78)

It is clearly apparent that, in this regard, Selfridge is worthy of commemoration, being ahead of his time – and indeed, arguably, ours – in terms of concern for the well-being of his staff. Sanders does note, however, that while Selfridge believed that "with proper training, the stockboy might work his way up the ladder within the store to become a high level managerial figure," such encouragement could not be extended to its many female employees. These, although appreciated for the contribution they made up to head of department level, "could never attain a commanding position" (*North Eastern Gazette*, 25th June 1912). This aspect of the store's policies must be rewritten to make them palatable to modern viewers, of course, as I will discuss. But the ways in which "Selfridge introduced revolutionary methods into the Dickensian world of British department stores' industrial relations" are foregrounded in the show itself, which represents the store as an idealised workplace where dedication is rewarded (Lanchester, 1995: 74). Indeed, so effective is the social and financial support that his staff is offered that unionisation seems unnecessary, as the arrival of Huxton, a union rep trying to drum up support for his cause, displays in series 2:

[Huxton] We are here for you when no-body else is. In these uncertain times, who is looking out for the rights of the workers? How are you protected if not by us? Will the great Mr Selfridge look out for you? ... The rich are getting rich and the poor are getting poorer. It's time to turn the tables. Think about how Selfridge would treat you if you got ill. [Ed] Look Mr Huxton – the things you're promising us – we already have. The store has a full time nurse: the dentist comes every week; there's all sorts of schemes for betterment and education.... [Huxton] If you've got all this, why did you ask me here tonight? You're wasting my time. (*Mr Selfridge*, series 2, episode 2)

This is all rather reminiscent of *Downton Abbey*, which as I discussed in the previous chapter used the benevolence of the Granthams towards their employees to suggest that any kind of welfare state is unnecessary. *Mr Selfridge* does similar things with industrial relations, in a way which can be summed up by George Towler's response to the Union rep: the moderate porter "is all for unions – where they are needed. But I've been here five years, and we rub along just fine without one" (series, episode 2). Unions do have a place in society, then, and unlike *Downton*, this show devotes an episode to exploring them, but it comes rapidly to the conclusion that they are superfluous in such a caring workplace. Hence the union rep soon disappears, unwanted and unneeded, from the plot. Even his speech to the men of the store, quoted above, is not given a single focus: it is intercut and interrupted by scenes from a staff party that Selfridge has thrown to stress the democratic and caring nature of the store. Selfridge's address to those gathered functions as an answer to the Union: "it might be my name on the door, but behind that door, you are the ones that matter" (series 2, episode 2).

In this regard, *Mr Selfridge* does, despite Davies's protests, have a similar ideology to Fellowes's show. Both dramas represent large institutions in which employees and employers alike are deeply invested, and whose success depends on teamwork and mutual support. In this way Selfridge's store can function as a metaphor for statehood just as the Grantham's estate does in *Downton*. The wider, political implications of Selfridge's message are clear: all classes must pull together in order to survive hardship. This can be regarded as pertinent both to a store coping with War-inflicted economic problems, or an audience not yet emerged from global recession. We might not be convinced by his democratic version of paternalism any more than we might Robert's, however. Harry Selfridge may pay tribute to his staff's role in his success, but the show does not challenge a capitalist ideology, which maintains that the store is a product of the drive and vision of its owner, who justly deserves to reap its richest rewards for himself. Harry is admired and loved by all his employees – there is not even one dissenting voice, like that which comes courtesy of the excellent footman Thomas in *Downton* – and this may be because he has worked for his wealth, not inherited it. We still notice the often stark difference between his luxurious, indulgent life and the hardship often endured by those who work for him, however. His staff may not seem to begrudge him that difference, but a left-wing viewer might.

Having begun this chapter arguing for the progressive nature of *Mr Selfridge*, it would appear that I have not got very far before having to acknowledge problems with the show's ideology. Its didactic message – that loyalty and hard work will be rewarded, and that your employer will look out for you – can be viewed as an attractive but dangerous, anti-union fantasy, also shared by *Downton*. However, there is a crucial difference between this show and Fellowes's, and that is that Davies is working with a past which is not irretrievably gone. The store itself (and others like it) still survive today, and the excellent working relations it promoted then might still provide an example for a modern workplace to follow. Moreover, it is didactic as much for those in charge as those who work for them. Harry himself spends most of the first series learning how to be a better leader – even if no-one else in the show seems to think he has any failings in that way. His sense of himself as a loving and caring patriarch is threatened by the suicide of a former employee, who throws herself under a train after she is dismissed without a reference. As this happens at the same time as problems with his family escalate following his affair, the viewer sees the close links between Harry as husband and father and Harry as head of the store: the staff of Selfridges are after all a "work-family", and he believes it is his responsibility to look after them in the same way. The visit of Sir Earnest Shackleton, the Antarctic explorer who turned back from the North Pole to save his men, to the store in this episode is used by the show to facilitate a discourse about being in charge: "The thing is, when you are up to your unmentionables in trying to be a good leader, you'd don't have time to think about what that is" (series 1, episode 8). Shackleton is here made to voice the moral message of the show: that care for those who depend about you is more important than money, fame or achievement: "we don't always measure in terms of success.... My real purpose as leader was quite simple. To bring my men in from the cold, each and every day" (series 1, episode 8). In turn Harry becomes more paternalistic: "I let one of our own out into the cold. This can never happen again" (series 1, episode 8).

Even if we still have to consider *Mr Selfridge* as a "small c" conservative show politically, it is, nonetheless, very different from the other representations of Edwardian period discussed in this book, and in ways are quite unusual for a historical fiction. *Downton* is, as I have suggested, nostalgic for a golden, fictionalised past and anxious about change and modernity: *The Forsythe Saga* and *Parade's End* share this view, to greater or lesser extents. Now, *Mr Selfridge* is of course nostalgic in the way that most period dramas are nostalgic, given that the past they represent on screen is glossy and desirable and pleasurable to view. It is impossible not to be seduced by the spectacle created by lavish costumes, a glamorous set and a cocktail-drinking lifestyle enjoyed by good-looking actors (the casting's emphasis on youth and attractiveness makes *Downton* seem dowdy, or perhaps realistic, in comparison).

As Davies points out above, however, the show is not at all anxious about change: indeed, the plot is driven by it, as is the central character who constantly embraces and courts it in many ways. Indeed, Harry's success is largely based on his willingness to break with tradition and relentlessly pursue the next big thing. This comes across very strongly in the first series, in which each episode is based around his exploitation of the latest trend, beginning with the exhibition of the Bleriot just after it flies the Channel, and including motor cars, a visit from the aforementioned Shackleton and even a dabble in spiritualism, with accompanying séance in the store attended by Sir Arthur Conan Doyle. As a result Selfridges is a place in which fashions cultural as much as sartorial are displayed and frequently delighted in. It is really this, as much or more than the experience of shopping itself, which is at the heart of the show.

In this way *Mr Selfridge* is an interesting, even revisionist period drama: its optimistic hero and light-hearted tone allow it to be relentlessly positive about change and about the future – even if that is mainly because change, for Harry, always offers an opportunity to make money. It is thus appropriate that Harry's political views are shown to be similarly ahead of his time, both as regards his revision of working conditions already discussed, and his rewriting in the show as a forward-thinking feminist, who supports the suffragettes. The contrast with Lord Grantham, who fears any form of change and as a result is particularly unsympathetic towards women's rights, is striking. So, if the other shows I examine are concerned with nostalgia for a social class, a family, a stately home, a rural idyll, or just old-fashioned values and a simpler time, what is being preserved, captured and cherished from the past in *Mr Selfridge*, is rather different. "We are making history here" Harry proclaims to his staff in the opening minutes of the very first episode, and while this is a self-conscious, self-referential moment in the show, it might also make us pause about what exactly that "history" consists of. In fact, what Harry means is that his new store is about to open, and what becomes apparent in the series that follows is that it is the consumer revolution which this drama suggests is most precious and worthy of preservation about the past. In *Mr Selfridge*, and indeed also in *The Paradise*, it is the beginnings of late capitalism which become "heritage." Hence progress and modernity are, inevitably, represented in largely materialist terms. Higson's complaint that heritage drama usually reduces the past to a collection of artefacts and items is still true here, except that it is the future which is symbolised and marked by physical objects, namely the airplane, the motor car, new types of female dress and the arrival of cosmetics – which all take us towards our modern world.

The show represents consumer goods as the bearers of modernity from the first episode, which opens in an old-fashioned department store where Selfridges is researching shopping in London. In this first scene Harry is served by Agnes Towler, the impoverished shopgirl who will go on to become one of the central characters in the show. In a dark *mis-en-scene* typical of the (still) late-Victorian shop, Gamages, the pair of bright red leather gloves she offers him stand out as a symbol of vibrancy and daring, anticipating the light and colour of the glamorous and innovative new store which we see complete by the end of the first episode. Furthermore, of course, they have a kind of fairytale resonance for Agnes, for whom they signify the start of a new life working at Selfridges. For her, consumer capitalism and the change it brings is a transformative thing. Indeed, the gloves hint at Agnes's construction as a kind of Cinderella figure, who will be rescued, not by romance and marriage but by commerce. The Prince-Charming-like Harry buys them for her to thank her for her help but, in an anti-tale style reversal, it is she who tracks him down some months later, wearing them as a reminder, to request a job at the newly opened store. This early narrative arc symbolises the potential for change that consumer goods offer, and the ways in which identity is fluid and can be reconstructed through dress. Agnes's other clothes are inexpensive and uniform but the gloves (which she also wears on the first day of work) are a first step towards her new self, marking her out as someone different and special.

This subplot also introduces the other main concern of the show: female ambition and achievement, and the power of capitalism to offer women financial and personal independence. This theme is most clearly demonstrated throughout by Agnes, but is echoed by a number of the other female characters. Head of accessories Josie Mardle, her assistant Kitty, head of fashion Miss Ravillious and window consultant Valerie Maurel are all following with enthusiasm the opportunities that a department store uniquely offered women at this early point in the twentieth century. As Sanders observes, the "upward mobility of the shop assistant signified a promise for individual self-improvement" – something which was not true of all the jobs which women began to do at this period (2006: 24). Agnes may begin by having to beg Harry for a job as an accessories assistant, but is rapidly and steadily promoted until, by series 2, she is in charge of the overall visual display of the whole store. She has no formal training or proper education, but the store, under Harry, is a meritocracy and hence her talent is enough to secure her rise in the ranks. In this regard the show is faithful to the real Selfridge encouraging, democratic spirit towards his employees, as discussed above. It also, however, must rewrite and update it, to ensure the approval of a modern audience for the central character: there is no hint here that he does not intend women to progress beyond a certain level. Having removed the glass ceiling, however, the show is still not prepared to go too far in its representation of a successful female employee. Andrea Wright's reading of *Mr Selfridge* and *The Paradise* concludes that both shows "have an inherently conservative attitude towards women," partly because its representation of characters like Ellen Love "unquestioningly construct woman-as-object: she [woman] is a consumable pleasure" (Wright, 2014: 246 and 243). It is certainly true that Agnes's progress is largely a result of the patronage and support of Henri Leclair, who encourages and assists his protégé throughout series 1: her achievements always take place with his help and support and under his watchful gaze. Moreover, in season 2 when he leaves the store and Agnes replaces him the stress of leadership is almost too much for her: "I am finding it all rather daunting," she admits (series 2, episode 2). Hence she is relieved when Henri steps back into his old post, relieving her of responsibility, and they are once again working together: "I'm just not very good at it … Please come back. I need you, more than anything" (series 2, episode 3). This hints at the ideological ambiguity of *Mr Selfridge*, which although in many ways a show about the portrayal of female ambition and the ways it can be satisfied through capitalism, also has a deliberate and conservative way of controlling that ambition, with the aim of reassuring a certain kind of audience. This is not confined to Agnes's anxiety about leadership, either: perhaps more problematically, several of the other key female employees clearly love their jobs, but regularly imply that they would give them up for marriage, children and a family. Agnes is in fact on the verge of doing so at the end of series 2 when she accepts Victor's proposal and prepares to leave the store to support him in his family business. Harry Selfridge's forward-thinking attitudes are clearly apparent here when he offers to let Agnes stay on in her job even though "women in this country usually leave after marriage," but Agnes, somewhat inexplicably, turns down his offer (series 2, episode10). Indeed, it is Victor who recognises her innate ambition and calls off their wedding, acknowledging that it is not the future she really wants and that it would be a waste of her talents. Similarly, when Mr Grove observes sadly to his former lover Josie Mardle that he "always thought you were wedded to your work" she corrects him "I would gladly have borne your child ... how little you men know what we women really long for" (series 1, episode 8).

Of course such observations are likely accurate representations of the social ideology of the time, in which many women would have been working out of financial necessity rather than ambition and genuine love for their job, and the majority of whom still believed that being a wife and mother was their true vocation. After all, late Victorian and Edwardian shopgirls were culturally positioned in a "narrative of eventual marriage and departure from the labor of the shop to the imagined leisure of the home" (Sanders, 2006: 31). M Mostyn Bird, a historian of women's labour writing in 1911 and quoted by Sanders, observed that a shop assistant had:

> no sense of permanency, for of the two main roads that lay before her ... marriage is sure to be the one that she elects and expects to follow: therefore ... any work she does between leaving school and going to the altar as something of a temporary and stop-gap nature. (Sanders, 2006: 31)

In this regard Agnes and Josie, who both display little interest in women's suffrage or rights, are seen to be struggling with the beliefs and expectations attached to conventional Edwardian womanhood. The show does represent more strident views, mostly voiced by Miss Ravillious, the head of fashion, who is clearly identified as a New Woman, and acts as a kind of feminist conscience for the other staff. Hence she advises Agnes to "think of her career" rather than of romance, and also persuades Josie to attend a suffrage meeting (series 1, episode 8). She also eloquently reminds the viewer of the lack of choice which confronted women in this period: "It can be a difficult lot for us women. If you don't find the right man, you work forever. If you do find the right man you can't work. It's so unfair ..."(series 1, episode 8). Significantly, however, she never really becomes a key part of the drama, and does not return in series two. *Mr Selfridge* goes further than *Downton* in its representation of first-wave feminism, but will not commit its central characters to it.

All this could be said to be an accurate barometer of the conflicted and ambivalent attitudes of the women who entered the workplace in the early years of the twentieth century. The characters discussed here display women in different stages of their movement towards modernity: at times ambitious, at times drawn to domesticity: some feminist in approach, some not, some seeking equality, some content with the status quo – and most not consistent in their feelings from one episode to the next. (Of course the success of the show is partially based on its awareness that, in these regards, not that much has changed for its female audience in the intervening 100 years.) Such a devotion to historical accuracy is not extended to the male characters in *Mr Selfridge*, however, who display a positive attitude towards working women which seems highly untypical of the period. Indeed they are not only supportive, but they are often more perceptive about recognising drive and ambition in their female colleagues and lovers than those women themselves. In this way Josie's comment to Roger, above, is ironic: she is angry that he has misinterpreted her and that he is exchanging her for marriage and children with the conventional and maternal (and much younger) Doris – but ultimately it seems he is right. She is after all still happily working at the end of series 2, even after an inheritance makes her independently wealthy and work of any kind unnecessary.

Of course, a feminist critic would regard this as rather patronising: it is clear than most of the men in the *Selfridge* world always seem to know best, whether in work or emotional life (even the flawed and old-fashioned Roger, who does makes mistakes, always recognises this and rectifies them: see for example, series 2, episode 4). It also can be seen to offer a troublingly conservative gender perspective, reassuring an audience anxious about fourth-wave feminism that the show may feature "career women" but they ultimately and innately wish to return to the private sphere. (Even though, interestingly, the show does not represent the chaotic domestic life cheerfully chosen by Doris as nearly as appealing as the orderly, glossy world of work.) At the same time, however, this is also undeniably appealing to a female viewer of the "lean-in" generation. Male support is there at every turn: with the possible exception of the generally "bad" head of fashion Mr Thackeray, all the men in *Mr Selfridge* are positive about female ambition and female success, and understanding of the difficulties involved. It is therefore satisfying as a kind of female fantasy: an idealised workplace where misogyny does not really seem to exist. Furthermore, this support and understanding removes any burden of guilt from the female characters. Josie and Agnes are given what they really want – recognition and achievement in the workplace, financial and personal freedom, and new, more exciting and more illicit sexual relationships – but the responsibility for these decisions is taken by their respective lovers, out of their hands. Neither have to ultimately feel guilty about choosing an independent life over a domestic, family-oriented one, even though this is what they really wanted, all along.

## Sex and *Mr Selfridge*

Female guilt is generally not something this show has much time for, and if we must agree with Wright that there is some conservatism around its portrayal of workplace relationships for women, its representation of personal ones are much more radical. In most of the texts I examine in this book, sexuality is problematic at best and pathological and destructive at worst. *Downton* and *The Village* repeatedly associate sexuality with death; *The Forsyth Saga* links it to violence, possession and control. *Mr Selfridge* is different in that it is, highly anachronistically cheerful and accepting of sexuality and is particularly willing to celebrate female desire, as displayed by almost all the women characters. It is true that Harry's wife Rose, falling for a handsome young artist, will not allow their illicit relationship to progress further, but she is in the minority in the show – and her desire for him is clearly made apparent. Agnes, though initially virginal, experiences her sexual as well as artistic education in the store, by embarking on a romance with Henri. This is particularly suggestive, of course, because she does not wish or expect a long-term future from it, in the first series at least: "I like him very much, but I am not in love" (series 1, episode 8). Lady Mae enjoys many lovers, none of whom she seems to be actually in love with, and many of whom are younger than she. And perhaps most interesting, and exceptional, is Josie, whose passionate long-term affair with the married Roger Grove is treated sympathetically by the show. He leaves her finally for married respectability, but she is soon rewarded for her suffering by a handsome Belgian musician, nearly 20 years her junior. She experiences anxiety over the suitability of their relationship in terms of this age gap – but not, significantly, about its consummation. Indeed, why would she, given that sex in this show, for women, tends to be joyful and remarkably consequence-free: no unwanted pregnancies, no public judgement, no hint of censure.

Now Davies is well known for his "sexing up" of the repressed plots of nineteenth-century fiction: his adaptations of classic novels always foreground sexuality that is absent or only implicit in the source text. Critics have objected to this, but at the same time it is widely recognised as the reason for much of the popular appeal of his work:

> "I feel I am bringing out the sexual content which is inherent in the material," he told one interviewer. "It's just that in the 19th century it was the convention never to write directly about sexual matters. One of the things I've always thought is a drag in so many period

adaptations is that they are always buttoned up to the neck in so many clothes all the time. I'm always looking for excuses to get them out of their clothes." (Davies, 2008)

This is a valid point: of course desire has always existed and relationships – even very unsuitable ones – have always been consummated, whether or not they could be written about in the pages of a famous novel. Davies's perspective, and his highly successful foregrounding of sexuality from *Pride and Prejudice* onwards, can be considered as the catalyst for a sea change in attitudes towards sex in recent mainstream historical fictions. From the not-so virginal Queen *Elizabeth* (Shekhar Kapur, 1998) to explicit bonkbuster history in *The Tudors* (2007–10) and *Spartacus* (2010–13), it is now commonplace to represent the past as a place where people have a great deal of sex. They do not usually have it on Sunday nights, however: these more explicit fictions are not BBC or ITV period dramas. *Parade's End* is a progressive exception, as we will see in Chapter 5. And sex without repercussion is still rare in historical fiction, as when Sylvia's desire is punished by illegitimate pregnancy and social condemnation in the latter show. In particular it is unusual to portray historical sex taking place between older women and younger men. Middle-aged female characters in most classic novels are usually comic or grotesque, not attractive and sensual, and hence adaptations tend to reflect this. *The Forsyte Saga*, for example, features several women over 40 who are all overlooked in favour of the young and beautiful Irene – who in turn is replaced by the much younger Fleur as the narrative centre in series 2. *Mr Selfridge* here benefits from its unconventional source text – one wonders if Davies enjoyed the opportunity – responding to recent sexual mores and trends rather than being bound by textual fidelity. (*Downton* could do the same, of course, but does not: all its older women are consistently asexual.) The sexual appetites of middle-aged women now have mainstream appeal, as displayed by the success of modern HBO dramas like *Cougar Town*. Moreover, *Mr Selfridge* female characters do not just desire, they act on that desire: and discrepancies in age are irrelevant. In this way, the show not only gives a voice – albeit conservatively, at times – to female ambition, it also acknowledges middle-aged female sexuality previously "written out" of history. And, of course, the two are closely associated: perhaps the most radical thing about the show is the way it reminds us that sexual freedom and economic freedom are closely entwined. Equality, it suggests, is an aphrodisiac.

## A 'special relationship': nationality and patriotism in the show

I have been concerned so far with *Mr Selfridge's* view of capitalism as heritage and what it might reveal about class and gender concerns facilitated or shaped by consumerism. I wish now to look at a different aspect of the show: its relationship with nationality and nationalism. If series 1 was dominated by Harry's journey to become a better leader, series 2 is preoccupied by his determination to become more British, and this plot markets and celebrates Britishness as a result. Now, a nationalist subtext in a period drama is itself unsurprising, given that historical fictions have long been regarded by many critics to be packaging and marketing nationality, as Claire Monk notes: "British period films have often been closely equated in the eyes of the world with Britain's national cinema itself ... with a widely perceived status as projections of the nation" (Monk, 2002: 1). Monk and other critics like Lovell (1997: 241) are uneasy about such a link and the assumptions it breeds, but we can see its resonance not only in historical films but in television programmes which celebrate the English countryside and English past. *Downton Abbey* is as usual a classic example of this. Series 2 of *Mr Selfridge*, however, deals with nationhood more directly even than *Downton*, and less inevitably, given its urban setting and the fact that its central character is from the United States. What the show actually represents, in the first series, is an American bringing his skill, money and groundbreaking ideas to a dull England which is still stuck in many ways in the Victorian period, and consequently transforming it forever. In doing so Harry has to overcome xenophobia and prejudice and convince his backers, staff and customers of his intelligence and vision, which he does: his success is not accidental or easily won, but is a result of his innate superiority in many areas. The kind of reverse colonisation this implies risks being unpopular with a British audience, of course, especially as it is a reminder of the real-life dominance of foreign companies over the national and global marketplace. (At the same time, a patriotically minded American market might enjoy the dynamic.) In order to address this, then, the second series takes pains to reassure the viewer that despite his achievements what Harry wants, more than anything, is to be British. This is displayed through his support of the War effort, which begins with his desire to join the Procurement committee and leads to his somewhat unlikely recruitment by the British War Office as an industrial spy. At a time when other Americans are returning home to escape the problems created by the War, Harry wishes to immerse himself more deeply in the culture, values and politics of his adopted country. Indeed, he is deeply wounded by newspaper allegations that he is not a patriot – more so than he is by any other damaging publicity in the drama, including the embarrassingly revealing play written about his personal life in series 1. Soon Selfridges, which he has been at pains to construct as a "British store," stocks only British goods, and its marketing strategy and window displays follow patriotic themes. These begin with a celebration of produce from Britain and its colonies and then become a nostalgic revisiting of "the comforts of home." (Notably, an alternative campaign to turn the store restaurant into a cocktail bar is withdrawn by Harry after only one unsuccessful day – perhaps because the concept is American as well as rather too decadent for war-time patriotism.)

Of course the drama's representation of Harry's Anglophilia, if a little exaggerated, is based upon historical fact: the real-life Selfridge did embrace the Old World and became naturalised as a British citizen in the 1930s, as a gesture of his loyalty towards the country (Woodhead, 2007: 228). However the programme's preoccupation with British nationalism goes well beyond the attitudes of its central character. Loving support for the monarchy, for example, is suggested by the highly affectionate treatment of the King's visit to the store in series 1 and by the Royal-themed window displays which result. These are ideologically undercut, though, by Harry's identification by his staff in the same episode as "the King of Oxford street," a subversive reminder that financial and mercantile success and power are becoming more important than hereditary privilege. By series 2, however, nationalism is being constructed and represented in rather more disturbing ways. This is most easily seen through the store's celebration of the British Empire in episode 3, the representation of which is so unambiguous and uncritical that it feels highly unusual in a contemporary television or film drama. In order to raise morale at the outbreak of War, the store is decked out in Union flags, a large statue of Britannia is positioned in centre stage and maps of, and produce from, the colonies are on display throughout. Aside from Victor's squeamish reluctance to have a stuffed tiger in his restaurant, there is no negativity about this exhibition and no critical commentary is offered on this celebration of the Empire at its height. British power and military strength are embraced by all the characters, who congratulate Agnes and Henri on their work, and Harry in particular is delighted with the "truly incredible" result, from the "the sun never sets on the British empire" window display to the mannequin big game hunter with rifle (series 2, episode 3). Even though most viewers will have an uneasy awareness of the dark legacy of Imperialism, there is no sense of this within the drama: we are not invited to question the implied exploitation of the Colonies, but only to rejoice in the riches they offer.

*Mr Selfridge* offers a similarly uncritical view of the First World War. The programme is not really concerned with the portrayal of war in any detail; its focus remains concentrated on the store, and war exists only as an external reality which impacts upon trade. As one critic scathingly observes, "I had not thought about the war as damaging shopping until I watched *Mr Selfridge.*" Its other function, as we have seen, is to demonstrate Harry's loyalty to England. But we could note at this point that war is represented in a flurry of patriotism and excitement: as a party, with eager and willing volunteers. A scene in which the men of Selfridges are drilled by Mr Crabb and march in formation through the store before enlisting together, is at once moving and disturbing from a modern perspective. There is a striking contrast here with *Downton,* which as I have discussed previously had a much more muted and cynical, if perhaps more anachronistic, approach to the conflict. The Abbey was anxious and depressed about the outbreak of War, reluctant to let its staff go to fight, and sympathetic toward conscientious objectors and shell-shock victims. *Mr Selfridge* is probably more historically accurate in its capturing of the optimistic mood of the time, but is also unusual in its rejection of modern – as in late twentieth-century – popular opinion regarding the First World War. In other words, as with its celebration of Empire, it prioritises – and indeed celebrates – the values of the early years of the twentieth century over those of the twenty-first.

There are complex issues, then, surrounding *Mr Selfridge*'s view of the past. In one sense, it can be seen as immersing itself in the mood and attitudes of the time, without mediating them through a deliberate postmodern lens as *Downton* has done (even when it is at its most didactic and conservative *Downton* always seems to have a self-conscious distancing from its subject matter). On the other hand, perhaps it is more accurate to view it as entirely up to date, in that it reflects completely contemporary attitudes in Britain, manifested only over the last couple of years. *Mr Selfridge*'s refusal to comment critically on the War may be reflective of the views of recent revisionist historians who have challenged the dominant twentieth-century view of the conflict as a pointless and reckless waste of life. Popular historian Max Hastings, for example, recently published a book and made a BBC documentary – entitled *The*

*Necessary War* – in which he suggested that the assumptions we have made about 1914–18 are no more than a "Blackadder take on history." Hastings believes that the war was crucial in order to prevent a dangerous Germany dominating Europe as it threatened to do in the 1930s: "I am among those who reject the notion that 1914–18 belonged to a different moral order than 1939–45" (Hastings, 2013: xviii). This view has proved controversial, but is not without support: another recent account and subsequent television series, this time by Jeremy Paxman, also challenged "the default conviction that the First World War was an exercise in purposelessness" (Paxman, 2013: 10). Paxman does not set out to agree with Hastings about the value of the conflict, but is critical of the kind of "bitter disillusionment" expressed in verse by poets like Wilfred Owen, which he suggests was simply "not the prevailing view at the time."(Paxman, 2013: 8). Stressing the heroism of many soldiers and the British "stiff upper lip," Paxman is interested in the initial optimism, and when that faded, the patriotism and sense of duty, which led to support for the War both at home and in the trenches.[1] It is this that *Mr Selfridge* captures: it may be going too far to say that the series is revisionist and positive about the conflict, but certainly its characters are. It chooses to show us a society which "some people give the orders and other people obey them ... everyone is complicit in the chain of command" (Paxman, 2013: 137). This is as true in the Trenches of Flanders as it is on the shop floor of Selfridges. Those who support the War in this drama are not upper class, and may not be trained in patriotism and obedience at public school – but nonetheless, they still believe England is worth dying for.

I discussed in Chapter 1 the ways in which the First World War has been appropriated as a marker of patriotism in our twenty-first century culture, and that is clearly reflected here in *Mr Selfridge*, a drama which doesn't want to engage with the grim reality of war, but is careful to stress the strong nationalist feeling it inspired, alongside a celebratory representation of Empire. In a wider sense, however, *Mr Selfridge* is just one example of a number of extremely patriotic television programmes which form part of a nationalistic trend in the media at present. *The Great British Bake Off* (with its "particularly British, crumbly charm" (Rainey, 2012)), *The Great British Menu* (currently, and rather tastelessly, "celebrating" the first World War with its menus), *Great British Railway Journeys with Michel Portillo* – these are just a few of many popular, largely BBC, programmes which seek to celebrate, or even create, a certain type of national identity. Patriotism, as constructed by these programmes, is unthreatening, cuddly and nostalgic. The prevalence of this kind of television has been interpreted as a response to low national pride, or to the SNP and the possible break-up of Union. As one journalist notes "there is at least one place we can find a happy and harmonious Britain – and that's our state broadcaster. *The Great British Bake Off* is the glâcé cherry on a Victoria sponge of mild propaganda delivered nightly by the BBC" (Godwin, 2014). Godwin goes on to argue that the BBC is attempting to "placate its Conservative critics and fulfil its national brief by appealing to the one thing that its audience loosely have in common: Britishness" (2014). For my purposes, what is significant here is the implication that celebrating nationality is uncontroversial and unifying. It is not only television which displays a newly nationalistic mood, of course. The excitement which surrounded the 2012 London Olympics, and the return to popularity of the Monarchy (with a much-celebrated Royal wedding and the birth of a new Prince and Princess) after some years of controversy, also suggest a new fascination with, and fondness for, being British – of which the rise in popularity of extreme nationalist party the BNP is the darker side.

With this in mind *Mr Selfridge* may gain some of its popularity from falling in with a general trend. But while even left-wing reviewers seem to consider the kinds of reality shows I mention above fluffy rather than disturbing, the representation of nationalism in historical fiction has long been considered controversial by critics, as critics like Geoffrey Nowell-Smith and John Hill have acknowledged:

> It is a constant criticism of nationalism that it seeks to impose upon the nation not only a historically frozen and hermetically (or authentic) conception of identity but also an imaginary sense of unity which fails to take account of the variety of collective identities and forms of belonging (such as class, gender, ethnicity and region) which may exist within the national community. In the case of Britain this suppression of difference is all the greater in so far as there is more than one national community within the boundaries of the nation-state... (Hill, 1992: 15)

*The Great British Bake Off* does at least acknowledge a "variety of collective identities" through its choice of contestants, if not through its vision of village-fete-style "Englishness": period dramas, however, often do not. One of the criticisms of certain types of heritage films of the 1980s and early 90s was that the kind of white Englishness they usually portray was not at all representative of the diversity of a modern multi-cultural Britain. Recent historical fictions in both film and television – *Hunterby* and *Wuthering Heights* (2011) are good examples – have attempted to broaden this by inclusion of black British actors, however. And, as discussed in the previous chapter, *Downton* has taken pains to portray its version of an inclusive nation state with Irish, Scottish and Northern English characters, albeit with political emphasis placed on their contented and mutually beneficial co-existence. *Mr Selfridge,* in contrast, generally holds fast to a very confined view of British identity. There are no Irish or Scottish characters, even though there are several Irish and Scottish actors: they do, however, have to play English roles with BBC accents. A Welsh character is, however, brought in series 2, presumably because her presence need not disrupt the sense of unity in what I might call the "nation-store." With its many American, and one or two key French characters, *Mr Selfridge* is unafraid of exploring international relations – and clearly has a mind to appeal to an international audience – but nationality itself has to be proved and earned: if the second series is on a wider scale about the store's response to the First World War, Harry's own battle is to become and be seen publically as British.

## Conclusion

I began this chapter suggesting that *Mr Selfridge* was, in many ways, more innovative and more democratic than the other neo-Edwardian texts I will examine in this book. Instead of setting out to preserve as heritage the lifestyle and values of the upper classes, it chronicles with equal value and narrative attention the lives of working, if not-quite working-class, people who might not conventionally be at the centre of history. Hence porters, shop assistants, waiters – and especially – women occupy some of the most important roles in the drama. It is also alternative – though, thanks to a similar focus in *The Paradise,* not unique – in organising itself around a department store, a communal, shared space, rather than a country house and a family unit. And, perhaps most importantly, it represents the coming of modernity as a positive thing. From exciting new technology to women's rights, this series uses its forward-thinking eponymous character to promote and embrace change. This past is represented as a series of steps towards our future – not an escapist, Sunday night refuge from it.

There are certain issues surrounding this drama, of course. We might applaud the type of "history from below" the series represents, but it still sanitises and polishes that history – and seems to use it to put forward a conservative world view. Like *Downton,* the hierarchal and ultimately patriarchal organisation of the store has an ideological message, preaching a doctrine of social obedience and paternalism, in which loyalty to the business and its owner is strictly demanded, and generously repaid. If you are a good employee, you will be supported, encouraged and even loved: you need not worry about new government policies concerning workers (Lloyd George is not even mentioned by the show) and you do not need a union. The capitalist system in which you work is self-contained, insular, personal and all-nurturing. In this way, then, the show provides a pleasurable fantasy for a contemporary viewer, who, due to the increasing alienation, instability and anxiety that surrounds the modern workplace, is unlikely to have a similar, friendly experience of their own on Monday morning. We can appreciate the pleasure involved in this, but still be aware of the inherent problems involved in idealising the past in this way. Similarly, we can applaud the show's interest in, and promotion of, women's entry into the public sphere, while also recognising the ways in which it is wary about and tempers female ambition and success.

It is important to note, however, that it is inevitable that *Mr Selfridge* will be politically conflicted, just as it is inevitable that it, like *Downton*, represents an idealised view of human interaction and relations. Indeed, as Buxton has pointed out, most long-running serials are based around careful ambivalence and constructed optimism. This is because they are vulnerable to ratings: in order to be successful, and to continue, they:

> must rally a mass, trans-class, trans-gender audience around a positive project – at once economic and ideological – which is neither reducible to, nor explicitly against, dominant class interests. Series are not only commercially vulnerable but also ideologically vulnerable as previously convincing strategies and resolutions fall apart under the weight of their own internal tensions or are unable to resolve new anxieties of the viewing public ... Addressed to a mass audience of different political shades and class determinations, the series is objectively ambiguous. The defence of what are ultimately narrow class interests is displaced on to generalised popular values like the family, friendship, security, sexual and racial equality, worthy values which command a wide consensus. (Buxton, 1990: 19)

*Mr Selfridge* can be clearly seen to be adopting this strategy: in order to attract, please, reassure and ultimately keep a large audience, it offers an attractive, even utopian view of the workplace, which a majority of viewers can agree on and admire. As Sue Harper, writing about the popular film, observes, successful mainstream fictions "must provide textual comfort and a sense of optimism for their viewers" (1994: 3). Hence, in the onscreen Selfridges, discrimination – on the grounds of sex, age or class – is unknown: Agnes's gender does not hinder her rise through the store, nor does Victor's East-end accent, and Mr Crabb is thanked, not forcibly retired, when he reaches 60. Men are supportive of women, not threatened by them. Strict hierarchies of rank are set up and then crumbled through friendship and mutual support. In complete contrast to *Downton*, where characters are usually happy to maintain their current positions – and are punished by the plot for trying to leave – only the highest employees occupy the same role at the end of the second series as they do at the start of the first. All the others, from Victor to Kitty, have "bettered" their social and financial position, though ambition and hard work. This kind of meritocracy described by the show can be seen as a positive thing – even if it is not an accurate representation of most people's lives in the early twentieth century, even those fortunate enough to work in progressive Selfridge's.

The show's other "values" – in particular those which it is not "objectively ambiguous" about – may be slightly more problematic. Its writers seem to be in agreement that a celebration of Britishness can "command a wide consensus" among its audience, and given the surge of patriotic feeling currently apparent in the media they are probably right. We do, however, need to be cautious about the narrow, white national identity constructed by the show, and even if we can overlook that, we might certainly feel uneasy about the uncritical celebration of Empire it also contains. Davies's version of a nation-store makes an interesting counterpart to Fellowes's nation-estate, but in some ways it is even less inclusive and less self-aware.

Finally, the most accepted and uncontested, and the most central part of the show's ideology, is also its most interesting: its creation of shopping as heritage. Such a reworking is of course appropriate, given that the whole genre of heritage has been controversially dismissed as, in Richard Dryer's words, "film as conspicuous consumption": it is only a post-modern step further to assimilate film and consumption. Shopping-focused productions like *The Paradise* and *Mr Selfridge* exploit and examine the links between consumer capitalism, commodity fetishism and the representation of the past on screen. As Wright has argued, these shows offer "a nostalgia for a certain kind of shopping. By focusing on the pleasures of the retail environment, the goods, the display cabinets ... they recall an experience that is less important in modern retail, which is overwhelmingly characterised by cavernous hypermarkets and malls" (Wright, 2014: 239). Our past, as far is this show suggests, is as consumers: modernity itself is constructed around the consumer revolution. In doing so, it reinforces and validates capitalism – especially pertinent at a time in which, following the banking crisis, economic structures in the West have been questioned. The show portrays ordinary people learning how to shop, and asks why they should, as though to remind an audience of these people of the value of consumerism itself. As though speaking for this audience, Mrs Crabb, when first sampling the delights of the department store, anxiously inquires of Mr Selfridge as to the moral and social benefit of what she is doing: "It is good to shop, isn't it?" "Mrs Crabb, it's very good," he replies: it may well be the viewer he is reassuring (series 1, episode 8).

# 5
# A Return to "quality": *Parade's End* (2012)

Susanna White's 2012 *Parade's End* is undeniably the most "highbrow" period drama examined in this book. The soap-like elements of the popular Sunday-night television programmes I have discussed thus far are notably absent here, in Tom Stoppard's "unashamedly literary" 2012 adaptation of Ford Madox Ford's tetralogy (Dowell, 2012). Constantly favourably compared to *Downton Abbey*, this five-part mini-series has been embraced by critics, who found it "deeper and more truthful" than Fellowes's show (Simpson, 2012): a kind of thoughtful, perceptive "*Downton* for grown-ups" (Thompson, 2012).[1] Indeed, *Parade's End* was considered a reaction against, and rejection of, the "dumbing down" of the historical serial by Fellowes and the texts which followed in *Downton*'s wake. With its high production values, a starry cast, a passionate love triangle and a complex and brilliant canonical source text (or in this case texts) this had all the ingredients of a classic "event in television history" (Thompson, 2012). Its reception with the viewing public, however, did not quite measure up to expectations: its ratings (although high for BBC2) were modest from the outset and plummeted further after the first episode aired. If this is how we measure success, this is the least successful Edwardian drama I explore here, and the one which reached the smallest audience.[2] Nonetheless, of course, it went on to win several Emmys and BAFTAS, including Best Actress for Rebecca Hall and Best Writer for Stoppard. There is clearly an opposition here between the types of history which appeal to critics and those which attract the general viewing public. This adaptation, then, displays many of the tensions in taste and appeal which surround recent period drama, and this chapter will examine the gap between history as soap opera – created by the *Forsyte Saga* in the 1960s, but now epitomised by *Downton* – and history as art, as in *Parade's End*.

Deliberately attempting to capture the modernist complexity of its source text, *Parade's End* was clearly designed not to be lightweight popularist viewing: it requires concentration and commitment, and its comparatively low rating figures reflect this. With its fragmented narrative, abrupt cuts between scenes, and jarring changes of mood and tone, this adaptation acknowledges the impossibility of an accurate, coherent and didactic version of history. Instead it prefers to offer moods and snapshots of a subjective past. Indeed, in many ways *Parade's End* can be considered a self-conscious comment on the position of period drama today. Thus the contemporary viewer, with their (presumed) interest in the past, is aligned with the hero Tietjens and his love for the old order of things: a love which is ultimately futile, but captivating nonetheless. He is still enthralled by a rural, feudal way of life which is fast disappearing; he believes that the "C18th is preferable to the C20th," and his ideas about loyalty, honour and sexual fidelity are equally old fashioned – and ultimately doomed to disillusion:

> I love every field and hedgerow. The land is England and once it was the foundation of order. Before money came in and handed it to the swindlers and schemers. Toryism of the pig's trough. [I stand for] duty. Duty and service to above and below. Frugality. Keeping your word, honouring the past, looking after your people and beggaring yourself if needs be before letting duty go hang. (*Parade's End*, episode 2)

The value system Tietjens expresses here is that which we associate with traditional "heritage" fictions: he, like them, harks back to a past which fetishises the English countryside and consists of an ordered class system built upon duty, paternalism and respect on both sides. It is basically the *Downton Abbey* world he invokes here, but Valentine, to whom he is speaking, is quick to laugh at him. She represents the central premise of the adaptation, which is that nostalgia must be rejected and overcome in order to move forward toward the modern world. The viewer may sympathise with Tietjens's views, but they come to understand, alongside him, that the world he longs for is dead and that only the present matters. Of course, this journey towards being post-heritage is somewhat hindered by the way that this drama constructs the Edwardian period visually. From the beauty of the central characters, to the glamour of Sylvia's costumes, to the idyllic serenity of rural England: the past has never looked more sumptuous, even in *Downton*, than it does here. Yet this drama, ever contradictory, still wants us to remember the pettiness, cruelties and limitations of the past, and to follow Tietjens on his journey towards modernity.

This refusal – or at least attempted refusal – to fetishise the past has been picked up on by reviewers who much prefer White's drama to Fellowes's: "there are cheerful men and women in Britain making *Downton Abbey* just as there are nostalgists here who watch it. But nostalgia is a plague to history" (Thompson, 2012). (Nostalgia is, certainly, a plague to Tietjens, after all.) This comment implies that *Parade's End* is in some way a more authentic version of the past than *Downton*, because it is less rosy, less "cheerful" in its outlook. The Edwardian period offered here is one which confines and restricts identity and personal freedom: as Serena Davies has noted and as I will discuss, the adaptation gives us a "deeply sad sense of the richer lives people would have led had they been born into different times" (2012). But of course authenticity itself is highly subjective: for every critic who welcomes *Parade's End's* cynicism about old values, others, like this one in the *Mail*, cannot see past some anachronisms in language, manners and costume which they believe a period piece should never allow:

> The clergyman would not have been referred to as "the Reverend Duchemin," in the manner of an American Baptist preacher – he would have been "Mr." And it is going to get worse: a future episode shows Tietjens saluting a senior officer in the trenches while not wearing a hat. So it is not such a masterpiece after all. The BBC seems to struggle with period drama – at least from this era – because it can't help but impose the values of 2012 on the context of 1912. (Heffer, 2012)

This review does not expand on what "values of 2012" might be "imposed" on this drama, though it is likely that it refers to its acceptance of adultery, nudity and sexual content, and a post-modern narrative form which is difficult to follow. Rather than being the products of our time, however, these elements are of course all present in Ford's novels, as I will discuss. We could say that it is not so much the adaptation – the odd wardrobe malfunction aside – which is anachronistic, rather that its source interacts with modernism and modernity in ways we are unused to seeing in literary adaptations of this period. The cinematic versions of the novels of Henry James and EM Forster I listed in Chapter 1, for example, may deal with explicit and often illicit and extramarital sexualities, but there is usually a fairly clear moral code: marriage triumphs over adultery in *The Golden Bowl*, for example, and Helen and Leonard are eventually punished for their illicit coupling in *Howards End,* no matter how sympathetic they might be. Ford's *Parade's End,* in contrast, represents an adulterous union with Valentine Wannop as the natural and right ending to Tietjens's story, even though his wife still loves him, and White's version complicates its morality further though its sympathetic representation of all three of its central characters, including the badly-behaved Sylvia. As a *Time* magazine review approvingly notes, there are "no easily identifiable good guys. This miniseries doesn't tell you how to feel..." (Poniewozik, 2013). Moreover, it is more usual to see realist novels adapted for the screen: modernism is more difficult for a viewer to follow and to make sense of. Indeed, *Parade's End* divided reviewers into two camps, one which loved the drama and appreciated not being "spoonfed" (Snider, 2013) and the other which, like Heffer's above, preferred more conventional "heritage" fare, and resented the confusing, labyrinth turns of the narrative. Assuming that the average viewer will agree with him – and many did – Heffer concludes that "if you like to understand what your Edwardians are doing, stick to *Downton Abbey*" (Heffer, 2012).

## Modernism on screen

This modernist source text, then, represents something of a challenge for adaption into period television. Firstly it is itself a historical fiction: written by Ford in the 1920s, the novels look back at the years between 1912 and 1919 from the post-War perspective. As a review in the *New Yorker* put it, they "were defined as much by the artistic and cultural changes that had taken place in the years since the War – the rise of modernism and the further dissolution of old class prerogatives – as they were by their vision of the past" (Anon., 2013). This adds an extra layer of "looking back" for the viewer: we are watching a version of history that was itself a version of history (and a judgement on it). We can see here how any notion of an accurate or right representation of the past is already complicated, and we can see why the kind of detailed period accuracy of costume and language criticised above may not be of primary importance to the creators of this drama. Indeed it frequently prefers to concentrate on the communication of mood through imagery, both romanticised and timeless: the scene in episode 1 where Tietjens and Valentine drive through the mist, emerging out of it to suddenly "see" one another emotionally for the first time, is one example. Ford was himself deeply aware of the unreliability of memory and of narrative and so *Parade's End* uses a kaleidoscopic camera device throughout to signify the fractured nature of representation. This visual technique is an unusual choice for the filming of period drama on television, but appropriate, for it was one that preoccupied Ford. For him, the kaleidoscope "signifies the complex multiplicity of British wartime psychology, one that depended partly on how the light (of experience, of understanding, or of narrative) was thrown" (Haslam, 2002: 88). The style of the adaptation hence deliberately invokes Vorticism, the British version of cubism, a movement which fascinated Ford and many of his contemporaries in the arts, and which reacted against realism in order to undermine certainties and absolutes both artistic and moral. Similarly the trajectory of the novels themselves is very far from linear or straightforward. Like many modernists, Ford experiments with narrative method: his "adoptive style is that of deepening the reader's understanding, making it more complex, rather than progressing it: he constructs parallel lines of narrative. These lines correspond to differing levels of consciousness, differing levels of communication" (Haslam, 2004: 53). Such a technique – where dialogue is intercut with introspection, and plots are returned to or explained pages or even chapters later – seems difficult to transfer to the screen, and is just one of the ways in which modernist fiction is difficult to adapt, either for television or film, as Halliwell has noted:

> When it comes to cinematic adaptations of modernist fiction filmmakers have often found themselves faced with major technical problems. The commercial pressures on mainstream cinematic production have historically ... demanded slick products that do not challenge viewers. Second, the interest among modernist writers in unreliable narrators, psychologically complex characters, fragmented perceptions and mythical allusions are devices that rarely translate smoothly into film. And third, the modernist distain of bourgeois culture does not sit comfortably with the liberal ideology that is usually upheld in commercial film. (Halliwell, in Whelehan, 2007: 90–91)

We can see how all this is true of *Parade's End*, which is more challenging, complex and elitist than the other neo-Edwardian texts in this book. This is something White deliberately embraces, however: she is determined that this adaptation "will make demands of the viewer as Ford makes demands of the reader" (White, interviewed by Davies, 2012). Furthermore, she argues that that this kind of complicated narrative reflects recent trends in high-end television: for her, *Parade's End* is *"Downton Abbey* meets *The Wire,"* referring to the hugely successful American crime drama which also demanded high levels of concentration and commitment from the viewer (White, 2012). White worked with *The Wire's* creator, David Simon, on his Iraq war drama *Generation Kill*, and has clearly adopted the same kind of fast-moving approach here: "You can happily go off and make yourself a cup of tea in *Downton Abbey* and pick it up again," she says. "You can't make yourself a cup of tea during *Parade's End*, or you'd be lost" (White, 2012). So *Parade's End* sets out to differ dramatically from what we expect from cosy Sunday night fare: it makes the viewer work, and in many ways puts the onus of understating the plot, and indeed the history it offers, on them.

It is also, as I have already indicated, a somewhat unusual choice for a literary adaption. Summing up the argument of Paul Kerr some years earlier, Sarah Cardwell has suggested that classic-novel adaptations "operate as part of an ideological project to elevate and perpetuate an elite literary culture, to maintain the distinctions between "good" (BBC) television and "trash" popular culture and to build reactionary nostalgia for a mythologised "ideal era in Britain's colonial past" (Cardwell, 2002: 78). We might consider how Ford Madox Ford fits into this definition. White's comments above – and indeed those of many (especially leftist) reviewers – construct *Downton Abbey* as this kind of "popular culture", almost if not quite "trash", and clearly regard *Parade's End* as its opposite: highbrow, sophisticated television. Yet simultaneously this production seems to be involved in the process of revising, or adding to, to, the conservative canon of "elite" British texts usually adapted by the BBC (among which was the project White worked on before *Parade's End*, *Bleak House*). Cardwell notes that traditionally:

> adaptations tend to draw on a small (though ever-expanding) number of texts by an even smaller number of "classic" authors ... In fact, there are fewer authors whose work is regularly adapted for television than authors whose work is included in undergraduate English courses of the Penguin catalogue: "adaptations of classic novels" is thus an even more restrictive category than that of "classic novels."
> (2004: 3)

Ford was, at best, on the fringes of this process: his best known work, *The Good Soldier*, had been adapted by Granada in 1981, and that was the only one of his many novels to be so, until now. Of course, the process of being adapted for the screen can also confer "classic" or canonical status, for, as Julie Saunders notes, "adaptation ... may in turn contribute to [the literary canon's] ongoing reformulation and expansion" (Sanders, 2006: 8). One example of such might be Elizabeth Gaskell, who as I have discussed elsewhere, was a relatively unknown literary figure before several well-received adaptations of her work made her much more of a household name (Byrne, 2013). It seems that the production team behind *Parade's End* were aware of the need to expand the "restrictive category" of sources for adaptation, and perhaps even to reclaim Ford Madox Ford from relative obscurity, as Stoppard himself indicates:

> Like many people, I only knew of Ford Madox Ford through a book called *The Good Soldier*, which is everybody's favourite Ford Madox Ford if they have one, but I came to read *Parade's End* when it was suggested via Damien Timmer of *Mammoth Screen* ... and thought "It's a sort of masterpiece, unusual and challenging." And it is set in a time and place which I found congenial as a writer. So I embarked upon it. (Stoppard, 2014)

Stoppard had acknowledged already that a television adaptation was the best way to rescue a literary work from oblivion and ensure it reaches a wider audience (Delaney, 1994: 190), and the *Parade's End* books were certainly in need of this. None of the cast, for example, had read Ford before becoming involved with this production: *Parade's End* is not usually taught on undergraduate syllabuses, and both White and Rebecca Hall (who plays Sylvia) "express something approaching embarrassment at having Oxbridge English degrees that never introduced them to this book" (Davies, "Interview," 2012, [sic]). Hence the choice of Ford's work as source – and it soon became a huge and expensive project, with 110 speaking parts, across 146 locations – reveals the willingness of the BBC to expand their repertoire of texts, albeit within conventionally "literary" limits, and not quite to the extent of ITV's unconventional choices (namely of a shopkeeper's biography in *Mr Selfridge*).

Their other departure from the usual heritage format was the choice of screening time: Friday nights on BBC2, instead of the customary Sunday night "period-drama" slot. Cardwell has noted out that "the scheduling of classic-novel adaptations has altered little" over the decades (2002: 81) and while she was referring to programming up until the 1990s, her point still holds true today. The success of all the other shows I explore in this book in that unchanging slot shows that is still signifies familiar, nostalgic and comforting viewing today: for viewers, period drama represents a "haven within the televisual" (Cardwell,

2002: 81). Hence *Parade's End* was taking something of a risk in marketing itself differently, even considering that recent technology means that television can be watched at any time. Indeed, this step was perhaps not successful – the scheduling has been blamed by critics for the drama's low viewing figures – but it does indicate the extent to which this series was determined to separate itself not only from the likes of *Downton* but from a decades-long tradition of period drama in this slot. The adaptation wishes to reject nostalgia in more ways than one.

## Fidelity

I have not yet talked about the screenplay of *Parade's End*, but much of the highbrow appeal – and critical expectation – placed upon the adaptation is a result of the involvement of famous playwright Tom Stoppard. This is not the first adaptation that Stoppard has been involved with: his most famous play, *Rosencrantz and Guildenstern are Dead* (1967), is a pastiche of *Hamlet;* he has in turn adapted this for the big screen (1990) and has written modern versions of plays by Schnitzler and Nestroy. Stoppard's long involvement in theatre has made him interested in the theory and process of adaptation and he has said that he believes that the "frontiers," as he puts it, of plays are and should be "movable." Presumably invoking Barthes, he has argued that there is always a point in staging a play at which the performance leaves behind the written text: "the author dies [and] when you are dead you've had your chance and its someone else's turn" (Stoppard in interview in Delaney, 1994: 202). He is more restrained, however, in his approach to adapting novels: in his view, some classics (and it is fair to assume that Ford's work can be included in this) are "not to be monkeyed about with" (Delaney, 1994: 190). We can see this respect for, even affection for, the classic novel in his screenplay for *Parade's End*. Stoppard's and White's version is not really a huge departure from its source text. Many of the most experimental aspects of the drama – those ways in which it seems to depart from typical period television – are actually present in Ford's novels. The repeated use of flashback, for example, feels like something of an innovation in heritage, but, as Rosemary Goring has noted, is mainly an appropriate cinematic means of representing Ford's complicated narrative mode, which rejects realism by revisiting and reworking aspects of the plot (2012).

The casting is also in keeping with the characters as Ford created them, although with a pragmatic eye for the attractive appearance of the production. Benedict Cumberbatch and Rupert Everett as the

Tietjens brothers, for example, are rather more handsome here than Ford's lumpen and silent Yorkshiremen. As discussed by Cardwell, however, the off-camera or intertextual existence of actors adds greatly to our understanding of their performance: "actors, especially well known ones, can never simply be viewed as the characters they play … they are associated with previous roles … interviews they have given, scandals they have been involved in, as well as the part they are currently playing" (2002: 89). Hence Everett's real-life identity as a gay man adds a neat subtextual explanation for Mark's unexplained refusal to marry and beget an heir. Similarly Benedict Cumberbatch seems a perfect choice for Tietjens, given that he has become famous for playing brilliant, but eccentric and socially awkward men with problematic – or non-existent – sex lives: Sherlock Holmes, Julian Assange, Vincent van Gogh and, most recently, Alan Turing. Cumberbatch does a nice line in tortured and vulnerable but still highly desirable masculinity, and in *Parade's End* manages to make the pursuit of Tietjens by two beautiful women believable while resisting the temptation to make him more dynamic than his source. The casting of Adelaide Clemens as Tietjen's lover Valentine Wannop is also faithful to the novel, though in her case her unfamiliarly to the audience of period dramas adds to the freshness and innocence she brings in this role of wholesome ingénue.[3] Critics have complained that the adaptation's Wannop does lack some of the feminist rebelliousness of the typical militant New Woman of the time, however: the *Telegraph* describes her as "the male fantasy suffragette" due to her gentle and long-suffering devotion to Tietjens (Harvey, 2012). (We might add that her abilities as a Latin scholar and bluestocking are played down slightly in the adaptation, though this might simply be that highly educated and intellectual women are less exceptional today than in Ford's time.) Like *Mr Selfridge*, this drama is interested in feminism, but quite careful and restrained in its representation of its organised form. It does wish to remind the audience of the struggles and achievements of the first-wave: at White's request "Votes for Women" marches take place in the background in the opening scenes, for example , and the slashing of the *Rokeby Venus* (Velazquez, 1647–51) by suffragette Mary Robinson at the National Gallery in 1914 is written into the narrative. At the same time, though, it shies away from some of the darker and more gritty realities of the suffrage campaign. There is no mention of hunger strikes or of the force-feeding of the suffragettes, or the famous suicide of Emily Davidson. Even Valentine's main protest – on the golf course where Tietjens is playing – is represented in a comic, even farcical way. So too is her suffragette friend's subsequent escape from the law. Indeed these incidents, and the (admittedly less lighthearted) harassment of Valentine at the Eton cricket match, are really catalysts for the love plot and temporary distractions from it. Susanna White is certainly a feminist and has herself spoken out about the sexism in the film industry, but the drama remains faithful to Ford's Wannop – a gentle suffragette that "only a man could have created" (Harvey, 2012). It is unsurprising that *Parade's End* is cautious about the suffrage movement, though, for it is consistently more interested in small and personal struggles rather than in bigger political conflict. Valentine may be "the face of the future" but the feminist focus of the drama is ultimately directed at a less likely source; her less political, but more subversive counterpart, Tietjens's wife, Sylvia (White, 2012).

I have so far been noting that what sets out to be an atypical or edgy period drama is actually a faithful rendering of Ford's plot, and that Stoppard, despite his history of approaching famous texts subversively (most famously *Rosencrantz and Guildenstern are Dead's* take on *Hamlet* and *Travesties'* on *The Importance of Being Earnest*) is reluctant to play around too much with a classic novel. This seems to be true here even though the novel in question is actually one which he is trying to reconstruct as a classic. Stoppard does acknowledge, however (while speaking about his version of a Schnitzler play, *Undiscovered Country*), that "helping" the original, is frequently desirable, for "you are not doing the author a favour if the adaptation is not vibrant..." (Delaney, 1994: 190). This is presumably why there is at least one very significant departure from the source text, and one which adds considerable "vibrancy" to the adaptation: the representation and portrayal of Sylvia. And it is Sylvia, not Valentine, who is most interesting to a feminist critic, for it is she who becomes the locus of gender struggle in the drama and who is the medium through which its critique of patriarchy really operates.

## Sexual politics in *Parade's End*

Ford's Sylvia has been greeted as one of the great monsters of literature: many critics have considered her a "corrupt beauty ... [a] cruel, ravishingly attractive temptress" whose passionate sexuality hides a "core ... [which] is cold and continent" (Meixner, 1962: 205–206). This is, arguably, an accurate representation of the later books in Ford's quatrology, in which Sylvia does become something of a stock villain if not quite a "devil" (Meixner, 1962: 219). Her attempts to keep Tietjens and

Valentine apart, for example, become ridiculously melodramatic: she pretends to be terminally ill when she is not, and later throws herself down the stairs in front of the reunited couple. (Her attempt to convince Tietjens of the former – while looking radiant with health – add to the moments of comedy, even farce, which punctuate the adaptation, but this scene is actually an abbreviated and downplayed version of her behaviour in *A Man Could Stand Up-*). Earlier in the novels, however, her beauty and cynical wit do make her an interesting and complex character, and even throughout *The Last Post* the reader stays with her subjectivity even while witnessing her obsessive behaviour. In this final book Tietjens himself only appears momentarily, whereas many chapters are devoted to the thoughts and plans of his tortured and torturing wife. Even recent critics have ignored Ford's continuing – if ambivalent – preoccupation with Sylvia, who remains a "horror" in many views, or is largely insignificant in others (Haslem, 2002: 111). Max Saunders's extensive critical biography simply notes her "demonic energy" and reminds us that she is a more "sporting" version of Ford's former partner Violet Hunt (1996: 266–267); Robert Green thinks of her as "sadistic" (1981: 143) but primarily sees her as a means of understanding and reading Tietjens (1981: 139).[4] Arthur Mizener's 1971 biography of Ford does hint at Sylvia's power, but at the same time condemns her as "systematically and ingeniously cruel" (369). Stoppard and White's adaptation takes the possibilities her character offers much further, however, recasting her as the real heroine of the drama, and the source of its heritage glamour. MacShane has noted that "by 1919 Tietjens had his fill of glamour and knew how worthless it would be in a world of no more parades,"(1965: 58) but in the adaptation he – and indeed the viewer – cannot fail to be captivated by Sylvia, who becomes "the driving force" of the story, no matter how badly she behaves (McNamara, 2013). David Thompson, for example, devotes much of his review to Rebecca Hall, whose Sylvia he considers the "knock-out owner [of *Parade's End*].... She is the most pressing reason for staying with this show ... it is so hard for a beautiful woman to be hateful in a movie. She may do bad things, but one sly glance at the camera and that game is shot" (2012).[5] Thompson judges, perhaps a little harshly (and rather naïvely, given Benedict Cumberbatch's considerable female fan base) that "Tietjens could hardly hold us for five hours" and so the books have been "improved" ("helped" in Stoppard's own terminology) by the repositioning of Sylvia as a sympathetic femme fatale (2012).

White is determined that we see Sylvia as a result of patriarchal oppression: "She could have been a harridan figure. I made her multilayered, a victim of circumstances. It's a big change from the book" (White, quoted in Brown, 2012). While in the first episode of the series Hall's Sylvia comes across as brittle, even hysterical, by the second the viewer understands that most of her behaviour is motivated by emotional and intellectual frustration. She is "bored" and unstimulated by her idle society life, and resentful of her husband's superior – inevitably, because he is a man in the early twentieth century – education, knowledge and opportunities. Her first aggressive act towards Tietjens in the drama is a response to his comments about the 1911 National Insurance Bill and by her mother's cutting remark that his intelligence outstrips her own. "You married above your intellect and don't take kindly to disadvantage," Sylvia is told just before she hurls a plate at her husband (*Parade's End*, episode 1). A modern viewer cannot help but feel some compassion here, for Sylvia is a reminder of the limited lives led by those who, unlike Valentine Wannop, had not yet benefited from the changes of first-wave feminism. For the rest of the adaptation we see her expending her considerable talents on the manipulation of those around her, as she has nothing else to do. In acknowledgement of Ford's own interest in Freud, this energy is largely directed at another source of frustration for Sylvia: her sexuality. From the opening moments of the drama Sylvia is shown to be victim of her own desires, unable to resist illicit and passionate (even almost violent) sex even though she is due to be married the next day. In this way she is "a new sort of female character" who is the very antithesis of the conventional heroine of period drama, whose desires are hinted at but rarely expressed (McNamara, 2013). She is clearly at odds with her Edwardian society (which is beginning to change but not doing so fast enough to accept her carnal appetites and illegitimate pregnancy) but at one with ours. As we see her embark on a number of extramarital and loveless affairs, her pragmatic attitudes towards sex reflect those of the modern world much more closely than the restraint and morality of the repressed Tietjens or his innocent would-be mistress. Now, one of the key attractions of period dramas to the modern viewer is the unconsummated, repressed and constantly deferred love affair of the central characters: Elisabeth and Darcy in *Pride in Prejudice* (1995) are only the most well-known of many examples of this. Virginia L Blum has written convincingly of the contradiction created by our modern belief that "sexual repression is one of the worst threats to personal fulfilment," which leads to a liberated and sexually open society that in fact seems less erotic than the repressed past (2003: 158). Thus we have a collective "fantasy of what we might recuperate via the adaptation of pre-Victorian and Victorian novels and our sense that we have lost the experience of desire that they had to repress" (Blum, 2003: 158–159). *Parade's End* plays around with the same conventions, except that its viewer's pleasurable frustration is echoed and acted out by all three of the central characters, and ultimately voiced by Sylvia. Her desire for the husband she has betrayed is true to the novel, but the adaptation leaves its source behind by complicating their triangle further. Hence the relationship between her and Tietjens, which Ford describes as almost entirely loveless on his side, becomes in White's version an ambiguous and entirely mutual mixture of desire, admiration and rage.

Needless to say, this conflicted relationship is much more compelling to the audience than more straightforward and suitable – if adulterous – romance with Valentine. In itself this is unusual: period adaptations frequently display love triangles but the central love affair is usually apparent, and the romantic resolution comfortingly predictable, to the viewer (even if they do not know it already from familiarity with the plot of the novel).[6] This version, instead, is able to exploit its less well-known source text and deliberately plays around with possible resolutions. For example episode 4 deals with Sylvia's visit to Tietjens at the Front, during which they have a kind of reconciliation. This incident also occurs – though is only accessed via Tietjens's description of it to another soldier – in Ford's *No More Parades*, but is represented rather differently there: one Ford critic described it as an "ugly episode in the Tietjens hotel room" in which Sylvia disgraces herself and her husband when one of her lovers is caught trying to visit her for sex (Meixner, 1962: 115). Stoppard's screenplay rewrites this, however, as a moment of revelation and honesty: Sylvia confesses that her bad behaviour is motivated by desire, and Tietjens apologises to her, with an awareness of his culpability which he never outwardly expresses in Ford's novels. It also becomes a love scene, albeit one which rapidly descends into chaos when they are interrupted by not one but two officers bursting into the room, but even this is a source of amusement for the lovers who recognise its air of farce. The exact extent of their reconciliation is, in keeping with Ford's narrative gaps, not revealed, but the episode concludes with Sylvia's triumphant declaration to the taxi driver who takes her away from Rouen that she "is the Captain's lady." With this in mind, the final episode, in which Tietjens is happily reunited with Valentine after the War, is more in keeping with Ford's ending than with the actual tone of the adaptation thus far. Even this happy ending – which critics have noted is more upbeat that the novels, for popular appeal – has a touch of ambivalence about it, however. Tietjens can only respond with slightly tortured silence to Sylvia's final appeal for him to leave Valentine and return to her: "Oh Christopher, Christopher. You can't mean it. Look at her. Is she a Girl Guide or something? Perhaps you do mean it..." (*Parade's End*, episode 5). He chooses only by remaining passive and allowing Sylvia to leave. And in this ending Sylvia is less bitter and more adaptable than in the novel, where only Valentine's impending pregnancy eventually stops her campaign for revenge. Her final rejection by Tietjens is accepted with fairly good grace – "Well, I wish you both nothing but happiness" – (*Parade's End*, episode 5) and she is already pragmatically planning her post-divorce future as General Campion's wife, like the resourceful woman she is (one of the most significant changes to all modern day heroines of literary adaptations is that they are much less constant than their source characters: we no longer expect women to remain permanently scarred by a lost love, even in fiction). This social and emotional survival mirrors Tietjens's emergence from the War: both characters endure and start over, but are not entirely unscathed.

That this rewriting of Sylvia as heroine is the main departure from Ford's text and at the same time one of the most successful aspects of the adaptation – almost every reviewer comments favourably upon it, and upon her – says a lot about the our modern expectations about the heritage package. Stoppard and White have foregrounded the most glamorous, lavish and consumerist aspect of Ford's novels: his tetralogy is generally about the rejection of artifice and display, about a return to simplicity and a more authentic way of life, and Sylvia's elegance functions as the antithesis of this. For Ford, her stylish clothes constitute her main appeal in the novels, but also signify her moral inferiority to the more austere Tietjens and Valentine. *Parade's End* takes a rather different approach, celebrating personal expression through clothing as a kind of art. This is something *The Forsyte Saga* also does, and Sylvia's costumes here also celebrate the kind of glamorous consumerism *Mr Selfridge* is focused upon. Sylvia's centrality and desirability serve other functions in the adaptation too, however. Thompson notes that she feminises what could appear to be a rather male novel by a male writer: "She has seized the opportunity and drawn Ford Madox Ford closer to those women's pictures where Bette Davis or Jeanne Moreau dominated proceedings" (2012). Women are still the main audience for period drama, and Sylvia's domination of the adaption may be in part a pragmatic way of ensuring their attention. She certainly provides necessary glamour, escapism and relief through the misery and tension of the war scenes which dominate the later episodes of the drama, to which I will now turn.

## The First World War in *Parade's End*

I have discussed the representation of the war throughout this book, and the methods of approach to it are surprisingly diverse. *The Forsyte Saga* chooses to avoid the conflict entirely, which also true to its source text, but surprising: an Edwardian drama which does not engage with the conflict feels like it is missing an important element. It is, after all, the First World War which signals the end of the Edwardian era and gives it its meaning and its poignancy. *The Forsyte Saga* does, however, represent a different, earlier conflict: the Boer War, which takes place entirely off screen, but which costs young Jolyon his son. *Downton Abbey* in contrast devotes a whole series to wartime, but clearly supports the dominant modern view that the conflict was a tragedy and a waste. As a result, rather than engaging with politics of the war, or the battlefields in any detail, it prefers to concentrate on the treatment and convalescence of soldiers at home in the Abbey. Their damaged bodies constantly remind us of the high price of warfare, while avoiding the need to directly confront the horrors of the trenches. *Mr Selfridge* also remains on home soil for those episodes set during the War, but takes an entirely different perspective, choosing to represent the patriotic and optimistic attitudes of ordinary people. Hence the enlisting of excited volunteers, for example, is an emotional but upbeat event, and the only other war narratives include the spy-story sub-plot of Selfridge doing secret war work, and the safe return of Agnes's missing brother. I have suggested that this may be signifying recent revisionist readings of the First World War as a positive or at least a "necessary" event, and that it certainly reflects the surge of patriotic feeling which surrounded the centenary of the conflict, as discussed in Chapter 1. *Parade's End* is, significantly, much more cynical of this kind of patriotism, and is much closer, both geographically and emotionally, to the Front, even though Stoppard has insisted that the love story came first in his interpretation:

> I said very firmly, look this is not a First World War story, it's the story of a man caught between two women who he has loved and loves. They're very different from each other. And he's a unique and most unusual gentleman. The war itself is something which is happening

in the background from the second episode onwards. But we don't visit the war until later and even then, much of it is from a camp behind the lines. So the First World War, as one always understands that phrase in drama, which is to do with soldiers in trenches, shells falling upon them, charging across No-Man's Land, occupies relatively few minutes, but of course the war is a huge fact. And it changed society irredeemably. (Stoppard, 2014)

Stoppard's interest in the War, then, lies mostly in its potential as a catalyst for social change, and he implies here that it is a secondary part of the plot (perhaps also to differentiate it from *Birdsong*, the BBC's last First World War adaptation, which focuses on the conflict and in which it is the love story that is background). Ford's own perspective was slightly different, for like many writers in the 1920s he saw fiction as a means of coming to terms with the psychological trauma that resulted from the recent conflict. TS Eliot would take a similar approach in *The Wasteland*, as would Virginia Woolf in *To the Lighthouse* and *Mrs Dalloway*. Ford found it difficult – even agonising – to put the experience of war into words, but was enough of a Freudian to understand that remembering it, and writing about it, was "necessary to exorcise the suffering" (Saunders, 1996: 197). Thus two of the four novels are taken up with wartime, and all investigate its effects on the human psyche. For a war novelist, however, Ford is in one way particularly accessible and suitable for adaptation for modern television, for his overall approach is to view the conflict though a personal lens. In other words, he uses the battleground of heterosexual love and modern marriage as a foil for his navigation of the war:

> like Lawrence and other modernists preoccupied by the significance of individual and private lives in the alien public space, Ford figures the trauma of the historical conflict very much in terms of a trauma in personal relationships.... The tragedy of World War One is reflected by the "sex war" being enacted at home. (Matthews, 2004: 80–81)

Hence the adaptation is able to acknowledge what has become a frequent approach to this conflict by period television: viewing this traditionally male history from a female perspective. Recent medical drama *The Crimson Field*, for example, represents trench warfare as seen through the eyes of a group of young, female nurses, and is located almost entirely within their field hospital. Similarly *Downton Abbey*, as we have discussed, constructs its war mostly as an experience for those who remain at home, albeit nursing its casualties there. This is not just a twenty-first century trend, either: *Upstairs Downstairs* and the *Duchess of Duke Street* followed the same pattern in the 1970s. *Parade's End* does have a number of scenes set at the Front, but its interest is also to show how Valentine and Sylvia cope with the war at home, in England. They, like the viewer, are removed from the direct experience of conflict. Critics complained about the rapid cuts between the battlefield and the drawing rooms of the upper classes in the drama, but the slightly schizophrenic nature of the narrative is reflective of its attempt to balance Ford's examination of the War with the experience of it from a distance, by women (Goodman, 2013). In this way, these period dramas remind us of women's narratives and perspectives which have tended to be left out of traditional "his-stories" of the war.

As I have indicated already in this book, there has much debate about when the war came to be regarded as a senseless horror. Some historians point out that at least by the publication of Wilfred Owen's poetry in the 1920s, society had reacted with condemnation against the carnage and the value system that unpinned it. Others believe that until the 1960s it was a trauma not much spoken of:

> The change began with the publication in 1961 of Alan Clark's *The Donkeys*, which by ridiculing the military leadership of the British Expeditionary Force offered a satirical perspective that Joan Littlewood and her company took full advantage of in the musical *Oh, What a Lovely War!* at Stratford East in 1963. A more general enlightenment had to wait until the war's 50th anniversary in 1964, when the BBC showed its now celebrated 26-part documentary *The Great War*, which every week for half a year returned us to the trenches, the field guns and the great naval fleets via flickering scraps of silent film interwoven with interviews of survivors, many of whom were then aged well under 70. It was a superb, eloquent achievement: prompted by Wilfred Josephs's sombre music, a suppressed national memory took shape and rose weeping from the mud. (Jack, 2013)

Interestingly, in both cases this construction was largely a literary one. Hence revisionists – most famously Max Hastings – who have recently argued for the significance of the conflict, and the extent of the popular feeling which supported it, have condemned what has become known as "the poet's view." This has which has been "caricatured as a post-war invention, a cultural artefact of the 1920s and 1930s, when a steady stream of published poems, diaries, memoirs, and novels created a new anti-war consciousness (Faulkner 2013)." *Parade's End'*s representation of the war itself is also interestingly conflicted, invoking both views, while seeming to acknowledge that neither is the full story. Hence Tietjens himself is supportive of the war, constructing it – initially at least – as the defence of the old world against the new: "If we'd stayed out of it, I would have done over to France, to fight for France. For agriculture against industrialism. For the C18th against the C20th" (episode 2). He goes to war in order to preserve England – viewed by the camera in full peaceful, rural panoramic beauty, at the end of episode 1 – exactly as it is. He fails, of course: the country he returns to after the War is a very different place, as symbolised by the cutting down of Groby Great tree, and that is both tragic and liberating for him. For the modern viewer, his patriotism might be reflective of revisionist views of the conflict, especially as it has been romanticised after much remembrance. Valentine is instantly dismissive of this kind of outdated, romantic idealism: "you are as innocent about yourself as a child. You would have thought all the same things in the C18th" (episode 2). In fact, it is the female characters who anticipate the horrors of the conflict. Sylvia, Valentine and Valentine's mother are all appalled by the War, and grief stricken even though they are not personally bereaved by it. For them, and for most viewers, the war is "pain and torture," an abomination (episode 2). Even the usually flippant Sylvia is distraught, "strangely unable to bear the horror of war" (Davies, 2012): "I can't sleep at night now because the pain is worse in the dark. It spreads into every corner. Black, like ink. Printer's ink. Newspapers dripping hate and lies, every day" (episode 2). Significantly, while her opposite in most respects, Valentine says almost exactly the same thing. We might be reminded here of Virginia Woolf's famous description of 1914–18 as a "preposterous masculine fiction" (Woolf also blamed the "dammed newspapers" for misinforming the public about the War, as Karen Levenback has noted (1999: 13)). For the female characters in *Parade's End*, it is men who created, believed in and mythologised this conflict, and they are completely wrong to do so.

This tension between male and female ideology continues throughout the rest of the drama, in which male characters usually support the War, by their actions if not their words, and women remain pacifists and are often condemned by society for being so. (Sylvia gets into trouble for sending presents and supplies to her German friends, for example.) Tietjens, however, undergoes a change in opinion and perspective as the years of fighting pass, and indeed as his mental health declines. In the novels, this is specifically constructed in gender terms: psychoanalytical critics have noticed that he undergoes a kind of feminising through his care for the troops he commands, and especially through his awareness of his own failures as leader and "father." This is most apparent in a scene in *A Man Could Stand Up-* in which he pulls a junior soldier out of a mudslide, which Sara Haslam has identified as a crucial moment of crisis for Tietjens's masculinity:

> He has failed his charge, one who looked to him as a father.... Thus he is impotent; the all-powerful, all seeing officer cannot even protect his own ... Tietjens also becomes intensely affected by the "femininity" historically associated with "passivity" and with the hysteric. In an extraordinary way, though, Tietjens's madness is caused by femininity that becomes more than passive; it is actively portrayed by Ford. Aranjuez has been buried, as we have seen. But Tietjens, and then two colleagues, pull him out of the viscous mud to safety ... Aranjuez is reborn, with Tietjens presiding as midwife. How much more concrete can the abstract become? Having let him down as omnipotent father, Tietjens becomes a mother, "he felt tender, like a mother, and enormous," as he carries the boy. (p 639) (Haslam, 2002: 97–98)

Tietjens's interiority here cannot be fully communicated in the adaptation, but there as in the novel, this moment is the climax to his war. White represents this scene as the last one set in the Trenches, for following this incident General Campion (appalled to find Tietjens plastered in mud) sends him back from the Front. For Campion, with his narrow conception of class and manliness, Tietjens is inadequate as an officer and a man, and his career as a soldier is over. He has, after all, failed to measure up to the standards of Edwardian masculinity which forms the mythology of war. For the modern viewer, however, this can only be a good thing, for the war has been exposed throughout to be the very opposite of heroic. As one critic noted, "the war sequences are intriguingly contrarian and unpatriotic, subtly lampooning Britain's military might as a bumbling bureaucracy" (Stuever, 2013). Certainly, the entire action of episode 4 of the series is devoted to the portrayal of the War as a manifestation of a pointless inefficiency bordering on farce. Orders are given and then immediately countermanded; troops are under-resourced and inadequately provided for; trains don't run when they should, and those in command are more concerned with the behaviour of a man's wife than his performance as a soldier. Even the horses are victims of conflicting orders and foolish care. If the BBC's *Blackadder Goes Forth* is our main reference point for this conflict, it never seems more accurate than here. Only Tietjens – despite his short-comings in other areas – can be trusted to get his draft out on time, or to understand how the system can work most efficiently, even though he is criticised at several points in the drama, and by several different characters, as "no sort of soldier" (episode 4). Even the General, him-self also a target of the adaptation's criticism and satire, is moved to sarcastic exasperation at the ineffectual bureaucracy which is in charge of proceedings:

> So we have Captain Tietjens, who the War Office wanted in charge of the 19th Division's horse lines, going instead to the trenches to take over as second in command of the 6th Battalion Glamorganshires. And we have Captain McKechnie, who detests Tietjens because he consid-ers the second-in-command of the 6th Battalion Glamorganshires to be his by right, going instead to take charge of the 19th Divisions horse lines, which he sees, correctly, as a humiliation, and finally we have Major Perowne, last seen attempting to enter the bedroom of Mrs Tietjens, allegedly at her invitation, being sent back to his battalion as a punishment. And all I can say is, it takes a Movement Order of some genius to send these three officers up the line sharing transport. (*Parade's End*, episode 5)

Under these circumstances, where no-one is where they should be, no-one is doing the job they are suited for, and even their transportation is fraught with difficulty, pointless slaughter is not only likely, but inevi-table. The viewer is aware that if even simple things cannot be correctly organised, the difficulties of combat with a trained enemy is bound to wreak devastation. We do not actually witness this, however, for there is little direct confrontation of violent death on the battlefield, some-thing which is also true of other recent period dramas which deal with the war, including *The Village*, as we will see in the next chapter. The audience for the classic serial does not seem to have an appetite for the full horrors of conflict: we prefer "a war at one remove, where we could stand back and contemplate the abstract – its tragedy, its alienation, its despair – without getting too mired in the filth" (Davies, *Birdsong*, 2012).[7] Instead, we are witness to the mental rather than physical break-down of most of the men in the adaptation.

Post-traumatic stress disorder, as it is now known, is the aspect of warfare most of interest to the contemporary period drama, for "the shell-shocked soldier is one of the iconic trauma victims of the twentieth century" (Luckhurst, 2008: 50). Its diagnosis is a key plotline in *The Crimson Field*, for example, and it is explored in *Downton* and *Birdsong* as well. In contrast to those shows, however, in which one character is represented as suffering from "classic" shell shock, all the officers in *Parade's End* are, at different points, hysterical and incoherent with fear. No-one who actually spends any time in the trenches is immune. Hence shell shock is less a notable pathological condition than a daily reality for all the central characters, none of whom are really fit for active service, let alone at the Front. This world's lack of concern for them is clear, unlike the more sympathetic society portrayed in *Downton*, in which Lang is invalided out of the army after his breakdown, and in *The Crimson Field*, in which a physician risks his career to protect the vulnerable. In *Parade's End*, in contrast, no-one even sees a doctor. Their illness reminds us of the shortcomings of the past, and the painful lasting legacy of the War even for those who are physically unscathed. Their trauma serves as a signifier in other ways too, however. As in *Downton*, and *The Forsyte Saga* (although Soames's breakdown is a result of love and guilt, not the Trenches) mental illness is here symptomatic of the wider problems masculinity would face in the era of female suffrage and with the breakdown of old systems of land tenure. Even more generally, it is indicative of a new era, of, even, the modern world. Theorists of trauma have noted that psychological damage is the inevitable condition of modern life: "modernity has come to be understood under the sign of the wound" (Selzer, 1997: 18). (It is hence significant that Joe Middleton's suffering in *The Village* is constructed as the catalyst for a new, more equal post-War society.) As Roger Luckhurst has argued, the post-industrial city, new technology, and especially the arrival of the railways, all contributed to the "exhaustion and overstimulation" of the modern subject, long before psychoanalysis identified hysteria as a condition or the First World War gave a name to shell shock. In his dislocation from the natural, agricultural world he so loves, Tietjens in particular is psychologically damaged before he even arrives in war-torn France. Ford's novels are fascinated by the way in which "trauma disrupts memory, and therefore identity" for him, this fracturing of the self is the very essence of modernism (Luckhurst, 2008: 10). For the viewer watching the adaptation in a new century, the exhausted and isolated city dweller we see Tietjens as in the final moments of the drama is the very epitome of modern life.

## Art and the heritage drama

I began this discussion with the suggestion that *Parade's End* was trying to escape from the kind of soap-opera version of history offered by the subjects of my two previous chapters, and which has, with the popularity of *Downton*, come to dominate the representation of the past on the small screen. It attempts this through a range of strategies, which vary from a complex narrative structure to an unusual choice of screening time, but its difference from *Downton* and co. is perhaps signalled most directly by its deliberate construction of history as art. Barbara Schaff has written about the ways in which highbrow heritage fictions are aware of the complications inherent in their means of representing the past (because they are usually themselves adaptations of fictional texts), and how they use the pictorial to acknowledge this:

> Whereas authenticity in history films is labelled quite simply as "true to historical reality," in heritage films it seems to be a much more multi-faceted concept. Due to the intermediality of literary adaptations, reality in heritage film is always two-faced: it displays the reality of history and the reality of fiction. Many heritage films foreground this consciousness of a double or alternative reality by translating the fictional reality into images that show distinct references to art. Their iconography quotes certain historical modes of representation such as portrait, landscape, and genre painting, or tableaux vivants.... The meticulously displayed visual splendour, the pictorial lushness, aesthetic grandeur and tasteful reconstruction of the British past make many heritage films appear as a chain of carefully composed single shots, each of them a perfect work of art in its own right. (2004: 126)

Schaff's comments have real resonance with regard to *Parade's End*: this drama is full of shots which construct and frame the English landscape – and English women, namely Sylvia and Valentine – as beautiful works of art, captured by the camera for the pleasure of the viewer. That is typical of most heritage drama, of course. The camera in *Downton* also lingers lovingly on the Yorkshire countryside, as it does on the Peak District in *The Village*, but neither it nor *Mr Selfridge* (even with its still life window displays) have the same post-modern thematic preoccupation with painting which we can see in White's deliberately artistic adaption (although the 2002 *Forsyte Saga* does to some degree, as I discussed in Chapter 2). White herself has acknowledged the important role art played in the drama, which she suggests was an acknowledgement to Ford's own artistic interests:

> One shot of the battlefield at night is a direct quote from a Nash painting, brought to life with moving flares and explosions. Ford Madox Ford was involved with the Cubists and Vorticists and there are references to paintings throughout. The era is the end of the Pre-Raphaelites and the costumes have a lot of the rich colours associated with that movement, particularly Sylvia's. We went for a much more subdued palette for the trenches and the images become more fractured as the characters' Edwardian values are shattered. The three mirrors of the opening titles, modelled on Vorticist photographers, become a recurring motif as things start to break down. (White, Broadcast, 2012)

As I have already mentioned, Ford's own modernist fascination with Vorticism informs his narrative style in the novels, and hence its inclusion here is appropriate as well as being one of the most innovative aspects of the drama. There are, however, many references to art in the adaptation which are not at all Cubist and are not directly relevant to the source text. Sylvia visits an exhibition of the Post-Impressionists in episode 2, for example, but appropriately brings home an eighteenth-century landscape for Tietjens instead. Later, Valentine is sitting in the National Gallery when the *Rokeby Venus* is slashed by an angry suffragette: she has just been on a "Votes for Women" march, but escapes it to contemplate the painting in the gallery. This is a moment in the adaptation (it is not in the source text) which seems to be about to make a point about the objectification of women and the stridency of first-wave feminism, but is more interested in the power and beauty of art, instead. Hence Valentine only looks appalled at the destruction of something so beautiful, and the picture has made such an impression on her that, later in the drama, her sexual fantasies about Tietjens are shaped by it. As Stella Hockenhull discusses, we see Valentine imagining herself in the Venus's erotic pose while waiting for his arrival to consummate their relationship (2015: 199). And, on a darker note, as White indicates above, the adaptation took inspiration from Paul Nash's First World War landscapes when constructing its scenes set on the Western front.

What White does not mention above, then, is that the use of painting as a significant and recurrent motif in the adaptation serves functions beyond signalling fidelity to the source. Firstly, it constructs the drama as a highbrow fiction which demands a certain cultural knowledge and interest of its audience. After all, it educates the viewer about British and Spanish art and photography from the seventeenth to the twentieth centuries. It also, however, reminds us of the ultimate function of heritage productions, that they

> do not recreate or envisage the past, rather they construct the past as a work of art. What follows on from this emphasis on art is that heritage films are not authentic in the sense that they present the adaptation of a novel ... in realistic terms as historically truthful renderings of events. (Schaff, 2004: 1270)

Given the way our culture tends to measure historical accuracy and precision as a way of judging the value of historical fictions (as the reviewers I quoted at the beginning of this chapter indicated) it is necessary to remind the audience that period dramas are too complex to function as history lessons. In fact, *Parade's End*, with its interest in painting both modernist and classic, its rejection and reinforcement of heritage forms, and its lack of moral judgements, constructs itself as a work of art as multifaceted as a Vortican photograph.

## Conclusion

It seems surprising that Ford's beautiful but critically neglected *Parade's End* novels have not been adapted before now. Of course their complex form does not make for straightforward transferral to the screen, but their mix of nostalgia and contempt towards the past sums up many of the issues confronted by period drama in the twenty-first century. Ford was preoccupied with the effect of social change on "the inner life," and his tetralogy gives "insight into the political effects of disruption, the end of feudalism, and the beginning of the modern world, on his imagined characters" (Green, 1981: 134). His solution to the trauma of modernity, however, is to opt out of society. In the fourth and final novel, Tietjens and Valentine have retreated to the countryside to live and rear their coming child in rural isolation. The adaptation does not include *The Last Post*, and by stopping at the end of *A Man Could Stand Up-* it offers a different ending, both less bleak and more anti-heritage. In it Tietjens is, as I have suggested, drained and exhausted by the war, and returning to his family home, discovers that the future he had been fighting to stave off is now here. Tractors are ploughing the fields and Sylvia has had Groby Great Tree cut down in her final act of revenge.

Tietjens mourns the rural and feudal past symbolised by the tree, which has grown by his family's stately home for generations, and returns sadly to the city, bringing the remaining logs from it as keepsakes. These fragments of the past reminds us of the fractured self Tietjens has long been. But they are also, of course, just dead wood, as his less sentimental brother Mark reminds him when he throws *his* log on the fire. In the final moments of the drama Tietjens does the same, and in doing so signals his acceptance of modern life and his rejection of old, nineteenth-century values: he is about to begin an exciting, but unconventional, relationship with Valentine. It is only after the past is destroyed that he can move towards sexual freedom, personal happiness and the future, through this union. The message here seems clear: nostalgia prevents progress and it is dangerous to sentimentalise the past. When this ending is compared with the source text's, however, a rather more ironic subtext emerges. In Ford's novel, the foundations of the house itself are damaged by the cutting of the tree: Tietjens's final words in the tetralogy are to tell Mark that "half Groby wall is down." In the adaptation, however, the tree may be a tragic stump, but the ultimate symbol of tradition and privilege, the house itself, endures unscathed. Even in this experimental, innovative drama, heritage survives.

# 6
# "An ordinary epic": *The Village* (2013–)

The subject of this final chapter, BBC1's most recent Edwardian drama, *The Village* (2013–), is the antithesis of the other historical fictions examined in this book. Set in the period immediately prior to and following the First World War, it covers ground which is by now pretty familiar to us, but sees it through very different eyes. Peter Moffat wrote the series with the intention of making it an "ordinary epic, a narrative that is determined to be interested in life as it is lived" which examines the world as it was for the inhabitants of a fictional village in the Peak District (Cooke, 2013). This show sets out to challenge and subvert the version of history offered by shows like *Downton*, by focusing almost entirely on the working class and attempting to represent their lives with accuracy. The televisual tradition established by *Upstairs Downstairs* and continued by *Downton* established that, where the lower classes are represented on screen, the focus is of the show is – more or less – equally divided, between them and their upper class employers. This seems to assume that while the viewer may be interested in servants, they expect equal screen time to be given to their more glamorous social "superiors". *The Village* ignores this: the inhabitants of the local Big House are marginalised curiosities a world apart from the villagers, and it is the latter who occupy all the key roles. Such an approach makes a stark contrast with typical period drama, for it deliberately disregards nostalgia, there being little for a modern viewer to mourn about the passing of this often brutal way of life. In its absence of glamour, its dark and gritty realism, and its focus on poverty and hardship, the early twentieth-century world portrayed here is hardly recognisable as the same era I have discussed in the previous chapters – until we come to the portrayal of the First World War, at least. This final chapter will thus conclude my exploration of the "Edwardians on screen" with an examination of this very different drama, which contradicts most of our preconceptions about Edwardian Britain, and chronicles a parallel version of history in which the working class occupy centre stage.

Series 1 opens as a (fictional) current-day interview with the "second oldest man in Britain," Bert Middleton, who is telling the story of his life through a series of flashbacks. In Bert's opening lines he tells his interviewer that this is the last thing he will do in his long life, and that as a result the programme they are making needs to "do it properly. Make it honest" (*The Village*, series 1 episode 1). Right from this meta-fictional opening scene the drama announces its intention to provide an authentic view of history, while at the same time acknowledging in a very post-modern way that what it is about to tell is narrative, not fact. Each episode thus begins and ends by returning to Bert, and to the presumably present day, repeatedly reminding the viewer that the history represented here is a personal one shaped through one particular perspective. This kind of framing technique is a popular one in historical fiction. Ian McEwan's 2001 novel *Atonement*, which was adapted into film in 2007, and the 1992 film adaptation of Susan Isacc's novel *Shining Through*, are just two examples of texts which use similar "interview" devices to explore the relationship between memory and narrative (both are about remembering the Second World War). Here, this framing technique also has the effect of constructing Bert into a symbol of Britain: as a kind of celebrity or even national hero for his longevity. The drama makes clear that his history will be the history of the country throughout the twentieth century. Hence, series 2 charters his life in the 1920s, and Moffat plans to follow him further in future years, although I will only concentrate on the Edwardian series 1 in this chapter.

*The Village* is deliberately a micro-history, however: the big events of the twentieth century do happen to Bert and his family, but the focus is always on the personal and private, as reviewers have noted:

> In the series the camera never leaves the village. Births, deaths, love and betrayal, great political events, upheavals in national identity, ways of working, rules kept and rebellions made, sex, religion, class, the shaping of modern memory – all refracted through the lives of the villagers and the village. One man, Bert Middleton lives across the entire hundred years and his life story from boyhood to extreme old age provides the narrative backbone. His last great act of remembering is our way in to an examination of our recent past. (BBC Mediacentre, 2012)

This deliberately insular approach has echoes of *The Forsyte Saga* and of *Downton*, both of which also concentrated the viewer's gaze on the life of one family and rarely moved the action beyond their homes. Similarly, *Mr Selfridge* rarely moves it outside the eponymous store. Indeed, it could be said that this is now how we prefer our history to be, that we find it more accessible if it is personal and intimate, told through the eyes of the individual – it is just that that individual, unlike Bert, is usually middle or upper class.

This change to a working-class perspective is not unique to *The Village*, but it does represent a very recent evolution in costume drama. The BBC's 2004 adaptation of Gaskell's *North and South* was a sympathetic and stimulating portrayal of industrial workers, but saw them primarily through the eyes of its very bourgeois heroine. It is not until Channel 4's Victorian drama *The Mill* (2013–) that we see a period fiction devoted to the examination of the urban working class – and the rural poor are still nowhere to be seen. Hence *The Village* is very unusual in what it sets out to do, especially because it rejects many of the conventions of Edwardian drama that we have come to recognise following *Downton Abbey*. Indeed, this world does not feel at all Edwardian in the way we have come to understand the term, and as it has been explored elsewhere on screen. The few scenes in the big house apart, there is no luxury here, and no commodification of the past: costumes are drab and the interiors in which most of the scenes are shot are bare and dark. Furthermore, the Edwardian period is traditionally associated with the coming of modernity, but here that change is very slow to arrive, given that the village is so cut off from the rest of the world. Only the arrival of the first bus and the approach of war reminds us of the date, for the changes we associate with the period – the motor car, the telephone, changing dress for women – are modernity as it was known to the privileged minority. It is also notable that the inter-class relationships represented are largely realistically remote and devoid of *Downton*-inspired affection or respect. The exception is an unlikely coupling between Joe Middleton, Bert's brother, and Caro Allingham, the daughter of the local gentry. This encounter does, however, seem to exist more for its symbolic function than for realism, for it results in a pregnancy which will be a means of uniting the classes later on in the series. Otherwise, the Allinghams have little interaction with the poorer inhabitants of the village, and when the villagers are in need are at best witnesses who do not intervene. Lady Allingham watches sympathetically as a shell-shocked Joe stumbles around, for example, but she does nothing to help, and he is soon captured by the army and shot as a deserter. Lord

Grantham would be appalled at such a lack of paternalism, but it feels historically likely in the way in which *Downton* does not.

It is this kind of grittiness and darkness which gives a sense of authenticity to this drama, and distinguishes it from the more sanitised historical television I have already discussed. There are moments here too, however, in which our modern sensibilities are prioritised ahead of accuracy about the historical past. Perhaps most notable is a stresses on cleanliness and hygiene which seems to say more about the viewer's standards than it does about life in the early twentieth century. Washing is a frequent part of the plot: there are repeated scenes in which the hero, Bert, is shown in the bathtub, as his brother, and later when his schoolteacher is realised from prison a bath is the first thing he is offered by the Middleton household. Then there are repeated scenes – several per episode – which are set in the women's bathhouse in the village, which functions as a place of refuge and escape for the female characters, as well as a source of gossip and information for them. Significantly, this all-female sanctuary is the only place Grace "feels safe" (episode 1) but like the laundry that she is constantly occupied with, reinforces the message of the bourgeois cleanliness of even the most impoverished characters. Indeed, John Middleton seems to be the only character in the drama who is not battling to keep clean, which is unsurprising as he is also frequently the most unsympathetic to the viewer. It is permissible to offer a bare and comfortless world, it seems, but dirt is a step too far for a contemporary audience, even though, in this farming community, it is actually everywhere. Moreover, cleanliness establishes closeness to, and identification between, these characters and the modern viewer: the women in the drama are seeking a better life and social mobility, and this is signified by their determination to cleanse and purify the working-class body.

## Problematic patriarchy in *The Village*

Its working-class focus is not the only way in which *The Village* differs ideologically from the other historical fictions I explore here. Its representation of family life is also highly atypical. In *Downton* and *The Forsyte Saga*, the family functions as a place of refuge, a buffer and solace from the rapidly changing and modernising outside world (albeit one which, especially in the latter, brings its own issues). Here, however, the home is a site of tension, violence and even abuse, more than of love and support, and it is the head of the household who is generally to blame.

In the period drama I have examined thus far we have frequently seen benevolent father figures who, despite their personal flaws, are kind and paternalistic patriarchs. Robert Crawley is loved and respected by family and employees alike; Harry Selfridge, Christopher Tietjens and even Soames Forsyte may not be ideal husbands but they are caring and devoted fathers. This is, of course, significant given the family politic that operates in each of these dramas, for it signifies that the fate and future of England – which they are in different ways responsible for – is in good hands. In contrast, *The Village* offers a much less benign view of its patriarchs. The local landowner, Lord Allingham, is a grotesque parody of Lord Grantham: badly scarred in the Anglo-Zulu war, he is now mentally as well as physically unwell. As a result Allingham is a disturbingly Gothic figure to his servants and the other villagers, who turn their back when he approaches, out of respect for his facial disfigurement. Within his own household, when he is expected to offer wisdom or paternalistic support, he shows only a lack of grip on reality, though whether this is a result of his mental decline or his aristocratic status is unclear. For example, when informed by his son that war has broken out, his only response is to inquire whether the "bank holiday is over?" For the viewer this is a highly ambiguous remark, which may be indicative that his mind is now irrevocably broken, but which may also indicate that he is an extreme version of the upper-class dinosaur who thinks only of the pleasures of the privileged life and is now permanently detached from the modern world. This is, after all, something that in its darker moments *Downton* hints Lord Grantham can or may become.

Certainly, at no point in the series does Allingham offer any kind of support to his family, and perhaps as a result of this they all seem unhappy and frustrated, especially his unstable and unpredictable daughter Caro, whose irrational behaviour echoes his, as though their shared mental illness is hereditary. Unlike *Downton or Parade's End*, there is nothing noble or superior about aristocratic blood in this drama. Finally, Allingham descends into mania, first maiming and then slaughtering his own cattle in a horrible perversion of his duties as a yeoman farmer, and then shooting himself in their barn (series 1 episode 4). As a result of this his family are left floundering, and are soon at the mercy of a surrogate father figure, the manipulative and sadistic Doctor Wylie. He comes to the house initially to treat the now hysterical Caro via a rest cure, but through a mixture of abuse and seduction, and the strength of his will, ends up not only dominating her but the rest of the family as well:

"Understand this. I will make her better. Who is the ... the head of this household? Neither of you. It's her. She is attention seeking and self-pitying and you are just the audience for these theatrics..." [Edmund] "May I ask how you propose to cure my sister?" [Wylie] "No. All I need from you is to place all, and I mean all, your trust in me ... Do as I say and I will cure your sister." (series 1, episode 4)

Wylies's "cure" involves force-feeding and sexually abusing Caro, but, while he is feared and resented by the Allinghams, they seem incapable of resisting his patriarchal power. "I think you are after power for its own sake," Caro's brother George tells him angrily, but his attempts to intervene in his sister's treatment are ultimately futile (episode 4). Hence, after beginning a controlling relationship with Caro, and orchestrating George's departure to the Front, the doctor continues living with the family long after his medical services are no longer needed. (The characterisation of Wylie can be said to be typical of the cynical way in which this drama views any representative of the British establishment – from the medical profession to the law and the Army – a point which I will return to.) It is significant, then, that far from being in charge and control of this society, the aristocracy represented here are shown to be in disarray: vulnerable, mentally unwell and easily influenced, they are in need of leadership themselves, but seek it in the wrong men. They cannot even command respect from their servants, largely as a result of Caro whose mental illness makes her the subject of gossip and ridicule. Even their name suggests the "ailing" nature of their position.

In fact, men in general are not the answer in this drama: it is not only aristocratic patriarchy which is shown to be abusive and damaging. The working and upper classes may be very far apart here in most ways, but the problem of masculine control over the family is universal. Thus Bert's father John, played by John Simm, is as problematic in his own way as Lord Allingham, who he is closely identified with even though they never actually meet. Their narratives are entwined throughout: John is blamed for the cattle mutilations Allingham has in fact committed, and he too sets out to commit suicide, although, lacking Allingham's privacy, he is seen and rescued by his wife at the last minute. Initially a violent alcoholic who beats his wife and is feared and hated by his children, he reforms after this event, giving up drinking and beginning the process of reformation into a god-fearing and respectable citizen. He does, however, continue to be an ineffectual – if no longer a violent – father, and an inadequate farmer and provider. Instead, it is the women who provide leadership, support and love in this drama: many of the problems in this society are due to its failure to recognise their worth. Hence, as the first series progresses, it is Grace, Bert's mother, who emerges as the most important character and the catalyst for social change. She has always been responsible, almost singlehandedly, for the survival and wellbeing of the Middleton family, and by the end of the series she has also become the voice of the labour movement in the village – negotiating for better treatment for the female factory workers – and leads its anti-war sentiment, as articulated in the final episode. Indeed, her activism is such that it causes the men of the community to become anxious to silence her and "return her to the home," and they attempt to bribe her husband into encouraging her to do so (episode 6). In her increasingly rebellious attitude she is joined by the other central character, Martha, the minister's daughter and Bert's first love. Martha's religious zeal and philanthropic work first rescues John from drink and despair, and later saves Gerard Eyre from the Spanish influenza. Martha identifies herself as a suffragette but, like most of the other period dramas I discuss here, first-wave feminism is not given much narrative space in *The Village*. There is one scene in the first episode in which the campaign for the Vote is discussed over dinner, but that is all: feminism is here of secondary importance to the labour movement. That aside, however, this is undoubtedly a female-centric drama, which suggests that its female characters are fundamental to the progress and change that will take place in the twentieth century. *Parade's End* suggested something similar through its portrayal of Valentine Wannop, but ultimately was more interested in the future as represented by Tietjens: even Valentine only really existed as a catalyst for his changing view of the world. Patriarchy in *The Village*, however, has no redemptive, sensitive male saviour, but is always deeply flawed, destructive or inadequate. Instead, matriarchy offers some solutions to personal and social problems. Grace ensures the survival of her family and her farm, and, eventually, Clem Allingham begins to take charge of hers. Hence the meeting between these two in the final episode is a significant one: in order to heal the war-scarred village, Clem takes the – for her – unprecedented step of visiting the Middleton's cottage to speak to Grace about the war memorial. This gesture of female support and solidarity hints at the construction of a cross-class bond in which two powerful women come together to shape a new future, as symbolised by the illegitimate grandchild they both share.

## Anti-establishment politics

Its interest in working-class life is not the only way in which *The Village* reveals its left-wing credentials. The series not only critiques patriarchy, but is suspicious of authority in all its forms. As we have seen, any possibility of respect for the local aristocracy is undermined by their shortcomings: the Allinghams are not so much thoughtless or cruel as preoccupied by their own problems. I have also already indicated how respect for the medical profession is undermined in the drama by the sadism and charlatanism of Doctor Wylie, and this is compounded by the ineffectual village doctor, who is a source of neither aid nor comfort when the first scarlet fever and later influenza strike the villagers. In both cases, patients are saved by the ministrations of other family members, not of their medical practitioners. (*Downton* does also remind the viewer about the flaws and limitations of early twentieth-century medicine – but takes care to construct it as a rapidly evolving profession inhabited by dedicated individuals like Doctor Clarkson, as I have discussed elsewhere (Byrne, 2015)). The legal profession is equally suspect: John Middleton is unjustly incarcerated for Lord Allingham's crimes, and it is only the latter's timely suicide which reveals the truth. Most fundamental, however, is the drama's representation of the British Army, which it constructs as the real villains of this drama. From the moment officers from the army arrive in the village, they reveal their inhumanity: Gerald Eyre is a conscientious objector, but they ignore his moral scruples and violently assault him when he refuses the draft. Next soldiers nearly bring about the ruin of the Middletons by attempting to commandeer their family horse, even though she is essential to the workings of their farm. It is notable that John's only moment of triumph in the series occurs when he defies this authority and hides the horse in the local pub so she cannot be taken to France. The "war effort" as we know it is here constructed as unreasonable sacrifice by families and individuals: the Middletons have already given their son and should not be expected to give their livelihood as well. Most horrific of all, however, is the Army's brutal treatment of Joe Middleton, who although incapacitated by shell shock – and classified as unwell by two local doctors – is captured and shot as deserter without compassion or further investigation when he fails to return from leave. The diagnosis of shell shock forms a reoccurring sub-plot in First World War drama, especially *The Crimson Field,* where some, though not all, of the Army physicians are struggling to understand it. In the more cynical *The Village*, however, it is a mystery both to Ramsey the local doctor and to the fashionable "nerve specialist" Wylie. (Although it is notable that, in his only morally upright act in the drama, Wylie does refuse to let the army take his patient, literally barring their entry to the house: even the most sadistic character finds the military inhumane.) Neither the medical profession nor the Army seem to have any real sense of the psychological trauma caused by modern warfare, even though the invalided out veteran Bairstow, who is not a medical man, recognises it immediately. More damning still, the catalyst for Joe Middleton's psychological breakdown is not actually conventional conflict with the Germans, but the punishment he receives from his superior officers for sending a coded postcard to his little brother:

> They must have found out what I were doin'. They confronted me with it. I didn't feel like taking it from some pimply officer, so I pushed him. He fell backwards, lost his balance. You can't do that to an officer ... I might have been shot, for in ... insurb. ...What's the bloody word? What's wrong with me? ... They tied me wrists and me feet to the wheel of a cart. And left me out all night. In the open. Behind the lines, so there's no ... But you hear – everything. And you feel ... I just ... just ... I just felt so ... So exposed. ([sic] episode 4)

Joe survives the Somme and other battles which claim so many of his fellow villagers, but he cannot endure the torturous cruelty of his own command and it is this which finally breaks him, first mentally and then mortally. One way or the other, authority is destructive. The violence and cruelty of the soldiers who come to make the arrest is not only directed at him, either: both Grace and John are beaten when they try to intervene. And while the army's representatives who travel to the village are ordinary soldiers far from the centre of power, Bert tells us in the final episode that Joe's death warrant was actually signed by Field Marshall Haig, and so his tragic death reflects inhumanity at the highest levels.

The British Army is not the only institution criticised by *The Village*, then, but is the one most directly and repeatedly attacked, in the strongest terms. Anti-First World War sentiments are common in Edwardian drama, as I have already discussed. Even *Downton* was critical enough of the ideology behind the War that it refused to condemn characters who did not wish to fight, and *Parade's End* relentlessly lampooned the pointless and farcical bureaucracy of the military. In neither case, however, was the Army portrayed to be such a brutal and vicious organisation as it is here. At least *Parade's End* portrayed some officers to be sensible and intelligent, even If the system they served was not. Tietjens himself is a reassuring character who leads his men with sense and compassion, but there is no Tietjens, and no Matthew Crawley in *The Village*. Instead, there are only nameless servants of an uncaring military machine, which destroys the lives of all those with which it comes into contact.

Given its general suspicion about institutions and authority, it is unsurprising that this drama is strongly anti-military. It is also, more generally, strongly anti-war, and while this is something it shares with other neo-Edwardian fictions, *The Village* takes a slightly different approach by constructing the War in class terms. It presents the conflict as a result of decisions made by a section of the population who are very remote – geographically and socially – from the inhabitants of the village, and yet expect them to give up their sons as fodder. The middle and upper classes, in contrast, do rather well out of the War: Hankin and Edmund Allingham make money from it, and Allingham also uses it to further his political career. The perceptive local vicar sees this kind of class exploitation, and uses his sermons and lessons in the village school to remind his congregation that those they are fighting are just like themselves: "Look. Jesus Christ with a machine gun, mowing down German farmers and factory workers ... And look, Saint Peter thrusting a bayonet into the belly of German coal miners. God is on our side?" (episode 2). Early in the War, the Vicar is in the minority: by its end, all the villagers come to share his views, their belief in their country's leaders irrevocably destroyed. The change is foreshadowed by the closing scenes in episode 1, in which the village's young men leave for France with the whole community's support and encouragement, the sense of solidarity and the pleasures of patriotism clearly apparent. However, this moment is immediately followed by one in which an innocent pet (interestingly, Caro Allingham's dog, a creature as pampered and frivolous as she is) is stoned to death by local children because he is a "German dog" (a dachshund). The representation here of patriotism as an excuse for casual cruelty and destruction prefigures that of the War itself. It also epitomises one of the main themes of the drama: the end of innocence both general and specific – of course firstly for Bert, who begins the series as a young boy growing up, but also more widely, for the village, and indeed society as a whole:

> The Great War took place in what was, compared with ours, a static world, where the values appeared stable and where the meanings of

abstractions seemed permanent and reliable. Everyone knew what glory was, and what Honor meant. (Fussell, 1975: 23)

Episode 1, set in the summer of 1914, is reflective of this "static" world, where no-one has left the parish for generations, but modernity – in the form of movement and disillusion – is on its way. Throughout this book we have been accustomed to the First World War being constructed as a watershed, which marked the end of an era for the privileged classes. From *The Shooting Party* to *Parade's End*, the conflict heralds the end of a pleasurable, luxurious way of life for the lucky few (only *Downton* represents, with unquenchable optimism, the aristocracy enduring with little change well into the 1920s). *The Village* has an alternative message, reminding the viewer that the First World War represented something rather different for the lower classes. For them, it was the end of unquestioned loyalty and service to King and country, and to their social superiors: obedience to those above did, after all, led to pointless slaughter on a huge scale. *The Village* makes clear that the Establishment, in its various forms, has little regard for the individual (especially if they are poor, or female), and so rebellion against those in authority can only be represented as a positive thing. This drama thus reminds the viewer that, while the war represented the end of a more innocent time, it was also the moment in which class structures began to break down. Hence, by last episode of the series, which is set in 1920, Grace is agitating for better working conditions in her factory, Bert is pursuing the middle-class hobby of photography, and they and other villagers are able to speak out against the decisions being made which effect their lives. Most controversially, however, the form this resistance takes is of reaction to the commemoration of the war.

## Remembering 1914

In Chapter 1 I discussed our current commemoration of the centenary of the First World War and the ways in which, in recent years, Remembrance Sunday and the wearing of the poppy have become crucial parts of British culture. I suggested there that patriotism and Britishness has become defined by the remembrance of the War, and that any reaction against this, like Jonathan Jones's condemnation of the Tower of London instillation or John Snow's refusal to wear a poppy on air, has been highly controversial. It is therefore significant that *The Village* chooses to interrogate the origins of this way of remembering, and exposes as controversial the decision to commemorate the dead on

the 11th November – a decision initially unpopular as it replaced the
original plan to bring home the bodies of the dead:

[Edmund] "The government, in consultation with the King and with
the most senior figures in the armed forces, has decided that there
will be no repatriation of the fallen."[Norma] "November the 11th
will serve as a day of remembrance for us all". [Grace:] "That's wrong.
Everyone's grief is different." [Norma] "It's more meaningful if we join
together." [Grace] "It costs less. And they can tell us what the history
will be. Do you want the generals and politicians who took us into this
war to tell us how to mourn our dead after it?" (*The Village*, series 1,
episode 6)

Grace's anger here is shared by the whole village, but is especially bitter
for her family because Joe, as a deserter, does not have his name on the
village war memorial (Lady Allingham, in the spirit of goodwill towards
the man who fathered her grandchild, has it inserted at the last minute).
The army, the King and the government – represented here by Edmund
as the local MP – have decided on collective remembrance in an attempt
to smooth over the individual rage and grief that followed the War, and
channel it towards patriotism. But that the only true war enthusiast and
eager jingoist in the drama is the sadistic schoolteacher speaks volumes
about the drama's view of the conflict and its aftermath.

Inevitably, this strong anti-war bias proved one of the most controversial aspects of the drama as Christopher Steven's scathing comments
in the *Mail* suggest:

Worst of all, writer Peter Moffat badly misread the country's attitude
towards World War I as the centenary approached. He assumed
viewers subscribed to the cynical, Islington-Lefty notion that the
war had been for nothing, that the gullible troops were betrayed
by the toffs. In fact, as an array of inspirational documentaries and
dramas has been proving for months, Britain is more proud than
ever of the sacrifices that millions of men and women made, on
the Home Front and in the trenches. The carping and whingeing
of Moffat and co was so misplaced, it was an embarrassment to the
BBC. (2014)

Such a virulent reaction to a negative representation of the War reveals
the extraordinary patriotic zeal that surrounds this conflict today,
100 years after it began. Clearly, the debates around the understanding

and the view of the First World War, which I have explored throughout this book, are far from resolved.

## "Life connected to the land": rural life in *The Village*

Throughout this chapter I have been suggesting that *The Village* is not simply "post-heritage," as *The Forsyte Saga* and *Parade's End* try to be, but in its rejection of nostalgia and its refusal to commodify the past seems to have gone beyond the conventions of heritage criticism altogether. There is one regard in which it still closely resembles traditional period television and film, though, and that is in its portrayal of the English countryside. The Peak District as represented here is as unspoilt and beautiful here as the landscape in any heritage film, and indeed occupies a more central place than in any of the other dramas explored in this book. The executive producer of *The Village*, John Griffin, has noted this, suggesting that: "the spectacular landscape is truly the star of the series" (Artsbeat, 2013). The drama is bleak in its portrayal of human lives but the countryside remains a – indeed the only – positive and exhilarating presence throughout. I will therefore conclude this chapter with an examination of this drama's tribute to rural England both past and present.

From *All Creatures Great and Small* (1978–90) to *Born and Bred* (2002–05) British historical television has long had a fondness for the representation of British village life. The popularity of this from the 1970s onwards is perhaps best summed up by the now iconic series of television advertisements for *Hovis* bread, beginning with the "bike-ride" advert in 1973 (1973–79). As de Groot has noted, this "presented an idealised version of Englishness" to the viewer/consumer, in the form of a sepia-tinged village street from the early twentieth century, which marketed nostalgia so successfully that this was voted the nation's favourite commercial in 2006 (de Groot, 2009: 8–9).[1] The Hovis commercial is still, significantly, repeatedly invoked by critics reviewing *The Village* (Cooke, 2013; Lawrence, 2013, *The Scotsman*, 2013) who note that the show exploits its visual closeness to "Hovis Britain" in order to set up expectations about sentimental cosy television which it then destroys. In fact, one sarcastic review in *The Scotsman* points out that Moffat's show "feels at times like a deranged Hovis advert," with its "mournful brass and harmonium soundtrack" combined with unrelenting period misery (2013). This desire to undermine cosiness aside, however, there still seems to be real affection in the drama for village and agricultural life, as Rachel Cooke has discussed:

Moffat has strained his every sinew not to gild his fictional village with what he has called a "Ready Brek glow": crops fail, families go hungry, and a scrap of tripe in milk is thought a feast fit for a king. It's no bucolic idyll. But even so, the romantic in him won't, or can't, dispense with the idea of the bond between his characters and their land. (Cooke, 2013)

Hence John Middleton, while a fundamentally inadequate farmer, still loves the land he owns and is determined to instil that love in his sons, reminding Bert that his family have worked this farm for generations: "five generations of this family have stood [here] ... this is our floor. This is our farm. And I will not let it go" (series 1, episode 1). This is a love that the viewer, too, is invited to share, as they are seduced by beauty of the Peak District in almost every shot. And the few sentimental and even uplifting moments in the drama tend to surround farm animals (not pet ones, significantly, given as we have seen the horrible fate of Caro Allington's small dog). For example, the Middleton family cannot save their son from the war, but they are able to prevent their horse, Big Molly, from being taken, much to Bert's delight. Similarly, John's redemption from alcoholism is symbolised by his purchase of a dairy cow, rather than drink, with Bert's savings. The dairy herd represent the opportunity for a new start for the family, and one of the few moments when they all work happily and productively together is when they spend the night stripping the field of wild garlic to keep the milk fragrant. Although frequently harsh, farming is restorative and brings its own pleasures and compensations.

This romanticism of agrarian life and agricultural animals is not unique to this series: we might recall here *Parade's End*, in which horses represent the bucolic life the luddite Tietjens longs to preserve and protect (his tenderness for them also signals his kindness and compassion, itself at odds with the cruelty of modernity). In episode 1 of that drama Valentine's horse is wounded by a motor car while pulling her trap, in a literal collision between the old world and the new, and the episode ends with Tietjens cradling the animal in his arms and sobbing for a past that is slipping away from him. Of course, his nostalgia is unsurprising in that the life he mourns is one of privilege, and *Parade's End* presents the beauty of the English countryside as just another part of a glossy heritage past. Here, however, it is at odds with *The Village*'s general refusal of nostalgia: this is after all a drama which seeks first and foremost to remind us that the past is not only another country, but one which we do not want to reside in. But it makes an exception for the land. Some critics have praised *The Village* for its "refusal to foist contemporary relevance on its audience" (Lawrence, 2013) but in its affection for the agrarian life, *The Village* is saying a great deal about our present, as Rachel Cooke has argued. She sees this one rose-tinted aspect of the show as indicative of a wider cultural pre-occupation, of "Britain's continuing fascination with a life connected to the land":

> Our love of the idea of the village, if not the reality, shows no sign of letting up. We cleave to it through thick and thin, for all that most of us live in cities and suburbs; for all that so many villages now have only half-lives, thanks to second-home owners and post office closures ... My own hunch is that this longing is to do with sense of place, a connectedness that is increasingly elusive in our cities, which all look alike, and whose inhabitants come from everywhere and nowhere. (Cooke, 2013)

Hence it is appropriate that *The Village* has an idealised view of rural life, for its audience does too. Indeed, Cooke's suggestion may explain part of the appeal of period drama for a contemporary audience, for we can certainly see that farming and villages have become constant features in recent historical fictions. Joe Wright's 2005 reworking of Austen's *Pride and Prejudice*, for example, re-imagines the Bennet's home as a small farm, complete with livestock wandering through the kitchen[2] (2005), and Andrea Arnold's recent *Wuthering Heights* emphasises the earthiness of the Earnshaw's rustic dwelling (2011). In an Edwardian context, even *Downton Abbey*, while primarily constructed as a place of employment, is after all also a working estate (even Lady Mary is seduced into the farming life when she saves a litter of pigs in series 4!). We might recall here that Tietjens, when goaded about his anti-patriotic feeling, indignantly responds that he "loves every field and hedgerow" of England (*Parade's End*, episode 2). Clearly, in period drama, Britishness and rural life are bound up together, and hence it is unsurprising that even the most anti-heritage of historical dramas cannot repress a nostalgia for, and celebration of, the countryside. But of course this does result in that same countryside becoming a commodity: the Peak District's tourist board is hoping for increasing numbers of visitors, and increased revenue, as a result of *The Village* (Artsbeat, 2013).

## Conclusion

Given its determinedly anti-authoritarian and left-wing stance, it is unsurprising that critical response to *The Village* has been mixed. Many of the critics I have quoted so far have embraced Moffat's attempt to do something different with the period drama format, and his determination to revisit the Edwardian era from a working-class perspective. Others have found this gritty view of the past depressing and humourless: Sam Wollaston in *The Guardian* found it "as bleak as bleak" (2014) and Christopher Stevens in the *Mail* was appalled at what he described as "boring Lefty claptrap" being brought back for another series (10th August 2014).The viewing public seemed to agree up to a point: the initial ratings of just over 8 million did tail off dramatically after the first episode, but the 5.48 million who remained were considered substantial enough for the BBC to bring the show back for a second series. The contrast with the viewing figures for *Downton* and *Mr Selfridge* is, of course, dramatic: audiences want certain things from their Sunday night viewing, namely "to end the week on a high not a low" (tweets quoted in Cox, 2014). It is tempting to speculate, however, that the ambivalent response from the public – after initial enthusiasm – is also because *The Village* portrays early twentieth-century England very differently from how the period usually appears on screen. There are already a number of Edwardian period dramas which examine history through the eyes, or through the lives, of the middle and upper classes: from "man of property" Soames Forsyte to the aristocratic Grantham family, there is no shortage of wealth and privilege on our televisions. There is, however, a real gap when it comes to representing the lives of the poor who made up the greater part of Britain's population and especially the rural poor, far from the urban centres of power. Thus it seems to me politically important that this kind of history is offered to us, even if it is, by necessity of accuracy, bleaker and more depressing than we might like. The stories of ordinary people may not allow us to escape our present in the pleasurable way *Downton* does, but they might make us thankful for it, and for the positive changes time has brought. In this way *The Village* encourages the viewer to experience the very opposite of nostalgia. At the same time, however, it reminds us of injustices and oppressions which have not changed much over the last 100 years. And this drama does, finally, expose the truth about the image of the Edwardian period which has remained in popular memory over the course of the century. In the last episode of the series, Grace, arguing with Edmund Allingham, reminds him how her version of the past differs from his:

[Edmund] "We are all making adjustments. We all remember before the war as being another time – a kind of golden age." [Grace] "You had more servants. That's what was golden about it. It wasn't a golden age for me, or for Margaret Boden, or for Agnes. Or for anyone else I've ever spoken to outside of your class." (*The Village*, series 1, episode 6)

It feels like Grace is not only answering Edmund here, but also the audience who enjoy glossy, heritage television set in the early years of the century. I began this book with this image of the Edwardian era as a golden summer, a time of pleasure and innocence before the War changed the world forever. Hence it seems appropriate to finish it on this reminder that the dramas which we all watch, and which perpetuate this attractive myth, can only do so because they close their eyes to ordinary people. They make us nostalgic for this "golden age" because they usually ignore those who, like Grace, were not part of it: those who need to hope that the future is sunny, for their pre-War past was not.

# Conclusion

On the 1st January 1901, one of *The Times's* leading articles greeted the arrival of a new century:

> The twentieth century has dawned upon us, and as we float past this quiet landmark on the shores of time feelings of awe and wonder naturally creep over us ... To Englishmen, Scotsmen and Irishmen, the first of all considerations must be – How will the new century affect the moral and material greatness of their country and their Empire? ... We enter upon the new century with a heritage of achievement and of glory older, more continuous, and not less splendid than any country in the world. Our national character, as the ordeal of this last year has abundantly shown, has lost nothing of its virility and dogged-ness when put to the proof of War ... We have a reasonable trust that England and her sons will ... live and prosper, one United and Imperial people, to be "a bulwark for the cause of men." (Read, 1973: 10)

This love letter to Englishness at the dawn of a new era sums up much of what we still associate with the Edwardians today: jingoism, faith in Imperialism, belief in British values and democracy, and optimism about the future. Above all, perhaps, is a sense of a great legacy of progress and prosperity, which originated with the Victorians and now is to be passed down to the generation that follows. This world is confident about its future and about the way it will be remembered, secure about its "heritage." By the beginning of 1914, the same kind of New Year greeting in *The Times* would be undercut with anxiety about degeneration and decadence – but still have the same confidence that "the fibre of the race is unimpaired (Reade, 1973: 10)." By the autumn of that year, all those beliefs would be irrevocably shattered by the First World War.

This book has set out to examine the "heritage" of the Edwardian period and the way this short but significant period of history is reconstructed and remembered today. Through a series of centenaries, it is a past which has recently come very close to us: with its sense of being the first really modern era, it lacks the remoteness of other moments in history. It is lent poignancy by its identification as the last days of innocence before a terrible War, and excitement and glamour by being the age which saw the arrival of the motor car, the invention of the airplane and the rise of the department store. It was a time of great social progress: its political changes included the Insurance Act and other early elements of the Welfare State, and the (rather long) path to the Vote for women. Yet it was also a time of huge social disparity and the last era in which the aristocracy were secure and unchallenged in their wealth and privilege. The British Empire was still at its height and yet, with the Boer War, cracks were just beginning to show.

With all this in mind, it is unsurprising that our society, also at the start of a new century, is fascinated by the world of 100 years ago. Yet this is far from the first cultural revisiting of the Edwardian age. The clothes of its dandies were worn by Teddy boys in the 1950s, and its style and literature was picked up again in the 1970s. The "Edwardian revival" in this decade also saw a preoccupation with the period on its newly available television screens, which made the past suddenly accessible and visually identifiable to all. It is here that this book began: with the start of what would become a long tradition of televisual representations of this period. Period dramas have usually been considered a conservative form, but classic serials like *The Forsyte Saga*, *Upstairs Downstairs* and *Shoulder to Shoulder* were all, in different ways, ground-breaking television, which used the problems and conflicts of an earlier era to reflect on their own. They were also historical without being especially nostalgic: from the cold and uninviting bedrooms of the maids in *Upstairs Downstairs*, to the prisons in *Shoulder to Shoulder*, the spaces of the past in these fictions are not places we long to revisit. As a result the 1970s viewer feels grateful for their more enlightened present – even while noting that there are many similarities between the then and now. Poverty, social inequality, sexism and social unrest were all part of the landscape of the 1970s and these dramas are social criticism first and foremost. For them, the Edwardian period, like their own, is a time of possibility, where a cook can become the owner of a hotel, and a married woman can commit adultery without judgement, where change is just around the corner.

The recent period dramas that I examine here are also interested in learning lessons from history, but they do not share that Edwardian optimism about the future, perhaps because that future is now here, and its promises – from sexual freedom to gender equality – are still problematic. They also tend to demand more things from their historical fiction: not only social critique, but escapism, glamour and romance, as well as – often – violence and grittiness. For them, the Edwardian period has the variety and contrast which makes fast-moving, plot-driven period television. Heritage fictions might traditionally offer us a simpler time, but Edwardian ones show us the complicated beginnings of our own society. In *The Forsyte Saga* and *Parade's End*, scenes move from peaceful, unspoilt rural England, to recognisably modern city life, with all the diverse charms of both displayed for the viewer. *Downton* celebrates the arrival of the telephone, *Mr Selfridge* the airplane and even *The Village* greets the arrival of the first bus with enthusiasm. Technologies that we take for granted now are freshly discovered and defamiliarised as we see them as though for the first time, and freedoms we now enjoy are still being fought for.

Hence our picture of this past is seductively complete, given that we now know – or feel we know, because we have been shown – a great deal about different facets of Edwardian life. We are familiar with the luxurious world of the aristocratic family holding on to power in *Downton*, and the life their servants lead below stairs. *Mr Selfridge* shows us the inner workings of the department store, revealing the thought and labour that goes into its display of glamour. Similarly, *Parade's End* reveals the bumbling errors and petty jealousies that make up the bureaucracy behind the British Establishment and, in particular, behind the First World War. All these dramas are about history as performance, and about people who are well aware that they are playing a role of class or gender – often against their will. And the viewer has a privileged part in this, for we are allowed to look "behind the scenes," sometimes in very personal ways. We witness Irene using a vaginal douche to prevent pregnancy in *The Forsyte Saga* and Sylvia complaining about having to use an old-fashioned chamber pot in *Parade's End* (in a rather post-modern moment, which reminds us of an inhabitant of *The Edwardian House*). We see into the dressing rooms and bathrooms of the past and its most intimate secrets seem laid out before us. Kleinecke-Bates has discussed this, and notes that "this look into what is kept private, secret and hidden, is used to depict a past that is, even though not necessarily more authentic, more interested in a certain kind of authenticity," the authenticity of personal rather than the public (2014: 39). She also suggests that such moments "provide a gateway into the past," that is, "enabling a bond" between the viewer and history. It is true that we are privileged with knowledge in these dramas, which even other characters are denied, and through that knowledge we feel that we have access to "real life." But of course this is an illusion: the real secrets of the past – that it may have been dirty and disease ridden, that there were lice and fleas, that people had huge families they couldn't feed and died of minor illnesses we can now cure – is still hidden from us here. That is not the kind of historical fiction we want on our screens.

That may be changing, however. *The Village* is the first neo-Edwardian drama to represent working-class life in the kind of gritty way we saw kitchen sink drama do in the 1950s and 1960s. It is possible, then, for even this idyllic past to become less seductive, less sanitised. And *Downton* and *Mr Selfridge* both insert the working classes back into history, albeit in, at times, very problematic ways. *The Forsyte Saga* and *Parade's End* do not, however: servants are only in the background of these dramas and it is the rich, privileged and beautiful whose lives we follow. But while I have complained about the class conservatism inherent in most of the dramas examined here, in their representation of gender they are much more progressive. All seem to be part of an ongoing media attempt to write the feminist movement back into history. Even *Downton* cannot ignore the Equal Suffrage campaign, although it associates it with damage and destruction when Sybil, attending a rally, receives a head wound which literally knocks such ideas out of her head. *Mr Selfridge* suggests that feminism is the future and must be embraced if one is to survive: Selfridge's window displays remain intact only because they display support for the Vote. And *Parade's End* constructs feminism as the panacea to old England's ills, in the form of sympathetic suffragette Valentine. Healthy, beautiful and intelligent, she represents Tietjens's future and hence England's, too. There is still a hint of ambiguity about the feminist movement, however, when in an adaptation lovingly preoccupied by art, the Rokeby Venus is slashed before Valentine's horrified eyes. The suffragette who commits this crime does so complaining about the objectification of woman, but we must expect her to be unsympathetically treated by a drama which, no matter how sensitive to gender politics, delights in female beauty (and nudity) and lingers on Sylvia's in every scene. But it is important to note that this series, like all I examine here, makes its most important, most memorable characters female: from Lady Mary to Agnes Towler to Grace Middleton, televisual history has become the story of women's lives.

It is interesting to speculate whether our fondness for the Edwardians will endure once the centenaries that remind us of them are past. After all, even *Downton*'s dominance of our television screens is to end soon, and as Fellowes turns his attention to the late Victorian period, the popular gaze may well follow. Period dramas are notably cyclical in their preoccupations, after all. As we move further away from the anxieties and tragedies that marked the first years of our own century, we may lose our cultural appetite for the mix of escapist glamour and impending doom that so defines the Edwardians. Unlike the Victorians, their time is short, and will be curtailed by the trauma of total war. But although we know how their world ends, we enjoy it while it lasts.

# Notes

## Introduction: Neo-Edwardian Television, and "Heritage" Today

1. See also the Comic Relief two-part parody *Upstairs Downstairs Abbey* (BBC, 2011). For further discussion of historical comedy, see Leggott (2014: 37–50).

## 1  The Edwardians in Popular Memory

1. The first episode of *The Village* attracted a very healthy 6 million viewers, but ratings fell throughout the gritty first series: only. 4.1 million watched the season finale.
2. *Ripper Street* was cancelled after its second season due to low viewing figures, although it is soon to be resurrected by Amazon; *Great Adaptations* got 6 million viewers for its Christmas slot, but this is still shabby compared to the 10 or 11 million the *Downton* Christmas special usually attracts.
3. See the falling – but still healthy – viewing figures at http://en.wikipedia.org/wiki/List_of_Downton_Abbey_episodes#Christmas_Special_.282012.29.
4. A recent decision by the BBC to ban the wearing of poppies on BBC World – arguing that the flower does not have the same resonance abroad – was also the subject of much criticism.
5. Interestingly, Ruth Prawer Jhabvala's screenplay shirts the action of The Golden Bowl to take place between 1903 and 1909 – even though the novel was published in 1904 – possibly to include a greater sense of modernity, as one interviewer noted.

## 2  An Adaptation of an Adaptation: *The Forsyte Saga* (2002)

1. Damian Lewis also emphasised his lack of reliance on the BBC version – while stressing his close knowledge of Galsworthy's novels. See http://www.pbs.org/wgbh/masterpiece/forsyte/ei_lewis.html.
2. See http://www.screenonline.org.uk/tv/id/1071033/ for this and other details about the 1967 production.

## 3  Class and Conservatism in *Downton Abbey* (2010–)

1. For more details on the awards *Downton* has received, see http://www.imdb.com/title/tt1606375/, accessed 2nd February 2012). For rating figures see http://en.wikipedia.org/wiki/Downton_Abbey#Reception.
2. See http://brielise.hubpages.com/.

3. See for example guardian.co.uk Thursday 17th November 2011. www. guardian.co.uk/culture/2011/nov/17/downton-abbey-kirstie-new-boring, accessed 10th March 2012.

4. *Downton* has even borrowed costumes from *A Room with A View*: see http://www. mirror.co.uk/tv/tv-news/downton-abbey-amazing-secrets-behind-155785.

5. For a discussion of the intertextuality created by the repeated use of the same actors in period drama – working to "assert the existence of a distinct generic microcosm – the world of the classic novel adaptation" – see Cardwell (2002: 89–93).

6. Several legally-trained fans have discussed the inheritance plot of *Downton* online: in particular James F Nagel has pointed out the similarity between the Grantham family's entailment and that in Austen's fiction. See http:// austenprose.com/2011/01/14/downton-abbey-entailed-understanding-the-complicated-legal-issues-in-the-new-masterpiece-classic-series/.

7. Moorhouse, 2014.

8. By, among others, the *Daily Mail* on several occasions: see for example http://www.dailymail.co.uk/tvshowbiz/article-2022645/Downton-war-Britains-favourite-drama--bloody-battles-arent-confined-trenches.html.

9. For a discussion of the darker direction the show takes once it leaves the Edwardian period behind, see Byrne, 2014.

10. See the cover of *Private Eye*, no 1275, 12th November–25th November 2010.

## 4   From *Downton* to the Department Store: Sex, Shopping and Heritage in *Mr Selfridge* (2013–)

1. For a detailed discussion of Paxman's argument – which is not quite revisionist but puts great stress on the faith the Edwardians had in the war as though we should share it – see Ian Jack's review in the *Guardian* (2013). This suggests that the main theme of Paxman's argument is to make the reader understand "why so many people at the time believed [the War] to be not only unavoidable but even necessary": Jack points out, however, that "we can understand this and still believe the war to be futile."

## 5   A Return to "quality": *Parade's End* (2012)

1. See also Serena Davies, who believes it is "the finest drama the BBC has given us all year" (2012).

2. Its ratings are around 2 million per episode, compared with 6 or 7 million for *Mr Selfridge* and 9 for *Downton*.

3. Prior to *Parade's End*, Clemens had appeared in *X Men Origins: Wolverine* (2009) and in television programmes like *Love My Way*, (2004–07) but, unlike most of the rest of *Parade's* cast, not in any period drama.

4. There are some (albeit not very recent) exceptions: see for example Frank MacShane's *The Life and Works of Ford Madox Ford*, which notes some of the complexities surrounding Sylvia, a spoiled society woman who is torn between the old world and the new (1965: 179).

5. Further positive responses to Hall's Sylvia include Ben Dowell's review in the *Guardian* (2012), James Poniewozik in *Time* (2012) and Serena Davies in The

*Telegraph*. Only Simon Heffer in the *Mail* is unsympathetic, dismissing her as "manipulative, adulterous and generally ghastly" (notably, he does not like White's direction either).

6. See for example Elizabeth's dalliance with Wickham in *Pride and Prejudice* (1995) or Margaret Hale's with Henry Lennox (2004) or even Cathy's marriage to Linton in *Wuthering Heights* (most recently adapted in 2013). A rare possible exception is Fanny Price's half-romance with Henry Crawford in *Mansfield Park*, but Rozema's 1999 adaptation makes clear that Edward, played by Jonny Lee Miller, is the real love interest and romantic lead (something Austen's novel is less certain about).

7. Davies is here reviewing the 2012 BBC adaptation of *Birdsong*, a more gritty portrayal of war than we see in *Parade's End* or *Downton*, but like those shows, it chooses not to show us "the full horror of war" (Davies, 2012).

## 6 "An ordinary epic": *The Village* (2013–)

1. The street featured in the original advertisement was meant to be in an industrial Northern town, but was actually filmed on Gold Hill – now known as "Hovis Hill" – in the picturesque Dorset town of Shaftesbury, which has become a popular tourist destination since. Partly because of this, and partly for the sense of a small community they invoke, the adverts became associated with rural rather than with city life: a later one in the series consolidated this by shifting the location to a deserted country road with beautiful views over the Yorkshire Dales.

2. For further discussion of this see Dole, 2007.

# Bibliography

Anon. "The Saga Continues." *Sydney Morning Herald*, 28th August 2003. http://www.smh.com.au/articles/2003/08/27/1061663840567.html?from=storyrhs (assessed 13/01/2015).

Anon. "TV preview: *Doctor Who* | *The Voice UK* | *The Village* | *Life's Too Short*". *The Scotsman*, Saturday 30 March 2013.

Baggott, Rob. *Public Health: Policy and Politics*. Basingstoke: Palgrave Macmillan, 2000.

Ball, Vicky, and McCabe, Janet. "The Nearly Forgotten 40 Year-old BBC Mini-series, *Shoulder to Shoulder* Reminds Us Why the Struggle for Gender Equality Still Matters." *London School of Economics Online*, 4th June 2014. http://blogs.lse.ac.uk/politicsandpolicy/why-remember-shoulder-to-shoulder/ (assessed 27/01/2015).

Barker, Dudley. *John Galsworthy: the Man of Principle*. London: Heinemann, 1963.

Barr, Charles. *All our Yesterdays: 90 Years of British Cinema*. London: British Film Institute, 1986.

Barrett, Frank. "Touring the French Battlefields: On the Trail of the Real-life *'Downton Abbey'*." *WWI Hero*. *Mail Online*, 24th October 2011. www.dailymail.co.uk/travel/article-2052408/Edward-Horner-The-real-life-Downton-Abbey-WWI-hero.html#ixzz3U6BvTOmR (assessed 27/01/2015).

Barthes, Roland. *Erte*. Translated by William Weaver. London: Random House Incorporated, 1975.

Baskin, Ellen. *Serials on British Television* Aldershot: Scolar Press, 1996.

BBC Media Centre. "*The Village*, new epic drama series for BBC One. 13th September 2012. http://www.bbc.co.uk/mediacentre/latestnews/2012/the-village.html (assessed 10/05/2015)

Beck, P. *Presenting History*. Basingstoke: Palgrave Macmillan, 2012.

Billen, Andrew. "The Secret Life of Rupert Graves." *London Evening Standard*, 27th March 2002. http://www.standard.co.uk/news/the-secret-life-of-rupert-graves-6305043.html (assessed 13/01/21015).

Bird, M. Mostyn. *Women at Work: A Study of the Different ways of Earning a Living Open to Women*. London: Chapman and Hall, 1911.

Blum, Virginia L. "The Return to Repression: Filming the Nineteenth-Century." In Pucci, and Thompson (eds), *Jane Austen and Co.: Remaking the Past in Contemporary Culture*. New York: University of New York Press, 2003.

Breithaupt Fritz. "Rituals of Trauma" in Chermak, Steven, et al. (eds). *Media Representations of September 11*. Westport: Praeger, 2003.

Brooks, David. *The Age of Upheaval: Edwardian Politics 1899–1914*. Manchester: Manchester University Press, 1995.

Brown, Maggie. "Parade's End Director Says Sexism is Still Rife in Drama World." *Guardian*, 8th September 2012. http://www.theguardian.com/tv-and-radio/2012/sep/08/parades-end-sexism-drama-industry (assessed 18/12/21014).

Buxton, David. *From the Avengers to Miami vice: Form and Ideology in Television Series*. Manchester:Manchester University Press, 1990.

Byrne, K. "Anxious Journeys and Open Endings; Family and Feminism in the BBC's *Wives and Daughters.*" In Loredana Salis (ed.), *Adapting Gaskell.* Cambridge Scholars Press, 2013.

———. "New Directions in Heritage: The Recent Dark Side of *Downton* 'Downer' *Abbey.*" In Leggott and Taddeo (eds), 2015.

Cacciottolo Mario. "Punks of '77: Still Angry After all These Years?" BBC News UK, 16th May 2012. http://www.bbc.co.uk/news/uk-17397222 (accessed 27/01/2015).

Cardwell, Sarah. *Adaptation Revisited.* Manchester: Manchester University Press, 2002.

Carter, Dan. "Fact, Fiction and Film: Frankenheimer's George Wallace." *Perspectives*, January 1998. http://www.historians.org/perspectives/ issues/1998/9801/9801FIL.CFM.

Coates, J. B. "Aldous Huxley." In Denys Val Baker (ed.), *Writers of To-day.* London: Sidgwick and Jackson, 1946.

Copelman, Dina. "Real Life History of Downton Abbey Season 2." *WETA, Public Television and Classical Music for Greater Washington*, 2013. http://www.weta. org/tv/program/downtonabbey/history/season2 (assessed 3/03/2015).

Copping, Jasper. "TV Aerials, Modern Conservatories – Viewers Spot Howlers in *Downton Abbey.*" *The Telegraph*, 24th October 2010. http://www.telegraph. co.uk/culture/tvandradio/8082752/TV-aerials-modern-conservatories-viewers-spot-howlers-in-Downton-Abbey.html (accessed 20/01/2012).

Cooke, Lez. *British Television Drama: A History.* London: British Film Institute, 2003.

Cooke, Rachel. "We Long for a Sense of Belonging that Village Life Offers." *The Guardian*, 31st March 2013. http://www.theguardian.com/commentisfree/2013/ mar/31/why-brits-love-villages (assessed 03/03/2015).

——— "*The Fall* – Misogyny in a Veil of Classiness?" *The Observer*, 16th November 2014. http://www.theguardian.com/commentisfree/2014/nov/16/the-fall-misogyny-gillian-anderson-tv (accessed 17/01/2012).

Cornell, Paul, Martin Day, Keith Topping. *The Guinness Book of Classic British TV.* London: Guinness, 1996.

Corner, J., and Harvey, S. (eds). *Enterprise and Heritage.* London: Routledge, 1991.

Cox, Laura. "*The Village* of misery lightens up: BBC drama set to show cocktail parties and weddings to try and win back viewers it lost during grim first series set in World War I". *Mail Online*, 24 July 2014. http://www.dailymail. co.uk/tvshowbiz/article-2704893/The-Village-misery-lightens-BBC-drama-set-cocktail-parties-weddings-try-win-viewers-lost-grim-series-set-World-War-I.html#ixzz3ZkwEXDVM (assessed 10/05/2015).

Craig, C. 2001. "Rooms Without a View." In Ginette Vincendeau (ed.), *Film/ Literature/Heritage*, 4–11. London: British Film Institute.

Crompton, Sarah. "Granada's grand undertaking". *The Telegraph*, 27 March 2002. http://www.telegraph.co.uk/culture/tvandradio/3575198/Granadas-grand-undertaking.html (assessed 05/05/2015)

Dave, P. *Visions of England.* Oxford: Berg, 2006.

Davies, Andrew, interview. "Andrew Davies: Champion of the Bodice Ripper." *The Telegraph*, 4th January 2008. http://www.telegraph.co.uk/news/ uknews/1574503/Andrew-Davies-champion-of-the-bodice-ripper.html (assessed 21/12/2014).

Davies, Serena. "*Parade's End*: Benedict Cumberbatch and Rebecca Hall, Interview." *Telegraph*, 12th August 2012. http://www.telegraph.co.uk/culture/tvandradio/9489975/Parades-End-Benedict-Cumberbatch-and-Rebecca-Hall-interview.html.

———. "*Parade's End*, Episode Two, BBC Two, Review." *Telegraph*, 31st August 2012. www.telegraph.co.uk/culture/tvandradio/tv-and-radio-reviews/9512852/Parades-End-episode-two-BBC-Two-review.html.

Davis, Deborah. *Strapless: John Singer Sargent and the Fall of Madame X*. London: Penguin, 2004.

de Groot, Jerome. *Consuming History*. London: Routledge, 2009.

———. "*Downton Abbey*: Nostalgia for an Idealised Past." *History Today*, 19th September 2011. http://www.historytoday.com/blog/2011/09/downton-abbey-nostalgia-idealised-past.

Delaney, Paul. *Tom Stoppard in Conversation*. Michigan: University of Michigan Press, 1994.

Dole, Carol M. "Jane Austen and Mud: *Pride & Prejudice* (2005), British Realism, and the Heritage Film." *Jane Austen Society of North America*, V.27, NO.2, 2007.

Dowell, Ben. "Have you been watching … *Parade's End?*". *The Guardian*, Thursday 20th September, 2012.

Dyer, R. "Nice Young Men Who Sell Antiques: Gay Men in Heritage Cinema." In Ginette Vincendeau (ed.), *Film/Literature/Heritage*, 43–48. London: British Film Institute, 2001.

Ebert, Robert. *The Shooting Party: Review*. http://www.rogerebert.com/reviews/the-shooting-party-1985. (assessed 3/11/2014)

Edwards, Sarah. "The Rise and Fall of the Forsytes: From Neo-Victorian to Neo-Edwardian Marriage." In Marie-Luise Kohlke, and Christian Gutleben (eds), *Neo-Victorian Families: Gender, Sexual and Cultural Politics*, 197–219. Rodopi, 2011.

*Elizabeth*. Shekhar Kapur (director). Gramercy Pictures, 1998.

Egner, Jeremy. "The Bodice Ripper that Started it All." *New York Times*, 21st September 2012. http://www.nytimes.com/2012/09/23/arts/television/the-forsyte-saga-and-downton-abbey.html?pagewanted=all&_r=0.

Faulkner, Neil. "How historians today are denying the reality of World War One". *No Glory in War*, 13 November 2013. http://noglory.org/index.php/articles/80-the-deeper-reality-of-the-first-world-war-poets-that-today-s-historians-want-to-deny?

Fellowes, J. "*Foreword*" to Jessica Fellowes, *The World of Downton Abbey*. London: Collins, 2001.

Freeland, J. "David Cameron's *Downton Abbey* Government." *The Guardian*, Monday 26th March 2012. http://www.guardian.co.uk/politics/shortcuts/2012/mar/26/david-cameron-downton-abbey-government (accessed 2/04/2013).

Friedman, Lester (ed.). *British Cinema and Thatcherism: Fires Were Started*. London and Minneapolis: University of Minnesota Press and UCL Press, 1993.

Frost, Laura. "Black Screens, Lost Bodies: The Cinematic Apparatus of 9/11 Horror." In Aviva Briefel, and Sam S. Miller (eds), *Horror After 9/11*. Austin: University of Texas Press, 2011.

Fussell, Paul. *The Great War and Modern Memory*. London: Oxford University Press, 1975.

Gabriel, Tate "*Mr Selfridge*, Series 2, Episode 1, Review." *The Telegraph*, 19th January 2014. http://www.telegraph.co.uk/culture/tvandradio/tv-and-radio-reviews/10580316/Mr-Selfridge-series-2-episode-1-review.html.

Gaddis, John Lewis."And Now This: Lessons from the Old Era, to the New One." In Strobe Talbott, and Nayan Chanda (eds), *The Age of Terror*, 1–22. New York: Basic Books, 2001.

Gaines, Jane, and Herzog, Charlotte (eds). *Fabrications: Costume and the Female Body*. New York: Routedge, 1990.

Galsworthy, John. *The Forsyte Saga*. London: William Heinemann Ltd., 1950.

Gibson, Pamela, in Robert Murphy (ed.). *British Cinema of the 1990s*. London: BFL: 2000.

Glennie, Alastair. "A Right Carry On in The Village." *The Mail Online* , 14th August 2014. http://www.dailymail.co.uk/tvshowbiz/article-2722373/A-right-Carry-On-The-Village-Fans-compare-costume-drama-one-films-series-two-opener-features-smutty-jokes-nudity.html (accessed 19/11/2014).

Godwin Richard. "It's the Great British Brand Corporation". London Evening Standard, 16th April 2014.

Godwin, Richard. "It's the Great British Brand Corporation." *London Evening Standard*, 9th August 2014. http://www.standard.co.uk/comment/richard-godwin-its-the-great-british-brand-corporation-9264005.html.

Goodman, Tim. "*Parade's End*: TV Review." *The Hollywood Reporter*, 22nd February 2013. http://www.hollywoodreporter.com/review/parades-end-tv-review-423406 (assessed 6/01/15).

Goring, Rosemary. "The Bleak Brilliance of *Parade's End* needs No Comparison to *Downton*." *Herald Scotland*, Friday 24th August 2012. http://www.heraldscotland.com/books-poetry/comment-debate/the-bleak-brilliance-of-parades-end-needs-no-comparison-to-downton.18662776.

Green, Robert. *Ford Madox Ford: Prose and Politics*. Cambridge University Press, 1981.

Grey, Edward. *Twenty-Five Years 1892-1916*. London: Hodder and Stoughton Limited, 1925.

Grice,Elizabeth. "Shock is Tempered as Soames Strikes Again." *The Telegraph*, 22nd April 2002. http://www.telegraph.co.uk/news/uknews/1391733/Shock-is-tempered-as-Soames-strikes-again.html (assessed 14/10/2015).

Groskop, V. "*Downton Abbey* Fans Brace for Farewell." *The Guardian*, Saturday 6th November 2010. http://www.guardian.co.uk/tv-and-radio/2010/nov/06/downton-abbey-itv-last-episode (accessed 19/11/2014).

Grosop, Viv. "Could ITV's *Titanic* Sink the Period Drama Ship?" *Guardian*, 26th March 2012. http://www.theguardian.com/tv-and-radio/tvandradioblog/2012/mar/26/itv-titanic-period-drama-series (assessed 20/11/ 2014).

Gross, Edmund. "War and Literature." *Edinburgh Review*, V.220, October 1914, 313.

Hanson, Ellis (ed). *Out Takes: Essays on Queer Theory and Film*.Durham: Duke University Press, 1999.

Hargreaves, T. "There's No Place Like Home: History and Tradition in *The Forsyte Saga* and the BBC." *Journal of British Cinema and Television* 6 (3), 2009.

Harlan, D. "Historical Fiction and the Future of Academic History." In K. Jenkins, A. Morgan, and Munslow (eds). *Manifestos for History*, 121–143. Abingdon: Rouledge, 2007.

Harrison, Paul. "On the Set of '*Mr Selfridge*'." *TimeOut*, 2013. http://www.timeout.com/london/film/on-the-set-of-mr-selfridge (assessed 1/08/014).

Harper, Sue. *Picturing the Past*. London: British Film Institute, 1994.

Harper, Sue. *Women in British Cinema: Mad, Bad and Dangerous to Know*. London: Continuum, 2000.

Harvey,Chris. "*Parade's End*: Valentine Wannop – the Male Fantasy Suffragette." *The Telegraph*, 21st September 2012. http://www.telegraph.co.uk/culture/9558459/Parades-End-Valentine-Wannop-the-male-fantasy-suffragette.html (accessed 18/12/2014).

Haslem, Sara. *Fragmenting Modernism*. Manchester: Manchester University Press, 2002.

Hastings, Max. *Catastrophe: Europe Goes to War 1914*. London: William Collins, 2013.

Heffer, Simon. "I Don't Want to Rain on the Beeb's Parade, But This is no *Downton*." *Mail Online*, 28th August 2012. www.dailymail.co.uk/news/article-2194477/Parades-End-I-dont-want-rain-Beebs-Parade-Downton.html#ixzz3LieytSgi (accessed 18/12/2014).

Heller, Dana (ed.). *The Selling of 9/11*. New York: Palgrave Macmillan, 2005.

Hewison, Robert. *The Heritage Industry: Britain in a Climate of Decline*. London: Methuen Publishing, 1987.

Hinckley, David. "*Mr. Selfridge*: TV Review." *New York Daily News*. Friday 28th March 2014. http://www.nydailynews.com/entertainment/mr-selfridge-tv-review-article-1.1736977. (acessed 2/01/14).

Higson, A. "Representing the National Past: Nostalgia and Pastiche in the Heritage Film." In L. F. (ed), *British Cinema and Thatcherism*, 109–129. London: University College London Press, 1993.

—— *Dissolving Views: Key Writings on British Cinema*. London: Continuum, 1996.

—— *English Heritage English Cinema: Costume Drama Since 1980*. Oxford: Oxford University Press. 2003.

Hill, John. "The Issue of National Cinema and British Film Production" in Duncan Petrie (ed.). *New Questions of British Cinema*. London: British Film Institute, 1992.

Hockenhull, Stella. "Experimentation and Postheritage in Contemporary TV Drama: *Parade's End*" in Leggott and Taddeo (eds), 2015.

Hodgson, Jessica. "Thumbs up for *Forsyte Saga*." *The Guardian*, Monday 8th April 2002. http://www.theguardian.com/media/2002/apr/08/overnights(assessed 14/10/2015).

Hynes, Samuel. *A War Imagined*. London: Pimlico, 1990.

Hubble, Nick. ""In the Twentieth Century, and the Heart of Civilisation": The London of the Forsytes". *Literary London: Interdisciplinary Studies in the Representation of London*, Volume 9 Number 1, March 2011.

Infante, Francesca. "A miserable start for *The Village*, the BBC's answer to *Downton Abbey*". *Mail Online*, 1st April 2013. http://www.dailymail.co.uk/tvshowbiz/article-2302163/A-miserable-start-The-Village-BBCs-answer-Downton-Abbey.html#ixzz3ZXL9duaE . (Assessed 8/05/2015)

Jack, Ian. "*Great Britain's Great War* by Jeremy Paxman – Review." *The Guardian*, Thursday 3rd October 2013. http://www.theguardian.com/books/2013/oct/03/great-britain-war-jeremy-paxman-review (assessed 29/01/2015).

Jardine, Lisa. "The Horror of War." BBC Radio 4: A Point of View, 12th September 2014. http://downloads.bbc.co.uk/podcasts/radio4/pov/pov_20140912-2100a.mp3 (assessed 17/11/2014).

Johnson, Paul (ed.). *Twentieth Century Britain: Economic, Social and Cultural Change*. London: Longman, 1994.

Jones, Jonathan. "The Tower of London Poppies are Fake, Trite and Inward-looking – a Ukip-Style Memorial." *The Guardian*, 28th October 2014. http://www.theguardian.com/artanddesign/jonathanjonesblog/2014/oct/28/tower-of-london-poppies-ukip-remembrance-day (assessed 10/11/2014).

Kagan, Dion: "Homeless Love: Heritage and Aids in BBC2's *The Line of Beauty*." *Literature/Film Quarterly*, V.39, NO.4, 2011, 276–296.

Kamp, David. "The Most Happy Fellowes." *Vanity Fair*, December 2012. http://www.vanityfair.com/culture/2012/12/julian-fellowes-downton-abbey# (assessed 02/01/15).

Kirk, Brian. *Great Expectations*. BBC, 2011.

Kleinecke- Bates, Iris. *Victorians on Screen*. Basingstoke: Palgrave Macmillan, 2014.

Kolko, Gabriel. *Another Century of War?* New York: The New Press, 2002.

Lancaster, Bill. *The Department Store: a Social History*. Leicester: Leicester University Press, 1995.

Lawrence, Ben. "*The Village*: The Most Accomplished New Drama of the Year So Far." *The Telegraph*, 31st March 2013.

———. "*The Village*, Series Two, Episode One, BBC ONE, REVIEW: 'Shackled by History." *The Telegraph*, 10th August 2014.

Lawrence, DH. "John Galsworthy". Rickword, Edgell, ed. *Scrutinies by Various Writers*. London: Wishart and Company, 1928.

Leggott, James, and Taddeo, Julie Anne (eds). *Upstairs and Downstairs: British Costume Drama from* The Forsyte Saga *to* Downton Abbey. London: Rowman and Littlefield, 2015.

Lee, V. "Countdown to Downton." *The Independent*, 20th September 2011. http://www.independent.co.uk/news/media/tv-radio/countdown-to-downton-your-essential-guide-to-the-tv-event-of-the-year-2348865.html.

Leese, Peter. *Shell Shock. Traumatic Neurosis and the British Soldiers of the First World War*. New York: Palgrave Macmillan, 2002.

Levenback Karen. *Virginia Woolf and the Great War*. New York: Syracuse, 1999.

Levenson, Michael. *The Cambridge Companion to Modernism*. Cambridge: Cambridge Univerity Press, 1999.

Levy, Ariel. *Female Chauvinist Pigs: Women and the Rise of Raunch Culture*. New York: Pocket Books, 2005.

Lewis, Damian. "Interview." *PBS* http://www.pbs.org/wgbh/masterpiece/forsyte/ei_lewis.html (assessed 12/01/2015).

*Little Dorrit*. Written by Andrew Davies. London: BBC, 2008.

Lloyd, T.O. *Empire to Welfare State*. Oxford: Oxford University Press, 1970.

Long, Robert Emmet. *The Films of Merchant Ivory*. London: Penguin, 1992.

Lovell, A. 'British cinema: The known cinema?' in R. Murphy (ed.) *The British Cinema Book*. London: BFI, 1997.

Lowenthal, David. "Fabricating heritage". *History and Memory* 10, 1 Spring 1998.

Luckhurst, Roger. *The Trauma Question*. Abingdon: Routledge, 2008.

MacShane, Frank,. *The Life and Works of Ford Madox Ford*. New York: Horizon Press 1965.

Matthews, Steven. *Modernism*. London: Arnold, 2004.

May, Elaine Tyler. "Echoes of the Cold War" in Dudziak, Mary (ed.). *September 11 in History*. Durham: Duke University Press, 2003.

Meixner, John. *Ford Madox Ford's Novels: A Critical Study*. University of Minnesota Press, 1962.

McNamara. Mary. "*Parade's End*, Review". *LA Times*, 26th Febuary 2013.

Mizener, Arthur. *The Saddest Story: a biography of Ford Madox Ford*. Cleveland: World Publishing, 1971.

Moffat, Peter. *The Village.* Dirs Antonia Bird, Gillies MacKinnon et al. BBC, 2013-.

Monk, C. "The British Heritage Debate Revisited." In C. Monk, and Amy Sargent (eds), *British Historical Cinema*, 176–198. London: Routledge, 2002.

—— "Pageantry and Populism, Democratization and Dissent: The Forgotten 1970s" in Leggott and Taddeo (eds.) 2015.

Moore, Frazier. "King of Adapters Reigns During Austen Festival on 'Masterpiece'." Vindy.com 2008. http://www.vindy.com/news/2008/jan/19/king-of-adapters-reigns-during-austen-festival-on/? (accessed 03/12/2014).

Moorehouse, Drucilla. "Doubting Thomas: '*Downton Abbey's*' Love-to-hate Character Loses His Charm." Today, 17th February 2014. http://www.today.com/popculture/doubting-thomas-downton-abbeys-love-hate-character-loses-his-charm-2D12107622 (accessed 30/01/2015).

Mottram, R. H. *John Galsworthy.* London: Longmans and Green, 1956).

Munslow, Alun. *The Future of History.* Baskingstoke: Palgrave Macmillan, 2010.

Paris, M. "Enduring Heroes: British Feature Film and the First World War." In M. Paris (ed.), *The First World War and Popular Cinema*, 51–73. Edinburgh: Edinburgh Univeristy Press, 1999.

Paxman, Jeremy. *Great Britain's Great War.* London: Viking, 2013.

Pike, Frank (ed.). *Ah! Mischief! The Writer and Television.* London: Faber, 1982.

Poniewozik, James. "TV Tonight: *Parade's End*." *Time*, 26th February 2013. http://entertainment.time.com/2013/02/26/tv-tonight-parades-end/.

Powell, David. *The Edwardian Crisis.* Basingstoke: Palgrave Macmillan, 1996.

Purnell, Tony. "Review." *The Mirror*, Monday 8th April 2002.

Pym, John. *Merchant Ivory's English Landscape: Rooms, Views and Anglo-Saxon Attitudes.* London: Pavillion, 1995.

Rackl, Lori. Lori's List. "'Surviving Jack,' Hannibal Buress, '*Mr. Selfridge*'." *Chicago Sun Times*, 23rd March 2014. http://www.suntimes.com/entertainment/television/26338249-421/loris-list-surviving-jack-hannibal-buress-mr-selfridge.html#.U8vls_ldV1Y (assessed 10/08/2014).

Rainey, Sarah. "Sacré Bleu, the French Will Flambé Our Bake Off Alive." *The Telegraph*, 8th October2012. http://www.telegraph.co.uk/culture/tvandradio/9594212/Sacre-bleu-the-French-will-flambe-our-Bake-Off-alive.html.

Raw, Lawrence (ed). *Merchant Ivory: Interviews.* Jackson: University of Mississippi Press, 2012.

Read, Donald. *Documents from Edwardian England 1901–1915.* London: Harrap, 1973.

Revoir, Paul. "I won't surrender to 'poppy fascism': C4 News host Jon Snow refuses to bow to viewer demand to wear the emblem" *Mail Online.* 3rd November 2010. http://www.dailymail.co.uk/news/article-1326063/Jon-Snow-poppy-fascism-row-C4-News-host-refuses-surrender.html#ixzz3ZY8dQx2K (assessed 8/05/2015).

Rigney, A. "Being an Improper Historian." In K. Jenkins, A. Morgan, and A. Munslow (eds), *Manifestos for History*, 162–172. Abingdon: Rouledge, 2007.

Robbins, Ruth. *Pater to Forster, 1873–1924.* Basingstoke: Palgrave Macmillan, 2003.

Roland, Peter. *The Last Liberal Governments: The Promised Land.* London: Barie and Rockliff, 1968.

Rosenberg, Howard. "A Seductive Remake of *'Forsyte Saga'."* *Los Angeles Times*, 4th October 2002. http://articles.latimes.com/2002/oct/04/entertainment/ et-howard4 (assessed 12/01/2015).

Rosenstone, Robert A. *History on Film/Film on History*.London: Routledge, 2006.

Sanders, Julie. *Adaptation and Appropriation*. London: Routledge, 2006.

Sanderson, E. *The British Empire in the Nineteenth Century*. London: Blackie, 1899.

Sargent, A. "Making and Selling Heritage Culture." In J. Ashby, and A. Higson (eds), *British Cinema, Past and Present*, 301–315. London: Routledge, 2000.

Saunders, Jennifer and Edmondson, Adrian. *Upstairs Downstairs Abbey* for *Comic Relief*. BBC1, 2011.

Saunders, Max. *Ford Madox Ford: A Dual Life Volume II*. Oxford: Oxford University Press, 1996.

Schaff, Barbara. "Still Lifes – Tableaux Vivants: Art in British Heritage Films." In Eckart Voigts-Virchow (ed.), *Janespotting and Beyond*. Germany: Gunter Narr Verlag Tubingen, 2004.

Selzer, Mark. "Wound culture: Trauma in the Pathological Public Sphere". *Serial Killers*, October 1997, 80: 3-26.

Sheffield, G. D. "Oh What a Futile War." In Ian Stewart, and Susan L. Carruthers (eds), *War, Culture and the Media*, 54–74. Trowbridge: Flicks Books, 1996.

Simpson Neil. "Why *Parade's End* is deeper and more truthful than *Downton Abbey*". *The Telegraph*, August 29th, 2012.

Smith, Rubert. *The Forsyte Saga: the Offical Companion*. London: Granada, 2002.

Snider, Nanette. Amazon Review of *Parade's End*. 2nd July 2013. http://www. amazon.com/Parades-End-Rebecca-Hall/dp/B00BOTCJXC.

Stevens, Christopher. "Oh No! The Beeb's Sentenced Us to 100 Years of Boring Lefty Claptrap: *Christopher Stevens* Reviews the Weekend's TV." *Mail Online*, 10th August 2014. http://www.dailymail.co.uk/tvshowbiz/article-2721334/Oh-no-The-Beebs-sentenced-100-years-boring-Lefty-claptrap-CHRISTOPHER-STEVENS-reviews-weekends-TV.html (assessed 22/12/2014).

Stewart J.I.M. *Writers of the Early Twentieth Century: Hardy to Lawrence*. London: Clarendon Press, 1963.

Stone, Norman. "Through a Lens Darkly". *The Sunday Times*, 10 January 1988.

Stoppard, Tom. "Interview". BBC Media Centre, 2014. http://www.bbc.co.uk/ mediacentre/mediapacks/paradesend/tom-stoppard (assessed 8/05/2015).

Street, Sarah. *British National Cinema*. London: Taylor & Francis, 2009.

Stuever, Hank. "HBO's. "'Parade's End': All Dressed up with Nowhere to go." *Washington Post*. 25th February 2013. www.washingtonpost.com/ entertainment/tv/hbos-parades-end-all-dressed-up-with-nowhere-to-go/2013/02/25/685e12cc-7d12-11e2-82e8-61a46c2cde3d_story.html (assessed 22/12/2014).

Tate, Gabriel. "*Mr Selfridge*, series 2, episode 1, review". *The Telegraph*, 19th Jan 2014.

*Thomas and Sarah*. David Askey (director). ITV, 1979.

Thompson, David. "'Parade's End': Ford Madox Ford's Masterpiece Comes to the Screen." New Republic, 2012. http://www.newrepublic.com/article/112212/ downton-abbey-grown-ups-ford-madox-fords-parades-end (accessed 11/12/2014).

Trodd, Anthea. *A Reader's Guide to Edwardian literature*. Calgary: University of Calgary Press,1991.

Voigts-Virchow, Eckart (ed.), *Janespotting and Beyond*. Germany: Gunter Narr Verlag Tubingen, 2004.

Voiret, Martine. "Books to Movies: Gender and Desire in Jane Austen's Adaptations." In Pucci, and Thompson (eds), *Jane Austen and Co.: Remaking the Past in Contemporary Culture*. New York: University of New York Press, 2003.

Walton, James. "Review of *The Forsyte Saga*". *The Telegraph*, Monday 2nd April 2002.

Warlow, Richard. *Ripper Street*. BBC, 2012.

Wheatley, Helen. 'Rooms within rooms: ITV and the studio heritage drama of the 1970s', in C. Johnson and R. Turnock (eds) *ITV Cultures: Independent Television Over Fifty Years*. Open University Press, 2005.

White, Susanna. Interview for HBO, 2012. http://www.hbo.com/parades-end/episodes/0/03-part-3/article/the-status-of-women.html#/ (assessed 19/12/2014).

Whitelocks, Sadie. "*Mr Selfridge* the new *Downton?*". *Mail Online*, 22nd March 2013. http://www.dailymail.co.uk/femail/article-2297131/Is-Mr-Selfridge-new-Downton-Abbey-PBSs-latest-British-costume-drama-set-Edwardian-England-thats-similarities-end-.html.

Whitelocks, Sadie. "Is *Mr Selfridge* the new *Downton Abbey*? PBS's latest British costume drama is set in Edwardian England - but that's where the similarities end... Mail Online, 22 March 2013. http://www.dailymail.co.uk/femail/article-2297131/Is-Mr-Selfridge-new-Downton-Abbey-PBSs-latest-British-costume-drama-set-Edwardian-England--thats-similarities-end-.html#ixzz3ZZFt7S89 (assessed 08/05/2015).

Wollastan, Sam. "*The Village* Review – Still Bleak But Now with Jazz." *The Guardian*, Monday 11th August 2014. http://www.theguardian.com/tv-and-radio/2014/aug/11/the-village-bbc-review-james-may-cars-people.

Woodhead, L. *Seduction, Shopping and Mr Selfridge*. London: Profile Books, 2007.

Woollen, Tania. "Over our shoulders: Nostalgic screen fictions for the 1980s" in Corner, J. and S. Harvey, (eds). *Enterprise and Heritage*. London: Routledge, 1991, 178–193.

Wright, Andrea. "This Wonderful Commercial Machine: Gender, Class and the Pleasures and Spectacle of Shopping in *The Paradise* and *Mr Selfridge*" in Leggott and Taddeo (eds), 2015.

York, Peter. "The 1970s Edwardian Reconstruction." *BBC Four*, Tuesday 7th August 2007. http://www.bbc.co.uk/programmes/b007hgh4

# Index

Printed and bound in Great Britain by
CPI Group (UK) Ltd, Croydon, CR0 4YY